THE TRUE CONFESSIONS OF A BADLY MISUNDERSTOOD DOG

"It has been a really, really long time since I read a book that caused me to both laugh out loud and get a little weepy, and Bill Rowe has done that with this book." — THE NORTHEAST AVALON TIMES

"This is an easy-to-read book that anybody who has ever had a dog can easily relate to. It's a story with warmth and humour."

— EDWARDS BOOK CLUB

"Durf's voice is full of affection and is, by his own lights, honest. And the tone is plausible and authentic. The writing is at its strongest when Durf is in some kind of exchange with That Man: '*No man is indispensable,' I heard That Man say one time about himself, and he got that right. But I never heard him say that no dog is indispensable.*"

— THE TELEGRAM

"Dog persons, likely even cat persons, will love this book. They will haul *Marley and Me* from their bookshelves and replace it with [*The True Confessions of a Badly*] *Misunderstood Dog*." — THE ADVERTISER

"[Durf's] misadventures are funny and sad, and always well-written. Definitely a book to read." — THE PEI GUARDIAN

THE MONSTER OF TWENTY MILE POND

"A fantastical novel with a mysterious creature and added thrill of a murder, Rowe creates a connection with the reader through sympathy, mystery and an overall amazing story." — TINT OF INK

"Rowe is an excellent writer and you can't really go wrong reading anything by him. This is one of his best." — THE PEI GUARDIAN

"Rowe's writing shines particularly brightly when his lawyer is chastising the (female) premier or other political discussions are underway, but the entire book is a rollicking ride with likable characters (except the skeets) in familiar settings." — THE NORTHEAST AVALON TIMES

"A well-constructed novel, weaving murder and monsters into a single speculative tale." — THE PACKET

THE PREMIERS JOEY AND FRANK

"A voyeuristic and tantalizing trip through the workings of the government by a man who was there." — THE PILOT

"Rowe's stories paint not only an interesting picture of Rowe's own life, but the lives of the two men in which the book is named, and in the process, their greed, power and lust." — THE MUSE

"*The Premiers Joey and Frank* is crack for political junkies and will be a welcome gift for even the marginally interested observer of the political scene." — THE TELEGRAM

ROSIE O'DELL

"*Rosie O'Dell* is one of those books with such brilliant writing as to lull you into forgetting you're actually reading." — THE PILOT

"Yes, it's Bill Rowe—back this time with his third novel, which I think is by far his best. Probably one of the better novels to come out in the past few years—depending on your own tastes, of course."

— THE NORTHEAST AVALON TIMES

"[A] deeply emotional page-turner by one of the country's finest writers." — MEGAN MURPHY, INDIGO

"This is a terrific story that hinges on a woman who is like quicksilver, running through all the cracks." — THE GLOBE AND MAIL

"It's well-written (Rowe is an experienced and accomplished writer), the characters are excellently drawn and much of the writing is just plain funny." — THE PEI GUARDIAN

"There is not a false note in this book. All the characters are drawn with skillful insight, the descriptions are so vibrant you can almost hear the water and feel the mist of St. John's, Newfoundland. Although it has elements of a thriller, this is no gothic soap opera, but rather a brilliantly crafted look into the hearts and souls of ordinary people who are thrown into extraordinary circumstances."

— ATLANTIC BOOKS TODAY

"This novel is a real page-turner, with lots of tension and mystery."

— THE TELEGRAM

DANNY WILLIAMS, PLEASE COME BACK

"I started to really appreciate Rowe's ability to narrow down a topic and come up with something pithy and witty to say about it, week after week." — THE TELEGRAM

"Like any columnist worth his salt Rowe is provocative and a number of the columns deal with topics whose lessons are still relevant."
— THE NEWFOUNDLAND QUARTERLY

"Rowe's columns on Williams's persona, bellicose manner and political antics truly shine. What Danny Should Do in the Crab War? (May 7, 2005) puts a delightful Shakespearian twist on Williams's strategic positioning; Is Danny a Dictator? (June 25, 2005) will stand as a classic." — THE CHRONICLE HERALD

"A brisk read and a fine book to have in your personal library."
— THE COMPASS

"[Rowe] does it all, of course, with his usual blend of droll good humour and common sense." — THE GLOBE AND MAIL

"With a mind—and a pen—as sharp as a paper cut, the elegant, affable Rowe remains Newfoundland's literary agent provocateur, provoking, teasing, sometimes coddling his subjects, but all the time digging towards truths that cause discomfort for the province's Who's Who and everyman alike." — THE BUSINESS POST

DANNY WILLIAMS: THE WAR WITH OTTAWA

"Interesting book about a successful Canadian politician . . ."
— THE GLOBE AND MAIL

"[Danny Williams] is captivating. [Bill Rowe] spares no punches."
— THE COMPASS

"The most interesting political book to be released in Canada in some time . . ." — THE BUSINESS POST

"Rowe's Ottawa chronicle [is] absorbing, humorous."
— THE TELEGRAM

"I quickly realized that this was not going to be a dry political memoir. To the contrary, not only is the book interesting and revealing of this contentious time, it is very funny in places."
— THE CHRONICLE HERALD

"An exciting read." — THE NEWFOUNDLAND QUARTERLY

"[One of] three of this year's most controversial and talked about political books." — THE HOUSE, CBC RADIO

"Rowe has a more humanistic side to politics. It is as if a citizen managed to be a fly on the wall while Danny Williams fought."
— CURRENT MAGAZINE

"An eye-opening, often hilariously funny, account of life among Ottawa power brokers and civil servants."

— CANADIAN LAWYER MAGAZINE

"Bill Rowe has a lot to say. There are dozens of interesting stories told, and comments passed on . . ." — THE NORTHEAST AVALON TIMES

"A fascinating and frequently funny read." — DOWNHOME

"Written with the knowledge and insight that only an insider could possess, this book (sub-titled 'The Inside Story of a Hired Gun') is a timely reminder of the duplicity of far too many of our elected leaders—no matter what their political stripe." — ATLANTIC BOOKS TODAY

"The writer's good English style—rare today—his knowledge of all kinds of personalities in the political world and his misadventures in getting a basic office set up (which took six of the eight months he was there) all make for amusing and exciting reading."

— THE PEI GUARDIAN

No Punches Pulled

The Premiers Peckford, Wells, and Tobin

BY BILL ROWE

NO PUNCHES PULLED

THE TRUE CONFESSIONS OF A BADLY MISUNDERSTOOD DOG

THE MONSTER OF TWENTY MILE POND

THE PREMIERS JOEY AND FRANK

ROSIE O'DELL

DANNY WILLIAMS, PLEASE COME BACK

DANNY WILLIAMS: THE WAR WITH OTTAWA

IS THAT YOU, BILL?

THE TEMPTATION OF VICTOR GALANTI

CLAPP'S ROCK

No Punches Pulled

The Premiers Peckford, Wells, and Tobin

BILL ROWE

FLANKER PRESS LIMITED
ST. JOHN'S

Library and Archives Canada Cataloguing in Publication

Rowe, William N. (William Neil), 1942-, author
No Punches Pulled : the premiers Peckford, Wells, and Tobin / Bill Rowe.

Includes index.
Issued in print and electronic formats.
ISBN 978-1-77117-590-6 (paperback).--ISBN 978-1-77117-591-3 (epub).--ISBN 978-1-77117-592-0 (kindle).--ISBN 978-1-77117-593-7 (pdf)

A CIP catalogue record for this book is available from Library and Archives Canada.

PRINTED IN CANADA

RECYCLED Paper made from recycled material FSC® C103567 www.fsc.org

This paper has been certified to meet the environmental and social standards of the Forest Stewardship Council® (FSC®) and comes from responsibly managed forests, and verified recycled sources.

Cover Design by Graham Blair Cover photos courtesy of CBC

FLANKER PRESS LTD.
PO BOX 2522, STATION C
ST. JOHN'S, NL
CANADA

TELEPHONE: (709) 739-4477 FAX: (709) 739-4420 TOLL-FREE: 1-866-739-4420
WWW.FLANKERPRESS.COM

9 8 7 6 5 4 3 2 1

We acknowledge the [financial] support of the Government of Canada. *Nous reconnaissons l'appui [financier] du gouvernement du Canada.* We acknowledge the support of the Canada Council for the Arts, which last year invested $153 million to bring the arts to Canadians throughout the country. *Nous remercions le Conseil des arts du Canada de son soutien. L'an dernier, le Conseil a investi 153 millions de dollars pour mettre de l'art dans la vie des Canadiennes et des Canadiens de tout le pays.* We acknowledge the financial support of the Government of Newfoundland and Labrador, Department of Tourism, Culture and Recreation for our publishing activities.

No Punches Pulled

The Premiers Peckford, Wells, and Tobin

A NOTE TO THE READER

The title, *No Punches Pulled*, refers to the forthright manner and style of these three premiers in advancing their ambitions, presenting their policies, and taking on their opponents. But it also describes how I've tried to write about them in a blunt, frank, and open way.

I knew all three during my years in politics, or law practice, or media, and these are my memoirs of their actions and personalities, their triumphs and blunders.

This is not a history. Like my book *The Premiers Joey and Frank*, the facts presented here consist of my personal memories, sometimes helped along by conversations, clippings, and notes, plus the occasional Google. My opinions come entirely from my own musings and are my responsibility alone.

I've endeavoured to be accurate and objective. But you may consider some facts to be wrong or only half-right, and some opinions to be ill-considered or half-baked.

I would encourage you to offer your suggested corrections for the public record and, if you wish, to contact me directly with your views at wrowe@nl.rogers.com.

Bill Rowe
St. John's
Newfoundland and Labrador
August 2016

ONE

My first serious contact with Alfred Brian Peckford concerned a clergyman's wife who'd been caught committing adultery with a high school student and now feared for her life at her husband's hands.

It happened not long after the 1972 election, when Brian got elected as the Progressive Conservative member for Green Bay District, and I was re-elected as a Liberal next door in the district of White Bay South. We both occupied offices on the ninth floor of Confederation Building, where the House of Assembly was then located. He was parliamentary assistant to the new premier, Frank Moores, and I was Opposition House Leader. Our offices were off opposite sides of the House, and there wasn't much interaction between us. We were political opponents, not pals, and we mostly stuck to our own turf.

One morning, I came to my office early to pick up a few things before driving across the Island to my district. I heard the elevator door opening outside and figured it was Brian arriving. He already had a reputation for being an early-morning workhorse. After a minute of silence, I heard a forlorn female voice calling out, "Hello, is anybody here?"

I went out and saw a woman standing by herself in the lobby, in front of the elevators. She looked vaguely familiar, but I was more taken by her confused state as she gazed around in an apparent daze. Thinking she must have gotten off at the wrong floor, I walked toward her to give directions. As soon as she saw me she lurched forward and spoke in a quavering voice: "Mr. Rowe, I need your help." Now I recognized her clearly; she was the wife of a rather dignified, older man, a highly regarded minister of the church, whom I knew fairly well from his home community hundreds of miles from St. John's.

I said good morning and held out my hand, but instead of shaking it, she seized the hand in both of hers like a lifeline. "The commissionaire downstairs told me you were up here," she said. That was in the days before security in Confederation Building became tight. "Please help me," she went on, "I need protection." Her tears started to flow. Her face showed panic and extreme fatigue. I was frankly shocked by her distraught look.

I led her into my office and invited her to sit down. She collapsed, exhausted, in the chair, and before I could ask her what was wrong, she burst out: "I think my husband is going to kill me."

I sputtered, "Kill you? Your husband? You mean . . . ?" I named him, to make sure I wasn't somehow mistaken about who she was.

She said yes and moved her hair from the side of her face to show a bruise below her temple and pushed her sleeve up to expose abrasions on her forearm. "He did that?" I asked, and when she nodded, I continued. "Where is he, now?"

She didn't know for sure. Perhaps he was still back home, or perhaps he had followed her here to St. John's. She had managed to grab the car keys last evening, she said, and then she ran out of the house and drove the family car all night until she reached Confederation Building this morning. But he might have borrowed another car and chased her here. "He's angry enough to," she said. "And he has every right to be."

"Well, no one has a right . . ." I said. "What caused all this?"

Haltingly, she unfolded the indecent drama to me. During her volunteer work around the school associated with her husband's church, she had grown close to a grade eleven student and entered into a sexual relationship with him. Everyone in the school found out about the affair, and soon it became common knowledge in her rural Newfoundland town. When her husband discovered she'd been unfaithful to him in this most humiliating and heartbreaking way, he felt so betrayed and shamed by her disloyalty as a wife, and her terrible breach of faith as a helpmate in his ministry, that he swore to her that he was going to kill her. Judging by his rage and his assault on her before her escape, she believed him. "But I don't even know why I'm running away," she said to me. "All night long driving here, the only thing I could think about was killing myself."

I asked her if the police were involved. Had they questioned her about her relationship with the student? She said no. I told her that, in addition to physical protection, she needed legal advice. The student was probably underage and, in any event, she had no doubt been in a position of trust toward him. Meanwhile, where could she stay where she would be safe?

She had no idea. She had no family here—she was from the mainland—and in the circumstances didn't feel she could appeal to any friends or acquaintances she and her husband had in common. This was at an archaic period in our history, when domestic violence was still largely considered a private matter, which police were reluctant to become involved in. It would be several more years before the Newfoundland Constabulary would receive its first female members, and nearly ten more years before the first shelter for abused women would open. Meanwhile, she was absolutely penniless, having spent on gas the few dollars she'd had on her. She possessed only the clothes on her back. And she had nowhere to go.

Outside, I heard the elevator door opening again. I told her to stay where she was while I checked. I closed the door behind me and geared myself up in case the husband had tracked her here and had found his way up. But it was Brian Peckford heading for his own office. After we exchanged a good morning, I went back to the woman and asked if she had any objection to bringing the premier's parliamentary assistant in on her situation. She said she knew of Mr. Peckford and would welcome his help.

I went over to Brian's office and explained the state of affairs in confidence. Would he be able to help? He could well have shown reluctance to get involved, deploring the woman's atrocious behaviour and dismissing her as the author of her own predicament. But there was none of that. He replied at once that he'd certainly do whatever he could. He was very familiar with government officials and programs in the Department of Welfare from his summer work in the field as a welfare officer. I brought the woman over.

In brief, Brian took the matter in hand and provided her with the advice and directions she needed for protection and assistance and put her in touch with the right officials. With the requests to the officials coming from the premier's parliamentary assistant, I knew there was no doubt she'd be safe and properly looked after while the legal side of her actions was navigated.

I was most impressed by the way Brian reacted to my request and the woman's distress. She constantly stated that her difficulties were all of her own making, but he disregarded that as before and simply acted with care and professionalism to make sure she would be safe, whatever the legal outcome of her tawdry action might turn out to be.

This was a side of Brian Peckford that was not usually evident years later, when, as premier of Newfoundland, he would be dubbed the Bad Boy of Confederation by *Maclean's* magazine: those years when he would become known throughout Canada for his finger-jabbing rants and for skewering local political opponents and prime ministers of Canada alike. But even during those later, so-called "bad boy" times, I found that his character had not changed from my earlier experience with him.

One example—and I know of others—involved a former colleague of mine, a Liberal Member of the House of Assembly who'd been a vocal critic of Peckford as premier. After my colleague left politics, he fell on hard times during one of the recurring recessions. Out of financial desperation he went to Brian, the man he used to criticize and attack all the time, and laid out his dire situation. Brian helped him to obtain contractual employment within his profession, no strings attached, and my colleague later went on to regain professional success under his own steam. He told me about it years afterwards and concluded simply, "Brian Peckford is a good man." There could be worse verdicts from a former political adversary.

I'd first heard of Peckford during the 1969 Liberal leadership campaigns that became a political bloodbath between Joey Smallwood and John Crosbie. I was in my district when I ran into Roger Simmons, who was principal of Grant Collegiate in Springdale and then became superintendent of the Green Bay Integrated School Board. He mentioned to me a teacher at the school who was an up-and-comer in the Green Bay Liberal Association, a supporter of Crosbie, and an excellent organizer: Brian Peckford.

Roger, who would later become an MHA himself, and an MP, and a Minister in Pierre Trudeau's government, was a sharp observer of the political scene. And he was certainly right about Peckford. I was recruiting leadership delegates for Smallwood in White Bay South, and one of the most challenging forces I had to contend with was a drive spearheaded by Peckford, from Green Bay, for Crosbie delegates. The Crosbie forces didn't succeed in electing any delegates from my district, but in some communities it was a close-run thing, owing to Peckford's efforts.

Later, after John Crosbie's defeat in the leadership, and he and Clyde Wells moved (or were moved by Joey) across the House of Assembly to sit as the Liberal Reform Party, I used to see Brian in the corridor on the other side of the House. He'd poke his head in through the door to pass a file or document to Crosbie, who then employed it to fuel his continual attacks on Joey.

Brian never looked very happy performing that activity. I think he was supposed to be Crosbie's executive assistant or research adviser, but his role seemed to be more of step-and-fetch-it or gofer. I got the impression his talents were not being used to their full extent. Or perhaps his dour demeanour had more to do with simply not being very happy with Crosbie himself.

I learned from Brian much later, after we'd both left politics, that John Crosbie had induced him to give up his promising position at Grant Collegiate to work as a leadership campaign organizer, with the assurance that, whether John won or lost, Brian would continue to be his paid political assistant for at least the remainder of the school year. But when Crosbie did lose the leadership and found himself drowning in hundreds of thousands of dollars of campaign debt, he told Brian he wouldn't be kept on in his position.

Shocked at the prospect of unexpectedly finding himself out of a job, and with no income for many months before the start of the next school year, Brian accosted Crosbie in his office and reminded him of his commitment. When Crosbie denied that he had guaranteed him employment after the leadership, contrary to Brian's clear understanding, Brian went aboard him verbally and threatened to go public over John's unreliability, if not his outright deceit. Brian's arguments must have been fairly persuasive, he laughed to me long afterwards, since Crosbie did keep him on.

Peckford's strong fellow-feeling for another human in desperate straits may have come, in part, from what he felt like himself that time when he found himself left in the lurch by Crosbie and had to demean himself with cajolery and threats. I got the feeling, watching Peckford, that he never really liked or respected the man. If any ulterior motive was needed for Premier Peckford's failure to pull his punches in his later attacks on Crosbie, or for his "lack of gratitude" to the federal minister, the bad memory remaining from those early days might be it.

Definitely, he never wanted anyone to consider Crosbie his political mentor or leader. After Crosbie finally abandoned all pretense that he was still a Liberal and announced he was joining the Progressive Conservative Party, bringing many of his followers over with him, Brian didn't appreciate being lumped in with those followers. It riled him whenever he heard statements from people that he had followed

Crosbie to the Tories. He was at pains to correct everybody, including Crosbie himself, by declaring that he had joined the PC Party two weeks before Crosbie did, and he had already announced he was running for the PCs in the next election. The importance of the point—who went over to the Tories first, and exactly how long before the other—was lost on many hearers, but it certainly seemed to mean a lot to Peckford: he was *not* a disciple of Crosbie; he was his own man.

I recall being surprised in the late 1960s, when I was a member of Joey Smallwood's government, on learning that Vic Young and Brian Peckford were first cousins. Brian had a lean and hungry look about him, sort of a rough uncut diamond, compared to the elegant, sophisticated-looking Vic. Brian seemed to parade and flaunt his bayman origins as a badge of honour, whereas Vic looked like a suave St. John's urbanite.

I got to know Vic Young as a young man in his twenties, when I was a minister on the treasury board in the government and Vic was the board's deputy secretary. He skilfully managed the board, consisting of several ministers, with his clear descriptions and analyses of the financial questions that had to be decided. I was not surprised to see him rise soon to deputy minister, special adviser to the premier, and, under cousin Brian Peckford, the chairman and CEO of Newfoundland and Labrador Hydro.

Later he would become chairman and CEO of Fishery Products International and chairman of the Royal Commission on Newfoundland and Labrador's Place in Canada, as well as a director of many local and national blue-chip corporations. I mention him here at some length because some armchair analysts regarded Vic and his family as a key to Brian's palpable ambition.

Vic was a son of Ross Young, who was well known in government circles before he died in 1970, in his sixties. I used to see him a fair amount around Confederation Building, and I heard a lot about him from Joey, and others, as a member of the Newfoundland Fisheries Development Authority. He'd been appointed by Joey years before at a salary which was high enough, I recall hearing, to astonish everyone around the cabinet table.

That affluence contrasted markedly with Peckford's outward appearance of financial modesty. Of the four sons I knew in the family produced by Ross, two became well-known medical specialists, Dr. Robert Young and Dr. Graham Young. And the other was brother Howie, who, through his Dale Carnegie course, transformed John Crosbie in the late 1960s from a political sow's ear into something of a silk purse.

Even ardent Crosbie supporters, including Peckford at the time, had been dumbfounded, leading up to the leadership convention, at how awful John Crosbie was as a speaker. On top of his horrible, boring monotone, he also closed his eyes as he droned on in front of his listeners. Howie Young succeeded in making him open his eyes, at least some of the time, and helped turn his hidden, hitherto private sense of humour into a life-long public asset, prodding him from being a shy, halting, mind-numbing speaker to becoming one renowned throughout Canada for his jests and wit. I remember Crosbie extolling Ross Young in the House of Assembly at the time of his death. And he dwelt on the merits of his four sons, as well he might: one of them had probably saved his long-term political bacon.

When Brian Peckford claimed to pride himself on his rural, outport background, teaching in Green Bay and living and serving as a welfare officer during summers in many rural communities, some people thought he was being a touch defensive, that he was projecting an almost pugnacious front: "I'm just as good as you (if not a damn sight better)!"

Some observers of a successful person's career always need to perceive some profound psychological reason behind his or her ambition. One amateur psychologist I know has seen a remarkable similarity between Brian Peckford's supposed modest status compared to his cousins, and that of Danny Williams in relation to his cousins. Both men, he opined, were motivated by the perceived superior station of these relatives to strive mightily, to succeed, and to outdo their hoity-toity cousins.

As I said in my book *Danny Williams: The War with Ottawa*, when I'd heard that analysis regarding Williams, I considered it nonsense. I have the same reaction about Peckford. I believe that, for the most part, a person either "has it" to excel or not. And knowing both these guys, I think they had it. Whoever the hell their cousins might be, they had within themselves the talent and energy and vision and sense of timing—the royal jelly—to propel them to success.

TWO

In the provincial election of 1972, when Peckford became the candidate for the Progressive Conservative Party in Green Bay District, the PCs under Premier Frank Moores won thirty-three seats and the Liberals under Ed Roberts salvaged nine. But despite this overwhelming victory for the PCs provincially, Peckford barely got himself elected. He received just over fifty-one per cent of the votes to nearly forty-nine per cent for veteran Liberal Harold Starkes. But Peckford's election there was in fact a political marvel.

Historically, Green Bay had always been one of the most Liberal districts in Newfoundland and Labrador. It was so Liberal that it had been one of only two districts to elect Liberal members in a Tory landslide election early in the 1930s. The once formidable Liberal leader Sir Richard Squires himself even lost his own seat in that election. So, by rights, Green Bay District in the 1972 election should have stayed Liberal with the other nine hardcore Liberal seats. But Peckford, as the Tory candidate, was able to squeeze out his improbable victory there.

And his effective style as a constituency politician would become even more evident three and a half years later, in the election of 1975. That time, despite the fact that the number of districts in the province had been increased from forty-two to fifty-one, Moores's PCs dropped from thirty-three to thirty and the combined Liberal and Liberal Reform and independent vote increased the number of opposition members elected to twenty-one. But Peckford bucked the overall loss of popularity of the PC Party and drove his personal majority in Green Bay up to more than seventy per cent of the vote.

Meanwhile, after his first election in 1972, Peckford started to make his mark on the House of Assembly. I didn't find him to be all "piss and wind," as Frank Moores would describe him to me once outside the House, but he did make himself felt as a presence from the beginning. He might not have always been among the most dignified of statesmen. He had a boisterous, slap-your-thigh laugh described by one of my colleagues in the Opposition as a hillbilly honk.

And gradually, when he was parliamentary assistant to Premier Frank Moores in 1973, and then as minister of Municipal Affairs and Housing, his speaking style in the House became more and more aggressive. That department was too dull to lend itself to many glamorous pronouncements or attention-grabbing antics, but then John Crosbie provided Brian with a better opportunity.

Crosbie was minister of the prestigious Mines and Energy department, but he finally got sick and tired of playing second fiddle to Premier Moores while having to hold his nose over Frankie Baby's well-known hedonistic lifestyle. So, Crosbie bailed out of provincial politics to seek the federal seat of St. John's West. Frank cried crocodile tears over John's departure—in public. In private, he did his happy dance: no longer would he have to endure Crosbie's dirty looks or jibes at his boozing, partying, hunting, holidaying, womanizing lifestyle.

The premier appointed Peckford to the Mines and Energy portfolio in the fall of 1976, but if Frank thought John Crosbie was being swapped for someone more manageable, he was miserably mistaken. Before long, especially when he was in his cups, people heard him muttering in good-natured despair about Brian as he used to do about John. One day, when I happened to encounter Frank in a corridor and mentioned something Brian had said, Frank laughed, "What's Peckie doing in the

PC Party, anyway? The man is an NDPer." And one afternoon, when I met him coming down the steps of Confederation Building, somewhat oiled, Frank inflated his description of Brian to "out and out fucking commie."

Whatever Peckford's core political philosophy might have been, he left no doubts from the start that he came into politics determined to seize back, from any other government or organization that controlled them, the management of our main resources and a fairer share of their revenues. These resources were the fishery, hydroelectric development, and offshore oil. Their proper management in our own best interests, he pronounced, would raise Newfoundland and Labrador's tiny population from the economic bottom of Canada right up to the top. He was not alone in these views; many of us in politics held them. But he was in a position—had put himself in a position—to try to act on them.

With John Crosbie off the provincial scene and no longer hogging the show as de facto premier, Peckford had a relatively free field of activity as minister of Mines and Energy. No one else in the cabinet, least of all Moores, was prepared to be as audacious, tireless, and dogged in his objectives as Peckford became. This was before oil was actually found at the Hibernia field on the Grand Banks. That discovery wouldn't happen for another three years, but sensing, from all the positive indications and data, the bonanza that lurked out there, he immediately joined battle with the Trudeau government to try to gain provincial government control over oil developments under the sea. And he took on the big oil corporations.

Peckford dragged the oil companies that were exploring and drilling on Newfoundland's continental shelf into the quagmire of "provincial management." He depicted, in gut-wrenching speeches and statements, the historic exploitation of the province's minerals and hydro power by outside forces. He was going to impose rules on the oil companies that would heighten our benefits and diminish the negative impact of social and environmental disruption.

Within a year after becoming minister of Mines and Energy, Peckford put out a wide-ranging package of protocols and procedures governing offshore explorations. They were designed to make sure, he said, that Newfoundland and Labrador would chiefly profit from the resource. In retrospect, it was pretty tame stuff. Included, for example, was a term that the oil companies would be made responsible for specified research and for spending money on training local people to work in the industry, failing which they'd be forced to pay for the cost of these items directly to the government. What could be more reasonable than that?

Yet, at any hint of meddling in their grab-all out there, the multinational petroleum corporations went bonkers: wasn't this capitalist North America? What the hell was this province doing, acting like those socialists over in northern Europe? Before this they must have considered Newfoundland to be a third-world county like, say, Nigeria, because they were clearly not accustomed to such impertinent behaviour. They blustered and then, stupidly, they tried to bully this upstart provincial minister and his colleagues into knuckling under by suspending offshore drilling.

The next year, though, they came to their senses. On top of realizing that this pit bull they were facing here was different from the usual lapdogs they routinely brought to heel elsewhere, they also grasped that the slanging match going on between the feds and the province over ownership and control was not even their fight. Although the battle seemed to position the companies uncomfortably between the two governments, it was in fact largely irrelevant to their own selfish interests. Whatever the outcome of the St. John's–Ottawa war—and they suspected strongly that the mighty (and sensible) federal government would win, anyway—the oil consortium's "fair" share of the offshore booty was sure to be secure.

Therefore, after they received from the government some face-saving tweaking in the regulations, the oil corporations agreed to the Newfoundland terms, and they resumed their drilling. But to the public in Newfoundland, the eyeball-to-eyeball confrontation between

Peckford and the giant multinationals had ended with the big guys blinking first and bowing to the provincial government's demands. Brian Peckford became a household name and extremely popular in the province.

His ongoing vociferous battle with the Trudeau Liberals in Ottawa over the actual ownership of the offshore petroleum resources added to his lustre. He made precisely zero progress against the federal Liberal government, but Peckford's three years as the "fighting Newfoundlander," heading the department of Mines and Energy, gave him the platform from which to launch his run for the leadership of the PC Party and the premiership.

Before that happened, though, Peckford often had to battle his own boss. Premier Moores, together with Wally Reid, the head of Newfoundland Hydro, met secretly for months with Quebec premier René Lévesque over a scheme to develop power on the Lower Churchill Falls. Until Moores called a big news conference in St. John's for March 1978 with Lévesque to be present, Peckford, the minister of Mines and Energy, apparently knew nothing about it. When he finally learned of the deal in the making, Peckford's reaction was outrage. Or, as one of his colleagues told me, "Brian went completely apeshit."

Among the proposed terms that appalled him was Newfoundland and Labrador's agreement to never try again to reopen the Upper Churchill contract. Brian barged into Moores's office and told him that, if he went ahead with his news conference, he would follow right afterwards with his own news conference, announcing his resignation from the cabinet and saying why. He added that most if not all of the cabinet would resign with him.

Perhaps the most unnerving aspect of this to Moores was how emotional Peckford became over the issue. He was shunted out of Moores's office temporarily and into the office of the premier's adviser, Peckford's cousin, Vic Young. There Peckford dissolved into tears of frustration, exasperation, and a sense of betrayal. The matter had obviously cut him to the core.

The drama ended when Moores backed down and Lévesque went home. Their Lower Churchill announcement was dropped into a garbage can.

Two things about that abortive deal have struck observers.

One, Moores had no guts when it came to holding firm on a difficult issue. His own supporters called him a coward. And he himself would come to see his cave-in to Peckford as a big mistake. There was no way, he thought later, that other ministers would have followed Peckford out of cabinet.

His timidity also extended, though he never acknowledged it, to a fear of involving the intelligent, independent thinkers in his cabinet in the schemes he was contriving. What world could he have been living in, if it apparently never occurred to him that Peckford, the minister directly concerned, would object strenuously to an important deal sprung on him at the last minute?

Two, Peckford's highly principled—perhaps too-principled—stand on the Upper Churchill came out. Some would consider it more like tunnel vision if he thought that prohibiting Newfoundland and Labrador from trying to open the Upper Churchill deal was giving away anything or would ever deprive this province of anything essential. Because, as subsequent events showed, no Supreme Court of Canada was ever going to cancel a contract freely entered into with Quebec, extolled by everybody at the time, involving a multi-billion dollar essential utility and affecting multitudes of interested parties and their investments.

I talked to a close representative of the Quebec Government later on the subject, and he was sure that the only reason Lévesque wanted the clause in the deal with Moores was for pure public relations at home and abroad: he needed everyone to shut up about trying to reopen the Upper Churchill deal, because the attempts only added to international uncertainty about the economy of Quebec under his separatist government.

As a result of that and other failures to deal successfully with Quebec, the Lower Churchill would not get going until Premier Danny Williams, more than thirty years later, would revive the old concept of the "Anglo-Saxon Route," without calling it that, to bring Muskrat Falls power across the Strait of Belle Isle to the Island of Newfoundland and thence across the Cabot Strait to Nova Scotia. We'll see how that works, scoff modern skeptics.

Some analysts continue to speculate that we would have been much further ahead by now if the deal put together by Moores and Lévesque involving Quebec, or something similar to it, had gone through at the time.

Back in the fall of 1977, after I'd been elected leader of the provincial Liberal Party and Opposition Leader, my colleagues and I in the House attacked Frank Moores and a couple of his more egregious cronies without mercy for months. We were substantially aided in this by the government sleaze and venality recounted in my book *The Premiers Joey and Frank*.

By the beginning of 1979, Frank Moores was fed up with being the target of this scandal-based fusillade of criticism. On January 19, he made a province-wide broadcast to confirm what everyone was speculating: he was getting out. He set a PC leadership convention for March 17, 1979, and proclaimed that he would be absolutely neutral and hands-off in the race.

The media surmised that Peckford's high profile from the offshore oil challenges had made him the one to beat, and many in the PC Party I talked to touted him as a good bet to take over. Some caucus heavyweights, after assuring themselves that Peckford was going to be the opposite of Moores in his methods (i.e. honest), joined his camp. But not everyone agreed he was the best for the job: some nine other worthies, most of them current or former colleagues of Peckford in cabinet, declared their candidacy.

Although by convention day he had attracted the support of the most caucus and cabinet members, it was by no means a cakewalk. Not only were some of the other candidates popular and reputable stalwarts in their own right, but Frank Moores had become a problem. I was hearing from infuriated Peckford-ites that Frank had reneged on his promise to remain neutral and was actively working behind the scenes for his good buddy Bill Doody.

MP John Crosbie had given private assurances of his support to Peckford, but publicly he was very tardy coming on side. Someone close to Crosbie told me he suspected John was hanging back trying to decide if he would run for leader himself. That would certainly have been in keeping with his well-known Julius Caesar syndrome, that it was better to be top man in a village than second man in Rome.

Peckford's own people figured Crosbie was jealous and couldn't stand the thought of Brian becoming premier instead of himself. This characteristic of Crosbie, as seen by Peckford to be somewhat less than dependable in his dealings with him—it was at least the second time now since the 1969 Liberal leadership—no doubt affected their future relationship for the worse.

On the first ballot at the PC leadership convention, Peckford received 200 votes, a shortfall of well over 100 votes from the number he needed to win. Bill Doody got 157, Leo Barry eighty-seven, Walter Carter eighty-four, Jim Morgan fifty-six, Ed Maynard twenty-six, Tom Hickey twenty-four, Ralph Trask two, Kenneth Prowse zero, and Dorothy Wyatt zero. People seemed surprised that St. John's mayor Wyatt didn't receive one single vote. She wasn't a voting delegate herself, but her own father was, and he didn't vote for her. She remained unperturbed. That was okay, she said, she wasn't in it to win but just to shake things up. One of her councillors, who was always in a racket with her at council meetings, said to me, "Dotty just wanted to be a shit disturber? Who knew?"

Although Peckford's forceful, hard-hitting methods as minister of Mines and Energy, in constant battle with oil conglomerates and Ottawa, had made him the darling of the rank and file in the provincial party, and of many in his caucus, it still took three ballots for him to win the leadership. Apparently, even back then, a substantial minority remained less than enchanted by his somewhat abrasive public personality.

When he did finally triumph, he would become, at thirty-six, one of Newfoundland's youngest premiers. I believe that only Philip Francis Little, who'd become colonial Newfoundland's first premier 124 years before, was younger. It was a magnificent achievement, just seven years after he was first elected, for the young Brian Peckford from South Brook, Green Bay.

THREE

Peckford's premiership began with a spate of good luck. The provincial Liberal caucus, of which I was leader, and which had been riding high during the last years of Frank Moores, was now experiencing dissension and disarray. (I recounted the background of this in *The Premiers Joey and Frank*.) However, as soon as Peckford became premier on March 26, I threw down the gauntlet, in a display of bravado, urging him to call an election right away. He didn't bite.

Instead, he announced he would hold off until he'd brought down a budget and reformed the rules of the House of Assembly. I knew he was only biding his time: in a few weeks he'd know the outcome of the federal election recently called by Pierre Trudeau for late May. Meanwhile, to clear up the discord in my own party, I arranged for a Liberal leadership convention to be held on July 6–7 and announced I'd be running.

The federal election yielded the result Peckford was waiting for and threw our provincial Liberal Party into a tizzy. On May 22, 1979, Joe Clark led the PC Party to victory over Trudeau's Liberals, winning enough seats to form a minority government of 136 seats, to Trudeau's 114. Three days later, on May 25, trumpeting the good news that, with the federal wing of his own party in power in Ottawa he'd be able to secure a good deal for the province regarding the offshore oil and other resources, Peckford pounced. He advised Lieutenant-Governor Gordon Winter to dissolve the legislature and hold a provincial election on June 18.

I'd discovered that a lot had changed in a few months. Before Frank Moores had announced that he was resigning earlier in the year, public opinion polls showed our provincial Liberal Party way out ahead of the Progressive Conservative Party. Then I asked a pollster to do a quick survey of Peckford's popularity soon after his leadership victory. I don't recall the numbers now, but I remember our pollster's conclusion: "They seem to really like this guy."

My own gut feeling was that the effect of a feisty new PC leader, plus the federal PC victory, on top of the dissension and discord in my own caucus, made a victory by the provincial PCs highly likely. Some Liberals tried to paint Peckford as dishonourable for calling an election in the middle of our Liberal Party's leadership campaign. But I didn't have the impression the argument cut much ice with the electorate.

On my birthday, June 4, Joe Clark's new federal PC government was sworn in with two Newfoundlanders in the cabinet: John Crosbie in the top post of Finance minister, and Jim McGrath as minister of the vital portfolio of Fisheries. Tory euphoria dubbed them "the fish and chips boys." Having more than one minister from this province in the federal cabinet was unprecedented. Nearly every day, it seemed, Peckford had something else positive going for him.

Don Jamieson, who'd been the powerful Liberal minister from this province in the Trudeau government, was now out of his cabinet job. Public speculation had already started on whether the political heavyweight, who'd hobnobbed as minister with the high and mighty in countries all over the world, might be available to become leader of the provincial Liberal Party.

Prominent local Liberal Len Stirling, former president of the party, concocted a slogan, "Bring Don Jamieson home for good!" It got considerable play on the talk shows, and the reaction seemed affirmative. Meanwhile, feeling keenly that, overzealous to do the right thing, I had mishandled a matter as leader, I called Jamieson in Ottawa and told him that, in the best interests of the party, I would consider vacating the leadership if he would accept the position. He pretended to be surprised and momentarily balked, but I already knew from his bagman that he couldn't believe his good luck at the prospect of becoming premier, just two weeks after being forced to step down as a federal minister.

With the blessing of most of the executive board of the party, I invited him to take the leadership. He accepted it in words that displayed no doubt he would win the election. He told the national media that he wasn't taking anything for granted, but private polls were showing that he'd easily be able to carry the province as Liberal leader. And every thoughtful, long-time Liberal I talked to, except for one, was convinced the great Don Jamieson would soon be our new Liberal premier. So prevalent was the feeling that one prominent Liberal, a good friend and supporter of mine, said bitterly even as he tried to dissuade me on principle from resigning, "After all our hard work, the premiership just falls into that blowhard's lap."

Joan Cook, a long-time Liberal activist, and later to be appointed senator by Prime Minister Jean Chrétien, told me I should not resign. She was the only person I talked to outside of family who thought I'd do better in the election than Jamieson. Everyone else rolled their eyes at her: no one could do better than our Don. One Liberal MHA got a good laugh when he said to our caucus that, after the announcement of Jamieson as new leader, Peckford would be asking the lieutenant-governor to please call off the election because he'd made a big blooper. Many people congratulated me for my "courageous" action in sacrificing myself for the success of the party.

After broadcasting to the media that there had been an "enormous draft movement" to make him leader, Jamieson arrived at St. John's Airport, where Liberals were gathered to greet him, and he came in surrounded by applause and cheers, with his extraordinary, pipe-organ voice blaring. Then the organizers led him out to a giant motorcade, probably the biggest political convoy of vehicles the city had ever seen.

Some thought Don's arrival was a victorious triumph; others thought it was way over the top. Even this early in the election campaign, some were expressing doubts. One prominent Liberal candidate shook his head and muttered to me, "He thinks he's the Ayatollah . . ." a reference to Khomeini's triumphant return from exile earlier that same year to take over as Supreme Leader of Iran.

After I went home that day, I received a pleasant and greatly appreciated visit. The doorbell rang and standing there were Rex Murphy and a friend from Placentia, dropping in on a purely private basis. We sat in the living room for an hour talking events over. It was a thoughtful act by Rex, done solely to provide companionship during what he knew was a somewhat difficult period for me. I have never forgotten how touched I was by Rex's generous and considerate gesture. Then I was off to Twillingate District to campaign for re-election.

As the canvassing went on, I was picking up some negative reaction to Len Stirling's mantra, "Bring Don Jamieson home for good." One man on a wharf on New World Island, a good Liberal supporter with a mind of his own, said, "Who gives a sweet shit if Don comes home for good? Is that what Jamieson thinks this election is all about—where he's going to live? Honest to God, no wonder Peckford is starting to wipe the floor with him." The man was zeroing in on the serious weakness in our election strategy: in the eyes of the electorate, our party and leader didn't stand for a damn thing, except for some weird concept of egotistical self-importance.

The contrast with Peckford was painful. The new premier knew exactly what he stood for and proclaimed it far and wide. John Laschinger was a great admirer of that quality. He'd been for decades one of the most highly regarded campaign organizers and managers in Canada. He'd organized Peckford's leadership campaign and was now managing his general election campaign. Years later I would have Laschinger on the air as a guest of my *Open Line* show to talk about a book he'd just written with Geoffrey Stevens called *Leaders and Lesser Mortals: Backroom Politics in Canada*. He told listeners that, for success, a candidate has to know and state clearly his or her reasons for wanting to become a political leader.

When he'd first met Peckford before his leadership campaign, he said, and asked him why he wanted that challenging job, Brian had a lucid and rational response. He covered, coherently, his position on energy, both hydro and offshore, and on the fishery, social programs, and cultural needs, and how they all wove together. In his book, Laschinger stated, "It was an impressive, impromptu performance by a raw, untutored young politician who in those days was mainly known for his fiery temper and burning ambition."

Peckford's impressive performance on where he stood, including distancing himself from his fellow Tory Frank Moores, was manifest in this 1979 provincial election. Jamieson's greatest asset was his bullhorn voice. Some detractors had even started to call him, as the new sound devices were becoming all the rage, "the human boom box" and "the ghetto blaster with feet." But his magnificent pipes gave out on him from all the roaring halfway through the campaign.

I watched him on television struggling his way through the leaders' debate. He spoke abstract generalities in barely audible whispers, while Peckford sounded knowledgeable and articulate and, unlike Jamieson, wholly in touch with the local scene. Laschinger would tell me on the air later that they had to tone down Peckford's normally histrionic speechmaking gestures for the debate on television by dressing him in a kind of straitjacket: they stuck him a suit several sizes too small in which he could hardly move, thus giving him more of the dignified, calmer posture of a statesman. Cute, but I doubted that it made much difference to the outcome.

Despite my own growing misgivings over the likely election results, I didn't believe what Peckford's top local organizer told me when I ran into him downtown by chance on a mid-campaign visit home to St. John's: he said their polls were predicting a big Tory victory and showed that I would have done better in the election than Jamieson. I replied that I found that information, especially coming from the PCs, hard to believe, because I'd heard that Jamieson's presence as Liberal leader was so powerful it had even scared some good PC candidates out of the race. One heavyweight non-candidate I mentioned was Corner Brook lawyer Tom Marshall.

But the PC organizer told me that his law partner, Clyde Wells, who was organizing and campaigning for Jamieson's election, had talked Marshall out of running by convincing the future cabinet minister, and interim premier, that their law firm had to come first.

As the election night vote count rolled in, I have to say that, in spite of the mounting doubts I'd been having, I was genuinely surprised at the results. And so was every Liberal candidate I talked to in person or by phone. Peckford gained fifty per cent of the popular vote and won a large majority government, winning thirty-three of the fifty-two districts. Thanks to the kindness of the people of Twillingate District, I was re-elected in my own seat, with an increased majority.

I felt sorry for poor Don. He and his followers may have connived at his return, but I had in fact eased his way by inviting him back. And here he was now, suffering the heartbreak of having lost two general elections in a row, federal and provincial, in the space of a few weeks.

He tried to keep a stiff upper lip, and he did become Leader of the Opposition in the House of Assembly for a while, but the good was gone out of him. And his situation only got worse for him. In just a few months, Finance Minister John Crosbie's federal budget, despite being praised by business writers and economists across Canada, caused a vote of no confidence in Joe Clark's government. The PCs were defeated in the House, and the ensuing election knocked them out of power early in 1980. The Liberals were back in. If only he'd stayed in Ottawa, Jamieson had to be brooding and fretting, he'd be riding high again now as a top minister in Trudeau's new government.

Short and fleeting as Joe Clark's administration was, two of Peckford's former colleagues were able to hit the jackpot. John Crosbie saw to it that the prime minister appointed Alex Hickman as Chief Justice of the Supreme Court of Newfoundland trial division, and Bill Doody to a seat in the Senate of Canada.

As soon as he'd been appointed premier, and even more so after his election, Brian Peckford made known his disgust with Frank Moores's practices. Some top supporters of his leadership also continued to push him to alienate himself unmistakably from Frank and his disreputable methods. Not that Brian needed the encouragement: soon after the election, he announced a review of any deals Frank had made during his declining days and compared him to Joey Smallwood in allowing himself to get sucked in by deal makers. (As we shall see, less than ten years later a similar accusation would be flung in Peckford's face.)

Then Moores found himself charged in court for building an illegal fishing lodge in Labrador, but he managed to get himself off that hook on a legal technicality. And the Public Accounts Committee of the House, on which Peckford had a majority of PC members, dragged Frank before it over allegations he'd used public money for party political polls. Frank could only bluster that the man he'd mentored and, in large measure, made politically successful, was resorting to "McCarthy-like" tactics. He stood astonished at Peckford's ingratitude.

Some people did see in these actions a mean and nasty streak in Peckford and a tendency to hoard up petty resentments. Unruffled, Peckford even expressed negative thoughts over Frank's use of Mount Scio House as the premier's official residence. (Before long, though, as if everything stupid in Newfoundland's political history is fated to repeat itself over and over, Peckford himself was being lambasted for converting the same house, at serious public expense, into his own official residence.)

Some Tories would consider it one of his petty resentments years later, when Frank Moores died in July 2005, that Brian Peckford did not attend his St. John's funeral. Hadn't he gone to the funeral service of his archrival, Joey Smallwood, over ten years before? Peckford did issue a news release on Frank's death, though, generously concentrating on his reforms after Joey Smallwood's reign. In it he even graciously held back the reality that some of Frank's ministers, like Peckford himself, were the ones who had to bring about the reforms, because Frank was really so uninvolved that he delegated everything to them.

Some Liberals would also consider it a petty resentment when Peckford allegedly refused former premier Smallwood any co-operation in getting the ownership of his Roaches Line ranch house back for him. Apparently, when he was premier, Joey had gone into a panic that the taxman was going to come after him for the elaborate house. His fear was perhaps realistic, in that it had been constructed from unbilled labour and materials donated by local companies.

To avoid the income tax morass, Joey donated the house to his dearly loved people of Newfoundland as some sort of a heritage structure, keeping only a life interest for himself and his wife, Clara. Later, after he'd retired from politics, Joey had second thoughts, and perhaps better tax advice, and wanted his heritage house back from the beloved people. Peckford said no—petulantly, some Smallwood-ites asserted. And it would be one of our later Liberal premiers, Wells or Tobin, evidently, who would say yes.

No mistake, Peckford certainly started out lily-white as new premier and determined to stick to his stated campaign positions against patronage. John Laschinger said that Norman Atkins, the president of the Toronto agency Camp Associates, which had worked on Peckford's leadership and election campaigns, thought he had the contract for the province's tourism advertising in the bag when Peckford was elected. But the new premier told him no. He was resolutely moving away, he said, from the old Frank Moores and Joey Smallwood ways. The Toronto agency wasn't even permitted to submit bids. Peckford was restricting the work solely to local firms. When the mainland operatives protested, Peckford asked them, with a surprised air, if they thought he was only joking when he'd promised the electorate he was going to do what he now in fact did. One of Brian's aides told me they looked at each other, flabbergasted, and blurted, "Joking? Well, yeah!"

This attitude was not something new for Peckford. He has recounted his dismay that, when he was one of Moores's ministers, the premier was always up to unethical, bordering on illegal shenanigans. One time Brian got wind of a behind-the-scenes scheme to sell the closed-down linerboard mill in Stephenville for peanuts to Consolidated Bathurst, owned by Paul Desmarais. Peckford barged into the premier's dining room, where the deal was being cooked up, and made it clear he would not support a rigged bid. The mill must go to the true best bidder. That was evidently accomplished later, when it was sold to Abitibi Price.

In addition to bringing his attitude against patronage into the beginnings of his premiership, Peckford also imported, and intensified, his earlier tendency to fed-bashing, and expanded it to include his own Tory partisans. That was unusual, if not unique, in federal-provincial politics, but the premier's lack of reluctance to nail even PC prime ministers and cabinet ministers was to become a hallmark of his career.

After Joe Clark's government came crashing down over Crosbie's budget, Clark dropped in on this province to campaign in the resulting 1980 federal election. He assured Peckford orally, as prime minister, that the federal government would agree to make Newfoundland and Labrador the owner of the offshore oil recently discovered at Hibernia. The resource would be treated the same as if it came under provincial jurisdiction on land. John Crosbie had engineered this great coup, which was the opposite of the Trudeau Liberals' hard-nosed stance of insisting on federal ownership and control.

Yet Peckford proclaimed publicly that he wasn't satisfied with Clark's oral commitment on the offshore oil ownership, and he insisted that the prime minister confirm his assurance in writing. Peckford probably felt that Clark owed him that much. After all, he had supported Clark's winning leadership bid in the 1976 convention, when other heavyweights from Newfoundland—Moores and Crosbie, for example—had supported rival candidates. But Crosbie was outraged now at Peckford's demand to Clark: he thought it was tantamount to calling his own federal Progressive Conservative leader and prime minister a liar who could not be trusted to live up to his word.

I figured at the time, though, that Peckford had merely sniffed the political breeze and concluded that Clark was probably going to lose the election. In that event, perhaps any commitment would be useless, but at least a prime ministerial undertaking in writing might hold more water with a new administration as an official government document.

Whatever he believed about the election result, Peckford was unapologetic about his offshore demands. Because next, he demanded as well, in the middle of the campaign, that Clark assure the province that the northern cod could be taken by Newfoundlanders and Labradorians only. Moreover, no outside factory freezer trawlers could be used, and only wet-fish trawlers would be permitted, which would require the harvest to be brought to the shores of the province to be processed, rather than being processed on board. When fellow Newfoundlander Jim McGrath, Canada's Fisheries minister, said he would consult with Peckford on those issues, the premier threw McGrath's offer back in his face. "He can consult all he likes," he snarled. "That's not good enough."

John Crosbie said publicly later, and privately at the time, that he was appalled at the way Peckford bit the hand that fed him during the election campaign, causing a war between two wings of the same party.

At least Peckford didn't discriminate in his attacks. He was an equal opportunities fed-basher, and he battled the Liberal government in identical fashion. He waged holy war against Trudeau regarding jurisdiction over offshore resources and the prime minister's failure to help Newfoundland and Labrador to rectify its contract with Quebec on the Upper Churchill hydro project. Not only did Trudeau fail to help, his government sided with Quebec when Peckford went to court to try to improve Newfoundland's position on the Churchill Falls deal.

In return, despite all the Alberta bumper stickers declaring, "Let the Eastern bastards freeze in the dark," Peckford, the most eastern premier of all, supported Alberta against Ottawa in Trudeau and Marc Lalonde's national energy program.

FOUR

Meanwhile, how effective Don Jamieson was being in his new job as Opposition Leader in the House of Assembly can be gleaned from Peckford's praise of him for the accommodating and obliging manner in which he supported Peckford's government agenda. He called Jamieson the best Leader of the Opposition in the history of the province, because he was non-confrontational and always looked for ways to co-operate with the government.

This was a little like the fox praising the chickens for putting up no opposition during his visits to their coop. Some of us in the Liberal caucus could not believe our ears. Everything fell into place when Don told us that he prided himself on never having knowingly made an enemy in his life. Some of us liked better the attitudes of the great leaders, Franklin D. Roosevelt, who said, "I ask you to judge me by the enemies I have made," and Winston Churchill: "You have enemies? Good. That means you've stood up for something, sometime in your life."

It's interesting to analyze Peckford's own actions in the light of Roosevelt and Churchill's criteria. He often took on frontally, and criticized publicly, other politicians of all stripes, like Joey Smallwood, John Crosbie, Frank Moores, Leo Barry, Clyde Wells, Richard Cashin, Brian

Tobin, Pierre Trudeau, Joe Clark, and even the leader he admired most, fellow PC Brian Mulroney, not hesitating to make enemies of them if he thought it necessary. Yet he got along famously with his actual official opposition, Liberal Don Jamieson. There may be a good insight there into the character and makeup of both men.

It was only much later that we got a hint from Peckford about why Opposition Leader Jamieson was so nice to the premier on the opposite side of the House. Peckford, when he'd been minister with Frank Moores, had already observed the effect on federal Liberal minister Jamieson, when the Tory premier provided him with helicopters and cars with drivers to transport Jamieson to his country estate in Swift Current, 100 miles away from St. John's. Evidently, a lot of federal largesse came back in return for the province whose leader had provided such personal goodwill.

Peckford recounts in his memoirs that in order to be friendly and get the co-operation of Opposition Leader Jamieson on a matter during an upcoming meeting in the premier's office, Peckford found out what his favourite Scotch was—a brand so superior, apparently, it was not available in this province—and produced it when he came visiting. And sure enough, according to Brian, Don was duly impressed. In any event, he thereafter displayed the obliging nature he was famous for.

Unfortunately for Peckford, Jamieson didn't last long. He soon resigned as Opposition Leader, and a couple of years later Trudeau appointed him to one of the plum diplomatic jobs he was made for, High Commissioner to the Court of St. James in London. I had the pleasure of being at Don's going-away party. We all had fun. I sought to add to it by insisting that he try on my sealskin parka in the hope that he could wear it in London and cause some excitement. Over there, protesters were lying in the streets dressed up in seal costumes pretending they were being brutally clubbed to death by barbarous Canadians. Regrettably, the fit was too tight, and he couldn't take it with him.

Also at the party, Jamieson had his host set up rows of chairs for his audience to sit in, with one chair in front, facing them. This chair Jamieson sat in and commenced to tell "jokes" and story after story to his captive listeners. He was really good at old-time storytelling. But one in the group groaned, got to his feet, and started to wander around, prompting Jamieson to order him amiably, "Sit down, Jim." Think what you like about Don's stories, "Jim" said to me later, but you could only admire Don's healthy ego.

Over in London during his two years at Canada House, Queen Elizabeth herself was reportedly entranced by his unparalleled store of hokey anecdotes. I never heard if he instructed Her Majesty, while on one of her walkabouts, to sit down and listen.

The brash, aggressive techniques regarding Ottawa of Newfoundland's third premier after Confederation could not have contrasted more with the easygoing, self-serving mode of operation of his predecessor, Frank Moores. Even Joey Smallwood, who had never hesitated to attack his political enemies up there, like Prime Minister John Diefenbaker and Newfoundland's Tory minister, Billy Browne, always took a conciliatory approach in public to his own federal Liberal Party.

Once, when he and the rest of his cabinet were completely frustrated with the federal Liberal government over an issue and some of us were urging him to "take the pricks on publicly," he mused to us, "Say you yield to the satisfaction of declaring war on your own party up in Ottawa. All right, then what? Answer: then nothing. That is the end. You have shot your bolt. You can only declare war on your friends once. After that, they are no longer your friends, and for the sake of that one moment of satisfaction, you're hamstrung forever regarding all further requests and talks." That never seemed to be Peckford's view.

As premier, Peckford allowed his obsession with gaining greater control and money from our prime resources, the fishery, hydroelectric developments, and the oil offshore, to dominate his agenda. That was entirely understandable. We possessed one of the greatest sources of protein in the world in the waters off our coasts and a world-class hydro project and further potential on the Churchill River, and many international economists were touting us as the next Kuwait in future petroleum developments. Hence, it simply boggled Brian's mind that Newfoundland and Labrador could still rank at the bottom, economically and financially, of Canada's provinces.

His stated and reiterated aim, over and over, was to regain some provincial control and management over these resources and end our have-not status. I recall that, during one of our many conversations on *Open Line*, we both imagined how pleasant it would be to turn on the national news some night and, just for once, hear a news story about our province that did not tack on somewhere in the piece the perennial label, "Newfoundland, *Canada's poorest province*."

Brian Peckford liked to participate in *Open Line* to get his ideas across. In the middle of labour disputes between the government and the public service unions, for example, the premier and the union heads would call up and make their points on the air, one after the other, arguing back and forth. They usually said that they wouldn't negotiate over the public airwaves, but of course that was exactly what they were doing.

Sometimes a difficulty between the parties would be overcome, or the basis of a new collective agreement arrived at, as a result of what was discussed by the principals on the show. Cartoons even appeared in newspapers where one or other of the parties would be depicted as advising that the labour dispute be sent to mediation . . . on *Open Line*!

When I first joined *Open Line* on VOCM as co-host with Carl Sterrett in the early 1980s, Brian Peckford told me during a chat at some function that he wouldn't have joined the show as a *co-host*, as I had done, but only as sole host, or not at all. I replied that my role suited me at the time.

I had visited VOCM Radio for an interview in 1983 when my first novel, *Clapp's Rock*, was published. Afterwards, Joe Butler, the president, and Elmer Harris, his right-hand man, asked me how I'd like to host the station's morning call-in show.

I was back practising law then and told them that, with preparation time, the show would cut into my practice too much. They suggested that I could co-host with the current host, which would mean far less preparation for me. On that basis, I accepted. But Peckford said he would still have done the show by himself; he couldn't stand sharing the top spot with anyone else. It was a good glimpse into his personality.

As it happened, Sterrett soon had to leave the show with congestive heart failure. The last time I visited him at the Health Sciences Centre, he was attached to a big oxygen tank, which he was going to drag to a family member's wedding he was determined to attend the next day. "This is a pain in the arse," he said to me, with a rueful laugh at his understatement. The next day, he was dead.

Though it was sad the way it happened, after I started hosting the show by myself, I never enjoyed anything work-related as much in my life. One time, I took a month or so off to pursue another interest, and well-known defence lawyer Jeff Brace sat in for me on the show. When I came back to resume the hosting, Jeff told me he was extremely disappointed to leave. He said publicly, "Bill Rowe has the best job in the world." You sit around for a couple of hours a day, he said, chatting with different people about interesting topics, and then . . . the station pays you! What was not to love in that scenario?

Peckford turned out to be absolutely right about going solo. Unfortunately, he was finding it difficult to arrive at anything near the same status regarding our lost provincial resources.

The roadblock to Peckford's progress regarding those resources was that two other equally determined, not to say fanatical, governments claimed the benefit and control. The fishery had been handed over to federal jurisdiction thirty years before at Confederation; the lion's share of the revenues from Churchill Falls had ended up, under the 1969 contract, in Hydro-Québec's coffers; and Trudeau's Ottawa was resisting with all its forces any provincial claim to offshore oil ownership.

The Churchill Falls deal was especially sickening to Peckford. From the start the federal government had left this province dangling in a politically powerless position vis-à-vis Quebec. When Joey Smallwood had approached his fellow Liberal government in Ottawa in the early

1960s to ask them to exercise their undoubted constitutional power to allow a transmission line across Quebec, Liberal premier of Quebec Jean Lesage sweetly responded with a rhetorical question to Prime Minister Pearson: "And sir, who is going to protect such a transmission line, running hundreds of kilometres through the Quebec wilderness, against sabotage?" The federal government's backbone turned to jelly in the face of the Mafia-style shakedown, and Pearson implored Joey, successfully, not to force the issue.

Peckford tried again and again to renegotiate with Quebec a better deal, but failed. And of course he was not able to persuade Ottawa to lift a finger in any way. That was exasperating enough when it came to the Liberal Québécois, Pierre Trudeau. But his fellow Tories, when they entered government in Ottawa, were equally useless.

I was an observer at the federal PC leadership convention in Ottawa in June of 1983, and I heard Brian Mulroney, who would be elected party leader on the fourth ballot, undertake to remedy for Newfoundland the unfairness of the Upper Churchill deal. But as prime minister after 1984, he did nothing whatsoever on the Churchill Falls file. In justice, though, it was probably the outrageousness of that contract that soon made his government take a different position from Trudeau's on an equally momentous resource matter, the offshore oil.

Before that, though, regarding the Upper Churchill, Peckford decided to play what many considered a mug's game: he went to court. But he had no choice, really. If he had not at least tried, the doubt that would have always remained from his inaction would have reverberated down through history. Still, the quixotic legal battles to somehow undo the worse aspects of the deal ate up provincial government time, energy, and money, and ended in abject failure.

Newfoundland argued strenuously in the Supreme Court of Canada that the deal struck under the Smallwood government in 1969 was unconscionable. It was tantamount to selling oil to Hydro-Québec at the unconscionably low price of $1.80 a barrel for forty years and then lower still, at $1.20 a barrel, for the next twenty-five years. But the provincial arguments availed us nothing: in 1984, the Supreme Court held that the contract governing the long-term sale of hydroelectric power from Churchill Falls to Hydro-Québec was binding, effective, and legally valid.

Again in 1988, after Peckford had launched another lawsuit regarding the Upper Churchill state of affairs, the Supreme Court of Canada came down on Quebec's side once more. Incidentally, one third of the nine judges of the Supreme Court of Canada must come from Quebec; since Confederation in 1949, there has never been a Supreme Court judge appointed from Newfoundland and Labrador. Of course, no judge is going to decide an issue in favour of his or her home province, against a correct interpretation of the law. (Some may doubt that statement in view of the 2016 decision of the Quebec Court of Appeal in favour of Hydro-Québec and against Nalcor.) But it would certainly give the highest court a better perspective on the country as a whole, if there were greater geographical diversity in appointment of judges.

In addition to regaining greater revenues from the Upper Churchill, Peckford wanted to build a power development on the Lower Churchill River, but naturally he could not obtain a route to transmit the electricity through Quebec into the American and Canadian markets. And no one in government in Ottawa, Grit or Tory, was suicidal enough to help him with that.

There was one matter the federal government was happy to help Peckford with, however: give Newfoundland the cash to let Ottawa get out from under their constitutional obligation to provide a railway service across the island. People could protest all they wanted, but everyone knew long before 1988, sadly, that it was no longer financially sensible or realistic to operate trains in any form or for any purpose across Newfoundland. The passenger service had already gone by the board nearly twenty years before.

Finally, therefore, Peckford agreed that his government would accept a bundle of money to let Ottawa off its constitutional hook. That year, both levels of government negotiated the Newfoundland Transportation Initiative, the "Roads for Rails" deal, which obligated Ottawa to provide $800.6 million over fifteen years to improve the highways and ports in the province and to provide pensions and severances.

The last "Newfie Bullet" ran that fall of 1988. As a Newfoundlander passionately interested in all aspects of our history and heritage, Peckford told me it broke his heart to have to oversee the railway, of necessity, disappearing. Over the next two years, all rails and ties were removed and sold or discarded, and some cars and engines were sold as far away as Africa and South America, to countries with narrow-gauge rail lines.

Later, the railbed became the linear park known as the Newfoundland T'Railway Provincial Park, our section of the Trans Canada Trail system. Some railway stations have been kept and maintained as museums. Occasionally, one spots an old freight car or caboose converted to a cabin or shed, prompting children to ask their parents what that thing is.

FIVE

Although historically the fishery was the reason Europeans had come to Newfoundland since the 1500s, and probably before, jurisdiction over this economic bulwark of rural Newfoundland and Labrador was passed over to Ottawa in 1949. And thereafter the federal government set fish quotas, gave out trawler licences, and decided nearly all other facets of fisheries policy.

During the constitutional negotiations called by Trudeau in 1981, leading up to the Canada Act, 1982, Peckford claimed that the province had historic rights to the fisheries that were not relinquished under the Terms of Union. He maintained that Newfoundland's historic and economic attachment to the fisheries gave the province a moral right to take part in their management, and he tried to use the constitutional talks to wrest some control of the fisheries away from the feds. He and Trudeau got nowhere on the issue, except on each other's nerves. "Don't put words in my mouth, prime minister," Peckford snarled on camera during one set-to. The other provinces were no help. He couldn't get enough support from the premiers to put real pressure on the federal government.

Peckford evidently didn't like Trudeau very much. He said he was never taken by him from the start; his demeanour always seemed to be a bit contrived and without much substance. That's an interesting description of a leader considered by many to have been among the most convincing of political actors and possessed of the best intellect of Canada's successful prime ministers.

Peckford also thought Trudeau inconsiderate, indifferent, and aloof. He was on firmer ground there. He recalled with disbelief when the prime minister appointed Lieutenant-Governor Anthony Paddon in 1981, without even a heads-up to Peckford, let alone any consultation. The premier of the province heard of the appointment of the new lieutenant-governor of his province on his car radio. This was either an instance of Trudeau's ordinary and natural discourtesy to provincial leaders or a deliberate, personal snub of Peckford. Either way, it was a bit nasty, unless he felt, perhaps, that he had good reason to behave like that with this particular premier.

Peckford has told of trying to make some progress at a meeting on the fishery with Trudeau and of being foiled. The failure was not caused by any disagreement but resulted from the prime minister wasting the meeting's timetable yakking about the European trip he'd just arrived back from. It was Trudeau's lack of interest in the fishery, Peckford claimed, that contributed greatly to the collapse and shutdown of the ground fishery just a decade later.

At that same constitutional conference in 1981, where Trudeau hoped to gain enough provincial support to patriate the Canadian constitution from the United Kingdom, an impasse occurred in the final session which seemed to doom all hope. Peckford has claimed that it was a compromise proposed by him which ended the stalemate. The evidence points to the famous patriation agreement being settled, not from notes on scraps of paper in the kitchen of the Hôtel Château Laurier by Attorneys General Jean Chrétien, Roy Romanow, and Roy McMurtry, as has been generally accepted as historical fact, but from a written proposal presented by the Government of Newfoundland.

That version of events has been vociferously disputed by some other participants. But by whatever method it was achieved, the fact is that Peckford was a Canadian premier who took part in, added to, and helped to conclude the historic deal that removed from the Canadian constitution the last vestigial remnants, except for the Queen, of colonialism.

He would become a constitution reformer again in 1987 when he signed, along with all the other premiers, the Meech Lake Accord proposed by the Quebec Government of Premier Bourassa and rubber-stamped by Prime Minister Mulroney. Just a few years later, he must have found it hard to watch that unanimous deal he was a begetter of, and a staunch supporter of, come to naught under the tender mercies of his own provincial compatriot, Clyde Wells.

In 1983, Peckford published a book entitled *The Past in the Present: A Personal Perspective on Newfoundland's Future*, in which he set out his views on Newfoundland and Labrador's dismal economic history. He argued that our poor economy was the result of past mismanagement of the province's resources and contrasted that malpractice with what he himself wanted to achieve here in the years to come.

When those aspirations were thwarted in the legal and constitutional arenas, he then strove to sway Ottawa with a barrage of political arguments and attacks, hoping thereby to shape some federal policies, particularly in fisheries. This approach looked more promising when, in 1984, the federal PC Party under Brian Mulroney formed the government in Ottawa and the powerful John Crosbie became Newfoundland's minister. But just how ineffectual Peckford continued to be over the years with both the Ottawa mandarins and the backroom boys in the Prime Minister's Office, even though his supposed kindred spirits were in political power, was soon to be seen.

It was bad enough when the Mulroney government granted a licence to a Nova Scotia company to operate factory freezer trawlers in the east coast fishery. Peckford reacted to that by stating in the media: "The honeymoon is over, the gloves are off!" And he maintained a sustained attack against his federal PC colleagues, Mulroney and Crosbie, over their fishery policy. But relations became even worse later when an event occurred which Crosbie said caused him his worst moment in the Mulroney government.

Ottawa signed a secret binding agreement with France, in Paris, that allowed French trawlers from Saint-Pierre and Miquelon to harvest "surplus cod" (a pure fantasy) in Canadian waters, off Newfoundland's south coast. Mulroney's senior adviser, the sinister Fred Doucet, had ordered the pact to be concluded in order to obtain brownie points for Mulroney at an upcoming francophone summit. It included an annual quota for the French from the already critically stressed northern cod. The deal was done without consulting or informing John Crosbie. And neither the Newfoundland Government, nor Fishery Products International, nor the Fish, Food and Allied Workers Union had any idea the agreement was being concocted.

When it came out, Peckford was utterly outraged and pronounced it a "disaster of monumental proportions." He attacked Crosbie as a liar and a traitor to his fellow Newfoundlanders and said that Newfoundland and Labrador was facing 1933, i.e. bankruptcy, all over again, unless Ottawa improved the province's place in Confederation with new regional development, better equalization, better funding programs, and fisheries jurisdiction.

He made his case on province-wide TV and in a pamphlet to every household in the province. He convened a meeting of seven premiers who publicly agreed with him. He must have known that John Crosbie had been caught flat-footed by the stupidity and duplicity of the Prime Minister's Office and the Department of External Affairs in the whole business, but that did not restrain him in his continued civil war with his province's federal minister.

Sometimes their battles got Crosbie into trouble with his own prime minister and colleagues. I'm not sure if it was at the time of one of the trawler rackets or when John Fraser, minister of Fisheries, resigned over the tainted tuna scandal, or some other inept fisheries action in Ottawa, but Crosbie came on my *Open Line* show on VOCM to talk about the issue and Peckford's reaction to it. During our conversation, I asked

Crosbie if the Prime Minister's Office was staffed by a bunch of dolts, and he replied that he wouldn't say they were dolts, but you could say they were not as politically astute as they should be. The national media were delighted, of course, at his perceived breach of solidarity. Some of them wrongly attributed my insinuation that there were dolts in the PMO to Crosbie himself, making his political life awkward with the gnomes in the PM's Langevin Block for a few days.

Crosbie often told me that he found Peckford completely selfish, and ungrateful and ruthless in his attacks, no matter what Ottawa did for Newfoundland and Labrador. Mind you, he would have the same complaint about Clyde Wells a few years later. He'd always say that both PC Brian Peckford and Liberal Clyde Wells were diabolically clever and skilled at seizing the credit themselves for anything good Ottawa did for the province, and brilliant at shifting the blame to the federal government for everything that went wrong, regardless of who was really responsible.

For his own part, Peckford would say later, when he finally got around to reading John Crosbie's autobiography, that it was full of false statements, half-truths, and selected comments ascribed to Peckford. The book was really nothing but an egocentric tirade, he remarked, and it merely proclaimed how good Crosbie was and how bad most other people were.

One time, when Crosbie and I were talking about the latest scrap between the provincial premier and the federal minister, he said he thanked God that Peckford had found himself a new woman after he and his first wife had split up. Now, he hoped, Brian might be a little more reasonable and human, and less contrary, bitter, and antagonistic.

Peckford's marital difficulties had begun to emerge in the public consciousness around the beginning of 1983. There was gossip in February, when one of his assistants made a statement about the premier's new living arrangements, after he returned from his vacation down south. Peckford was going to move out of his official residence, Mount Scio

House, the aide said, into smaller accommodations for reasons of cost. The premier's family was then living in South Brook, Green Bay, he explained, and thus the same need was not there.

A fuss had broken out earlier when renovations and redecoration, reported to have been planned by his then wife, Marina, had cost taxpayers $118,000. There were also questions about the unrevealed cost of erecting an electrified fence. It was all completely unfair to her. She had been requested to perform a service as the spouse of the premier, and now this private lady was coming under the glare of extremely uncomfortable publicity for doing so.

It had been after the 1982 election, the media disclosed, that Marina Peckford moved out of the official residence back to South Brook, where she opened a jeans shop. Now, in 1983, Brian Peckford was moving into an apartment complex where a number of middle-aged males of my acquaintance resided following their marriage breakdowns. Rather too sardonically, in a column in the *Evening Telegram,* I referred to this apartment building in which Peckford was taking up residence as Male Menopause Manor.

The Liberal leader at the time, Steve Neary, who'd been the lead critic of Peckford's living expenses, was reported to be pleased the premier had decided to "abandon his house in the Garden of Eden."

Peckford's marital problems made their way explicitly into print media in the fall of 1983. Even the mainland papers picked up on it. I recall a story in the *Montreal Gazette* in November that recounted how Peckford had returned from a day's cod-jigging on Hall's Bay to tell his wife of fourteen years, thirty-five-year-old Marina, that their marriage was over. The media quoted him as saying to her by way of explanation, "I am not appreciated."

Marina, who was reported to be two months pregnant with their third child at the time, said sorrowfully, "I married a teacher. It's a politician that's leaving me." She flew a flag at half-mast on their South Brook home, and her sister was rumoured to be planning to run against Peckford in his own district in the next election.

When Princess Diana visited Newfoundland with her husband,

Charles, the Prince of Wales, in 1983, she must have sensed that she had a sympathetic audience in Brian. This was part of their first regal tour of Canada ("The Canada Day Royal Visit") as a married couple, and the glamour that endeared her to the Canadian public was much in evidence. But so was her growing vulnerability and unhappiness. She told Premier Peckford that she was finding it very difficult to cope with the pressures of being Princess of Wales. Diana also disclosed to him her horrible feelings when the British tabloids wrote all those terrible things about her and her husband.

Horrible feelings about terrible things were also evoked in his victims by the presence of a local celebrity, Father Jim Hickey, during that royal visit. He was very much in evidence on television at the royal events, hustling about as a welcomer and organizer. It would later come out in evidence that leaders in the Catholic Church were aware of his sexual abuse of young boys during his career as a parish priest. In September 1988, five years after the visit of Charles and Diana, Hickey would plead guilty to, and be convicted of, twenty charges of sexual assault, gross indecency, and indecent assault against vulnerable teenaged boys. He was sentenced to five years in jail.

But back to Brian Peckford's public lifestyle during the mid- to late 1980s. His outward appearance and actions, to some eyes, started to become outlandish. He would be seen almost invariably puffing on a fat cigar like a highly successful used car salesman and dangling and jangling bracelets and chains from his wrists and neck. Commentator Rex Murphy remarked that he became egregiously vulgar, smoking cigars on the elevator, jaunting off to the Cayman Islands, hiring elite cars and drivers on government business trips, becoming notorious for huge tips, and sporting the ever-present bracelets and chains.

Murphy claimed Peckford had burnt himself out. In his last three years, he did everything possible to make people angry at him, said Rex, and he was brilliant at it. During his tenure, Peckford did not endear himself, either, to a long-suffering electorate by renovating the premier's office at a cost of half a million dollars.

Normally rather sanguine in his earlier dealings with the media,

Peckford began to react angrily. A feisty independent weekly, the *Sunday Express,* owned by Harry Steele and run by Michael Harris, started up in St. John's in the fall of 1986, and was soon taking Peckford on regularly. He countered by ordering his government to boycott the newspaper.

Both in his political as well as his personal style, Brian Peckford seemed to have altered enormously.

SIX

Still, government had to go on, including coping with the emerging disaster in the humble, unglamorous cod fishery. The coming catastrophe there would result from the overfishing permitted by Ottawa for decades, which continued largely unabated during the rest of the 1980s.

But when mismanagement would finally culminate in the utter collapse of the cod stocks in 1992, successive provincial governments could not be held blameless. Where the province did have some legal say, that is, in the issuance of licences to establish and operate fish plants, it allowed too many to set up. And it supported inshore and midshore fishermen in their understandable desire to compete more effectively by equipping themselves with larger boats and more advanced technology.

All of which contributed to the unbearable strain on the finite resource and led to the inevitable result of the competition between province and nation for the hearts and minds of 30,000 or 40,000 fishermen and their families. Disastrous federal and provincial political decisions outweighed the overfishing concerns voiced by numerous fishermen and scientists and independent investigators.

Peckford spread the blame around for the growing problems. He thought Frank Moores, as premier, didn't have the guts to take on the feds over the fishery, or the offshore, generally. And apparently he wouldn't even meet with Fish, Food and Allied Workers Union president Richard Cashin. He thought the union was in a conflict of interest because the FFAW represented offshore fishermen, inshore fishermen, and plant workers, all of whom had different, conflicting interests.

One can legitimately ponder whether Peckford, if he had in fact been able to gain greater provincial control over fishery management early enough, would have delayed the impending catastrophe or even staved it off altogether. Perhaps some form of joint management would have curtailed the fatal federal-provincial competition and lack of co-operation. But would it have been able to cope adequately with the so-called "tragedy of the commons"?

In its simplest terms, that economic theory covers a situation within a shared-resource system, like our fishery, where individual harvesters, operating independently and rationally in their own self-interest, act contrary to the common good of all and hence deplete the resource. The many aspects of the fishery made it more complicated than that, but surely it was a contributing factor.

The question of what Peckford's impact on the fishery might have been, under joint management, may perhaps be answered by the fact that he had very early recognized the dire need to preserve fish stocks: back in 1981, he called for a moratorium on the northern cod fishery. That was more than a decade before the 1992 crash, when the federal government would be then forced to replace conservation management with disaster management.

The offshore oil, from the beginning, should have presented a new opportunity for Newfoundland and Labrador to do something right with a lucrative resource, for a change. And Peckford did go at it with a vengeance. He had two strings to his bow.

His first was the political one. He tried to negotiate a deal with the Trudeau Liberals in Ottawa to share control over the offshore and to obtain most of the royalty revenues for the province. The attitude of the federal government would be shown by Jean Chrétien, after he became federal Energy minister in 1982: the feds couldn't accede to the province's demands, he reasoned, because they didn't want to "overheat the Newfoundland economy."

Even we provincial Liberals cringed in embarrassment at that one. At the time the province's unemployment rate was pushing eighteen to twenty per cent. For many it wasn't a stretch to imagine cynical laughter behind closed doors in Ottawa over Chrétien's bon mot. And of course Peckford's continued arguments and attacks remained fruitless.

He now decided to act on a well-rehearsed Newfoundland political strategy: if your electorate is starting to perceive you as ineffective in dealing with your own responsibilities, escalate your attack on the villainy of Ottawa; then hold an election on a simple-minded question: who were the voters for—the uncaring, faraway federal government, or their own true, fighting Newfoundlander government?

He was poised to call just such an election right after Valentine's Day, 1982, when tragedy struck. A hundred miles from where the *Titanic* had gone down, the terrible *Ocean Ranger* disaster occurred. On February 15, the gigantic rig, described by its owners, ODECO, as the world's largest semi-submersible oil rig, capsized and sank with the loss of eighty-four lives, fifty-six from Newfoundland.

That unspeakable event put a stop to everything—except the slanging match between St. John's and Ottawa. Relations were so bad that the provincial and federal governments could not even agree on holding a single joint, public inquiry into the catastrophe. Initially, each government set up its own inquiry, with separate chairmen.

But finally, as a result of public pressure, a month after the rig went down, the Trudeau federal government and the Peckford provincial government jointly established a Royal Commission on the *Ocean Ranger* Marine Disaster, chaired by Chief Justice T. Alex Hickman. It was directed to investigate three basic questions: why the oil rig sank, why nobody survived, and how similar disasters could be prevented.

Peckford felt free now to call his postponed election for April 6, 1982. Less than three years had passed since the last election, but he said he wanted provincial support for his offshore position. That was basically a mandate to continue his verbal assaults on Ottawa. The Liberals were led by Len Stirling, who had earlier brought Don Jamieson home for good. He was a decent man but no ball of fire. My memory of his biggest issue as leader was criticizing Peckford in July for increasing the salary of cabinet ministers by order-in-council instead of calling the House together for debate.

In the election, Stirling agreed with Peckford that Newfoundland and Labrador should own the offshore oil, but he faulted the premier's method of clashing with the federal government about it. He suggested that he himself could negotiate an offshore resource agreement with his fellow Liberal, Prime Minister Trudeau, by taking a conciliatory approach: "Make Work Not War" became his campaign slogan.

The Tories made fun of it, calling it the worst appeasement since Neville Chamberlain, and mocked the idea that paraphrasing a hippie mantra from the 1960s was better than Peckford's "fighting Newfoundlander" stance. They ridiculed the notion that "make-work" could equal the quality or quantity of jobs that would come from resource ownership and development.

I myself suspected we Liberals were done for when Peckford announced during the campaign that his polling was showing even historically staunch Liberal districts to be tending toward the PC side. He singled out my own, Twillingate District, as one of them. A small personal irony on that: when I'd been minister responsible for rural development in the early 1970s, I'd created a program to fund rural development associations around the province with grants so that each could hire a permanent worker. It was the director of the Twillingate District rural association, Ida Reid, who'd made herself widely known in the district from that post and then defeated me.

On the night of the election, no one was surprised that Peckford received more than sixty per cent of the votes cast and took forty-four of fifty-two seats in the House of Assembly. The Liberals clung onto eight. Stirling lost in his own district of Bonavista North and would resign as leader later that year.

Accepting victory that night, Peckford proclaimed that ". . . one day the sun will shine and have not will be no more." It would be a quarter of a century later, when Peckford was long retired as premier, and a resident of British Columbia, that his famous prediction would finally come true. At least, for a little while.

That same year, Peckford resorted to the second string to his bow regarding control of the offshore oil—legal action. He placed the question of ownership and control of the massive fields in the hands of the Newfoundland Court of Appeal. But Trudeau, in a pre-emptive stroke, superseded any coming decision of the St. John's court by referring the whole issue to the Supreme Court of Canada.

Peckford accused Trudeau of insulting the Newfoundland Court of Appeal and declared a day of mourning in the province. He and his colleagues put on black armbands. Adding to the feeling among many mainland commentators that he was tilting at windmills, Peckford dropped broad hints that, if the top Canadian court didn't side with his province's position on ownership of the offshore oil, he might take a page out of the Quebec separatists' songbook.

In court, the federal government maintained its long-held position that offshore resources fell under its jurisdiction. After all, a 1967 Supreme Court of Canada decision had already awarded seabed resources off the British Columbia coast to the federal government, and the Trudeau government argued that the decision applied equally to the east coast of the country.

The provincial government reasoned that international law had granted Newfoundland the ownership of mineral resources on the continental shelf before 1949, including that portion known for centuries as the Grand Banks of *Newfoundland*, and this had not passed over to Canada at Confederation. Their position was bolstered, the Newfoundland lawyers argued, by Section 37 of the Terms of Union, which stated in part: "All lands, mines, minerals, and royalties belonging to Newfoundland at the date of Union . . . shall belong to the Province of Newfoundland, subject . . : to any interest other than that of the Province in the same." It was a solid argument, not a flimsy tissue of blarney, as some opponents maintained.

In March 1984, two years after Peckford's magnificent election victory, which had accorded him a mandate to fight for the offshore, the centrist Supreme Court of Canada handed down its decision. Evidently they were not shivering in their boots over Peckford's hinted threats of separation, because they decided that Canada, not Newfoundland, had jurisdiction over the resource in the continental shelf off the nation's east coast. One of the lawyers who argued in favour of the winning federal government's case was Clyde Wells.

Undeterred, Peckford took the political route once more and tried to interest a largely apathetic country in giving his province joint management and the lion's share of the revenues from offshore oil. To that end, he travelled across Canada seeking provincial government backing for his own province's stance. He was met largely by a gigantic trans-Canada yawn and glazed-over eyes. It would be safe to say that, if the federal Liberals, by now under John Turner's leadership, had stayed in power after the 1984 federal election, Peckford would have remained out in the political wilderness, howling vainly for ownership, forever. But then he had one of his strokes of political good luck.

When John Turner called his federal election for September 4, 1984, the Liberal Party had a sizable lead in the polls. But Brian Mulroney's Tory Party went on to win one of the largest majorities in Canadian history and formed a new government. Part of his election platform was a fair deal for Newfoundland and Labrador on offshore energy.

During the campaign, Peckford had cajoled Brian Mulroney into promising, in writing, that, if elected, the Progressive Conservative government would give the province an equal voice in offshore management and make the province the "principal beneficiary" of the offshore resource.

No doubt the response of the Royal Commission of Inquiry into the *Ocean Ranger* Disaster helped bring the two governments together on an agreement over offshore oil. The commission's first report had uncovered unpardonable weaknesses in the way government and industry managed and regulated offshore developments. Inadequate emergency training, a flawed rig design, and ineffectually enforced safety regulations were disclosed as crucial factors in the loss of lives.

That tragedy-inviting situation had been further compounded by the unending political brawling between both levels of government for ownership and control. The unseemly struggle had diverted officials and politicians from setting up a sensible regulatory structure. As a result, separate federal and provincial agencies, plus the United States Coast Guard, "governed" the industry, leading inexorably to a convoluted and ineffectual and perilous bureaucratic hodgepodge.

The Commission recommended that a single Canadian agency regulate the industry, including drilling operations, the production of oil and gas, and standby vessels, helicopters, and other rescue craft.

Brian Mulroney's new administration began talks with Peckford immediately. Within six months, the prime minister and the premier negotiated the 1985 Atlantic Accord. Peckford went ecstatic with joy: "There is no other document, including the Terms of Union, that will come as close to achieving economic and social equality for the people of Newfoundland and Labrador as this. . . . We've got a document that every single Newfoundlander who can read and write will consider the most important in the history of this rock."

It was signed on February 11, 1985, by Mulroney and Peckford, and by federal Energy minister Pat Carney, provincial Energy minister William Marshall, and Newfoundland's representative in the federal cabinet, Justice minister John Crosbie. Brandishing his pen, Peckford prophesied that the Accord would allow "this province to catch up socially and economically to the rest of Canada." Mulroney took a slap at Trudeau's and Chrétien's fears of overheating our economy, intoning in his dulcet baritone, "I am not afraid to inflict prosperity on Newfoundland and Labrador."

The Accord elevated Newfoundland to equal partner with Ottawa under the new Canada-Newfoundland Offshore Petroleum Board (CNOPB) in decisions about offshore developments and their management. It replaced the federal agency and the Newfoundland and Labrador agency and the US Coast Guard as the single regulatory agency responsible for the offshore industry.

The 1985 Atlantic Accord was supposed to give Newfoundland a big cut of the revenues that would accrue to government: the province was empowered to collect taxes and royalties from petroleum resources as if it owned them, and equalization payments were protected for a twelve-year period. Peckford had been able to persuade Mulroney that the offshore oil, being a non-renewable and finite resource, would deliver only short-term gains and therefore did not reflect Newfoundland's real fiscal capacity. Hence, it should not be lumped in with renewable resources in applying the equalization formula. If the federal Tories had not agreed with Peckford on that, then oil royalties would have been factored in for the calculation of equalization transfers, which would leave the province spinning its wheels financially and getting no further ahead.

Ottawa paid $225 million into a $300 million offshore development fund that was set up to help the province prepare for industrial growth, and residents of Newfoundland and Labrador were to benefit from training opportunities and job openings. Employers connected with the offshore had to give first priority to qualified local workers. Developers were to chip in on local research and education programs and hire local businesses that were able to supply necessary goods and services for offshore undertakings.

In St. John's, the Accord was widely acclaimed as a brilliant accomplishment for Peckford, which would mark the defining moment of the turnaround in the province's economic fortunes. Just who was most impressed by the hoopla, though, might be grasped from an offhand remark to me from a person who walked across the parking lot at the Hotel Newfoundland on the morning of the signing. She had concluded, from seeing all the Mercedes Benzes and BMWs and Audis parked there, she told me, that a big celebration by rich people must be going on inside.

SEVEN

After the signing of the Atlantic Accord of 1985, Peckford dubbed himself the "Great Negotiator," and to benefit from this federal-provincial love-in, he called a snap election for April 2. It occurred less than three years after the previous election. Perhaps some of the electorate suspected he was manipulating them for his own political advantage, and certainly one large and vociferous segment, the public service employees and teachers, were lukewarm over his brilliant Accord. They were more impressed, and negatively so, by his government's two-year freeze on their wages.

Throughout the campaign they hounded him and vocalized their discontent everywhere he showed up. Fraser March, the president of the Newfoundland Association of Public Employees, lived up to his pledge to battle "every Tory in the province." Polls began to show the Liberals gaining support under new leader Leo Barry.

Barry had been first elected to the House of Assembly in 1972 as a PC and later became a minister in the cabinet of Frank Moores. In 1979, he was a leadership candidate against the ultimate winner, Brian Peckford. After that year's provincial election, Peckford appointed him minister of Energy, where he played a prominent role.

In 1979, as well, he and Peckford announced the discovery of the Hibernia offshore oil field some 315 kilometres off St. John's. They waved vials of offshore crude oil in the air and issued their projections of hundreds of millions of barrels available for commercial production. Barry invited Members of the House of Assembly to a boardroom where he described the significance of the find for the province. We, in the Liberal Opposition, figured our political goose was cooked forevermore.

Later, Barry resigned from cabinet in disagreement with Peckford about negotiations with the Trudeau government over Newfoundland's claim to offshore resources. Peckford said he'd been about to fire him, anyway, for not being a team player. Next, Barry crossed the floor of the House to join the Liberal Party, and he became party leader in the fall of 1984.

Just before voting day in this 1985 election, political surveys had the Progressive Conservatives and Liberals tied in popularity outside the capital city area. Inside the Overpass, though, in the metropolitan seats which were traditionally more Tory, and where the Accord was exerting greater economic impact on the minds of voters, Peckford was still ahead.

The election results would have delighted any other premier in the nation, but they were jarring for Peckford. His Progressive Conservatives ended up with less than forty-nine per cent of the popular vote, (down from sixty-one per cent in 1982) compared to nearly thirty-seven per cent for Barry's Liberals and over fourteen per cent for Peter Fenwick's New Democratic Party. Peckford's seats dropped from forty-four to thirty-six, while Leo Barry increased the Liberal seats from eight to fifteen, and Peter Fenwick surprised the province by winning a seat for the NDP. Significantly, the combined opposition votes had risen to a number greater than Peckford's PCs.

Armchair pundits walked all over each other in the media to account for the change. Some said it was as much a tribute to Barry's and Fenwick's campaigning as discontent in public service unions and gloominess in rural Newfoundland over economic stagnation. Some of us waxed cynical over the nature of provincial politics. The vote didn't seem to reflect the magnificent Accord between the province and Ottawa on future offshore oil developments or celebrate the resulting peace that had broken out between St. John's and Ottawa. We concluded that in politics, whatever you do, if you want overwhelming success as premier of this province, never broker a ceasefire with the feds. Always be attacking the Ottawa bastards with both barrels blazing.

Sure enough, not long afterwards, Peckford was going after his PC federal counterparts and colleagues again—this time by attacking Mulroney's deficit-fighting efforts and for generally ignoring the province's needs. Peckford even ordered his own caucus in the House of Assembly to join the Liberal Opposition in voting for a resolution denouncing the federal government for its hard-nosed budget.

Not for the first time, a dismayed Crosbie had to go public to declare astonishment at Peckford's assaults, especially in view of the fact that Ottawa was providing a good half of the revenues of the province's government. Crosbie felt that, "With friends like Peckford we'd never need enemies!"

Following in the tradition of nearly every purported breakthrough in the economic history of the province, Peckford's momentous 1985 Accord started to go wrong. The epoch-making document was signed not long before the price of crude oil plummeted internationally. It had spiralled up to more than $35 a barrel in 1980 (over $100 a barrel in 2016 dollars), and then it dropped in 1986 to less than $10 (about $22 in 2016). The low price stifled production ambitions, and it would be twelve years after the Accord, and eight years after Peckford had left the premiership, that first oil from Hibernia would in fact flow, in 1997. Brian Tobin would be premier by then, and I recall that the government's first royalty cheque from the consortium would be so low, Tobin was too embarrassed to publicly state its amount.

Nor, despite Peckford's best intentions, did his Accord even achieve its explicitly stated purpose of making the province the principal beneficiary of the offshore oil industry. Because production would progress much more slowly than expected, the result was low revenues when protection from the equalization clawback was at its greatest. Thus the provincial government would claim by 2003 that the province was in fact receiving only twelve cents of every dollar of offshore revenues, while the remaining eighty-eight cents flowed to Canada and the other provinces. These dismal figures would be backed up by John Crosbie, the federal minister when the Accord had been signed, who deemed the actual outcome to be outrageously contrary to everyone's intent.

Rectifying that perverse effect would have to become Premier Danny Williams's challenge in attempting to modify the Accord in the province's favour in 2005. Peckford's longed-for "have" status would not be achieved until 2008, over twenty-five years after his predicted "have not will be no more."

When that prosperous status finally did arrive, Peckford could proclaim that Brian Mulroney, whom he had attacked fiercely in the past, would go down in history as Newfoundland and Labrador's best friend. Mulroney's understanding of the Churchill Falls issue, he believed, made him support the province's position on the offshore. I agree. I always figured it was the pledge that everybody, myself included, heard him make at the leadership convention in 1983, to rectify the unconscionable Upper Churchill contract, that spurred him on. Mulroney's failure to deliver on that commitment must have forced his hand on doing the right thing regarding offshore oil.

Whatever the case, Peckford emphasized in his 2012 memoirs that "without Brian Mulroney there would be no Atlantic Accord, and without the Accord, Newfoundland and Labrador would not be a 'have' province today."

Contrary to the impressions of some, Peckford was not wholly preoccupied with getting control of our resources and obtaining a fair share of their revenues, or totally engrossed in the public animosities between himself and Ottawa and Quebec. Everything else was not utterly eclipsed. For example, he made our flag a burning issue.

Soon after his first election in 1979, he established a committee of the House of Assembly, under the chairmanship of MHA John Carter, to come up with a design for a new flag for the province. Within a year, in May of 1980, Peckford pushed a newly designed provincial flag on the legislature—with unseemly haste, some critics claimed. The flag was created by renowned Newfoundland artist Christopher Pratt, and Peckford professed to love it.

He and other members of his caucus, including the chair of the House flag committee, John Carter, as well as Pratt himself, went overboard in explaining what the design was supposed to mean. Perhaps the best point of all, though, was made by Carter when, during the rancorous debate inside and outside the House, he explained that the scientific term for the study and usage of flags was "vexillology," with the emphasis on "vex."

One critic said that, as explained by its promoters, the new flag carried enough symbolism to choke a bull moose. Some of that symbolism seemed blindingly obvious, while some consisted of strained and obscure gobbledygook:

The colour white on the flag, according to the explainers, symbolized the snow and ice of winter. Oh great, some said, a flag that reminds us every day of our winters.

The colour blue represented the sea, but on top of that, the triangles formed by the blue were a tribute to the Union Jack and the province's British heritage. Good try, but Anglophiles and lovers of the real Union Jack were underwhelmed.

The colour red on the flag signified, in some way, the effort and struggle of Newfoundlanders and Labradorians, and then, in a slight leap of logic, the two red triangles somehow represented the two areas of the province—Labrador and the island of Newfoundland.

Next, the gold colour symbolized the confidence that Newfoundlanders and Labradorians had in themselves, and the sharp end of the gold arrow pointed toward a brighter future. But when the flag is hung as a vertical banner, with the gold arrow pointing down, the arrow thereupon became a sword, venerating the sacrifices of Newfoundlanders in military service. This attempt at commemorative symbolism did not impress the provincial branch of the Royal Canadian Legion. They refused to recognize the new pennant as the flag of Newfoundland, contending that during both World Wars, Newfoundland soldiers had fought under the Union Jack. And they stated without equivocation that the Union Jack was the flag they'd continue to display.

Naturally, this wouldn't be Newfoundland if something designed to be a sacred symbol wasn't given an obscene spin by our local wags. Some of them argued that the arrow hanging down vertically did not represent a sword at all but that it clearly showed a man in a shower from behind, bending over to pick up the soap he'd dropped. I could be mistaken, but I do believe someone actually introduced that delightful image into the House debate.

Moving right along . . . those heavily burdened red triangles and that overactive gold arrow were not finished yet. Together they also symbolized the province's dependence on its fisheries and the resources of the sea. That became possible because, in addition to representing the Big Land and the Island, together with a bright future, plus a commemorative sword, they also formed—presto!—a trident.

But that wasn't all. The flag was also revealed to incorporate Beothuk and Innu ornamentation (no Inuit symbolism, apparently), plus a Christian cross, and an outline of the maple leaf, to boot. The reference to a Christian cross is curious. According to provincial government practice, flags representing particular religions are not to be flown outside Confederation Building. Hence we have the peculiar situation where, strictly speaking, our provincial flag, with its Christian cross, should not be flown in front of the province's government building.

But I digress. All that diverse symbolism was a hell of a lot to pile on one little provincial flag. Hearing it explained, Joey Smallwood denounced the flag as "the worst Newfy joke yet." Perhaps he was still mad at Pratt for leaving his artist's studio to actively support the Tories in the 1971 election, which had toppled Joey from the premiership.

My own objection had nothing to do with any notion that the flag was a bad joke or overweight with obscure symbolism. I simply didn't like its unbalanced and slightly too flashy look. I was and am a great admirer of Christopher Pratt and his phenomenal world-class art. I still remember the pride I felt as a law student in England, way back in 1965, when a reproduction of one of Pratt's new works, *The Lynx*, appeared in an international magazine. I showed it around to my appreciative fellow students: this genius, I declared, was my own Newfoundland compatriot.

In spite of my admiration generally, though, I rejected this particular artifact in the House of Assembly on aesthetic grounds. I don't think I was alone. I seem to recall others questioning it for similar reasons. But we may all have been wrong: the *Evening Telegram* extolled it at the time, editorializing that it was "striking and unique." I don't recall if any other Members of the House, besides myself, actually voted against accepting it as our provincial flag.

Since then I've learned that familiarity doesn't always breed contempt. Sometimes familiarity can breed, if not a warm and cuddly feeling, then at least tolerance. I've grown so familiar with the "new" flag, more than thirty-five years later, that I've almost come to identify with it as a Newfoundlander. I react these days whenever I see it flying among the other Canadian flags, not negatively but ambivalently—with a touch of pride mixed in with only a tiny remnant of a cringe.

But however anyone felt about the flag then, or reacts to it now, the fact is that Brian Peckford is one of those rare leaders who can count himself as responsible for having legislated into existence his jurisdiction's distinctive, identifying banner.

EIGHT

Peckford made other important policy decisions for which he may not be as well remembered as for his Atlantic Accord. In 1983, his administration introduced grade 12 to the school system, thereby bringing us up to modern standards. And in the same year, construction was finally begun on the long-awaited Trans-Labrador Highway.

In 1987, he achieved what many deemed impossible: he got the long-bankrupt Come By Chance oil refinery up and running again, under a new operator. The federal Crown corporation, Petro-Canada Exploration Inc., had bought it for $10 million in 1980. But when they later decided against reactivating it, that caused another battle royal by Peckford against federal minister John Crosbie and the Canadian government. Petro-Canada finally sold the refinery for a dollar to Newfoundland Energy Limited in 1986, and the upgraded refinery has operated ever since.

From the start, Peckford was progressive in his policies regarding gender equity. Right after his election as premier in 1979, he appointed the first female cabinet ministers in Newfoundland and Labrador's history. Lynn Verge had been elected to the House as MHA for Humber East, and he made her minister of Education. Hazel Newhook, elected from Gander District, was appointed minister of Consumer Affairs and Environment. Sadly, in view of his activist liberal attitude, his election juggernaut in 1979 defeated the first woman elected to the House after Confederation, Liberal Hazel A. McIsaac, of St. George's District.

Peckford quickly achieved some other feminist firsts. Soon after being elected as premier, he presented the province's first female pay equity policy, and in 1980 he launched the first Provincial Advisory Council on the Status of Women. No doubt he was listening closely to Lynn Verge.

A few years later, in 1983, the very first woman in our history, Margaret Cameron, was appointed as a justice of the Newfoundland Supreme Court. Peckford was not directly responsible, of course, since appointments to provincial Supreme Courts lie within the prerogative of the federal government. But his own actions certainly must have played a powerful role. Early in her career, Cameron had been in private practice (as it happens, as a member of my own former law firm, Thoms, Fowler, Rowe and Barry). So I was well aware of her superior intelligence, judgment, and ability. After she went on to become a solicitor with the provincial Department of Justice, I was not surprised when Peckford appointed her, in 1981, as associate deputy minister of Justice. And it was from that important and prestigious position that she was appointed to the Supreme Court of Newfoundland, by the government of Pierre Trudeau.

By coincidence, both she and her former colleague in private practice, Leo Barry, were under active consideration in 2008 for appointment from the Supreme Court of Newfoundland to the highest court in the nation, the Supreme Court of Canada.

In 1988, Peckford oversaw the official opening of the School of Fine Arts at Sir Wilfred Grenfell College in Corner Brook, which, together with his establishment of the Newfoundland and Labrador Arts Council back in 1980, confirmed his declared interest in fostering the arts in the province. He also established a book publishers' assistance program and a sustaining grant for the symphony orchestra. As well, he set up the first Environment Department, and he cajoled the feds into helping support a new campus for what became known as the Marine Institute.

During Peckford's time as premier, a nationalistic feeling, in the best sense, seemed to emerge among the new generation. Joey sometimes used to mention Newfoundlanders' inferiority complex and the nationalistic, even chauvinistic sentiment that sprang out of it. But what surfaced in the 1970s, and developed in the 1980s under Peckford, was different. Some observers called it a "cultural renaissance" in art, music, performance, literature, crafts, and the local celebration of distinctive traditions and heritage. And any assumption, here or on the mainland, that Newfoundland might be somehow substandard in any of those, was exploded by continuing bursts from the province of national achievement.

Peckford was a substantial agent of that change.

Leading up to the federal election of 1988, Peckford would not relent in his fed-bashing. John Crosbie gave out figures to show that spending by the federal government in Newfoundland and Labrador had gone up by hundreds of millions ever since he'd become a minister under Brian Mulroney. Still, when a reporter asked Peckford on national television if he'd campaign for Prime Minister Mulroney and the federal Tories in the federal election, his reply was curt: he would have to say no, he would not. This, in spite of the fact that he actually favoured the Canada-US free trade agreement that Mulroney would stake his election on, and win.

Besides his understandable feeling that the federal government never did enough, either financially or in structural changes, to lift his province out of its economic doldrums, perhaps part of Peckford's recurrent hostility to John Crosbie stemmed from the federal PC leadership convention back in 1983. He may have felt that Crosbie owed him a lot more because he'd put his neck on the line by supporting him against Joe Clark and Brian Mulroney. And he hadn't even done it for love or friendship. He frankly admitted he was doing it in the hope of having a Newfoundlander, who could benefit the province, as prime minister.

But whatever the case, while his former premier, Frank Moores, was pushing Mulroney, Peckford backed Crosbie to the hilt. His zeal even pushed him to approach Joe Clark, who was in first place (but stalled) after the second ballot, and ask him to withdraw in favour of third-place Crosbie. For his pains, the honourable premier of Newfoundland and Labrador received this reply from Joe Clark's wife, Maureen McTeer: "Fuck off, you nerd." He had to feel forever after that Crosbie owed him big time for that one and that the federal minister never fully paid his huge debt.

I don't know if it was hearing Ms. McTeer addressing him in such terms, or his feelings about his domestic difficulties, or simply a realistic appraisal of his province's place in Confederation, but also in that same year, 1983, he said that Newfoundlanders were lepers within Canada.

By 1987, most of Peckford's economic initiatives, after eight years of striving mightily, had come to naught. And he was starting to feel the political heat. The Liberal caucus had stabbed their leader, Leo Barry, in the back, causing a leadership convention to be called for June. Clyde Wells decided to run, and won it. Liberal MHA Graham Flight resigned his Windsor–Buchans seat to allow Wells to get elected to the House. But Peckford wouldn't call a by-election until December.

The Liberals claimed he was afraid that Wells would prove to be his downfall in the House. One Tory bigwig told me at the time, though, that Peckford was merely being cruelly mischievous. He wanted to keep Wells from getting elected, and from receiving an income as MHA and Leader of the Opposition, for as long as possible.

Meanwhile, a worldwide recession was making the province an economic basket case. Both unemployment and the provincial debt were the highest in Canada. There were ominous indications from fishermen in the late 1980s that mismanagement of the fishery was bringing cod stocks to the brink of collapse. Peckford's grand rural development visions had degenerated back to make-work schemes designed to qualify people for the pogey.

Critics were squawking that what the province needed for salvation was "economic diversification." The 1986 Royal Commission on Employment and Unemployment, chaired by Memorial University professor Dr. Doug House, had recommended that Newfoundland and Labrador "focus on small-scale resource development aimed partly at local markets. Agriculture is a prime example."

Enter the saviour, Philip Sprung, dragging with him from Alberta his fancy, high-tech agricultural scheme that would put its stain on Peckford's legacy forever.

In 1987, the Peckford government got excited at the thought of making a deal with Mr. Sprung, who headed an outfit out of Calgary, to construct a hydroponic greenhouse complex on the St. John's–Mount Pearl boundary. It was a method of growing plants, in this case cucumbers and tomatoes, using mineral nutrient solutions in water, without soil. The whole concept was a natural for us, one defender of the PC faith told me on *Open Line*, because our province had no soil but lots of water.

Philip Sprung alleged that the covering over his greenhouses was technologically unique and, together with his sophisticated hydroponics process, would grow plants more numerous and faster than orthodox methods. His greenhouses, he maintained, considerably hastened plant growth by uniting his specially created "biophotic" fabric covering, which enhanced sunlight, with a high-tech hydroponics method. Sprung's story was that his company had spent ten years in the development of his technologically advanced greenhouses at a cost of $35 million.

Peckford had made a grand tour of Sprung's operation in Calgary in late 1986 and soon afterwards dispatched a team of senior civil servants there as well, including agricultural and horticultural consultant Ross Traverse. Philip Sprung assured everyone that the proposed Newfoundland operation would grow 6.7 million pounds of cucumbers and tomatoes in its first year and produce 9 million pounds within five years. But the senior government advisers could not squeeze out of him any solid objective or independent evidence that such production figures were actually obtainable in the real world. His test operation, which had been in existence for a year or two, showed some production figures for cucumbers over the spring and summer months, but none for the colder months, and no numbers at all were provided for tomatoes.

Not surprisingly, for anyone familiar with Ross Traverse, the highly intelligent, plain-spoken agriculturist proclaimed his extreme skepticism over the whole shebang. Newfoundland's cold climate and limited sunlight from October to March, he predicted, would further limit the already dubious effectiveness of the technology. But the persuasive Mr. Sprung convinced the premier that his special artificial lighting system would solve that problem, and the province dived headfirst into the venture.

I would be amused, but not amazed, a few years later, when Ross Traverse, a member of the Atlantic Agricultural Hall of Fame, announced his retirement from the provincial civil service by publicly burning his bureaucrat's briefcase on television.

In May of 1987, Peckford announced one of our traditional, lopsided agreements in favour of an out-of-province adventurer. At $18.4 million for the jointly owned Newfoundland Enviroponics Limited, the government agreed to cough up over $11 million, while the Sprung Group of Companies put in $4 million. The company leased high-wattage, growth-inducing lights for $3 million. Philip Sprung became the CEO of the joint venture company, and the manager of the operation was his own youngish daughter, Dawn Sprung.

I had Ms. Dawn Sprung on my *Open Line* show as a guest a couple of times during this period, where she defended the project against its many mockers. She was your normal intelligent, charming, articulate young lady. But no one would have mistaken her for a rocket scientist, or even for an operator of an intricate and elaborate hydroponic greenhouse. She enjoyed it here in St. John's, she told me, living as she did in a high-end apartment in the Brentwood condominium on Portugal Cove Road. I got the impression that father and daughter were relishing the good life on substantial double salaries from the project.

It was a big operation both in physical size and its complement of workers. Eight greenhouses, each 800 feet long and nearly forty feet high, radiated out from a central control like an evil spaceship from *Star Wars*. Well over 300 workers were employed during its construction, and then, between a hundred and 200 employees were to grow and market the produce, mostly in the form of cucumbers, but with tomatoes thrown in for good measure.

The start-up was bumpy. It came at least three months later than projected, which increased expenses. It also meant that the first production of cucumbers hit the retail outlets in late spring of 1988, just as competition from the annual glut of greenhouse veggies from all over the world was at its worst, and prices therefore at rock bottom.

A cucumber from Sprung cost over a dollar to grow and market but fetched only half of that or less in local and external grocery stores. The result was that hardly a month went by, in 1988 and early 1989, that the Peckford government was not called upon to issue yet another line of credit or "loan" guarantee or "job creation" grant—a million here, a couple of million there. One Tory minister confided to me at the time that the province was being "dollared to death by this goddamned monstrosity."

Throughout all this, though, Premier Peckford and some ministers protested that naysayers from the Liberal Party and NDP and media were tantamount to traitors by the way they were publicly undermining Newfoundland's potential as an agricultural producer. They cited Dr. Doug House's Royal Commission recommendation for local development: "Agriculture is a prime example." Wasn't that exactly what the Peckford government was doing? Why couldn't Newfoundland grow cucumbers and tomatoes with the best of them?

I recall Liberal leader Clyde Wells dealing with that question as a guest on my *Open Line* show. No one was saying that Newfoundland couldn't grow greenhouse cucumbers, he replied. But at what cost? You could grow greenhouse cucumbers on the dark side of the moon, he suggested, if you were willing to spend the money.

Meanwhile, hardly a week went by in which the news from the

Sprung hothouses didn't cause hard-pressed Newfoundland and Labrador taxpayers to laugh or cry, usually at the same time. For example, on the subject of local markets, Statistics Canada reported that the average Newfoundlander ate one half of one cucumber a year, and the average local family spent $1.50 a year on their cukes.

Combined mirth and outrage ensued in the summer of 1988 after the media reported that the operation was producing so efficiently that tons of surplus cucumbers were being transported to farms as gourmet feed for cows and pigs and trucked to the dump at Robin Hood Bay as expensive pickings for the seagulls. This was the very month that the Peckford government granted Sprung an additional loan guarantee of over two and a half million dollars.

In the spring of 1988, as well, just in case there was any remaining doubt in the world that the entire province had gone mad, the government took it into its head to bring in double daylight saving time. This entailed moving clocks ahead, not by just the normal one hour, but by two hours. Apart from local jibes and lampoons that the government did it because they thought it would provide an extra hour of daylight for the greenhouses every day, there was a mixed reaction.

Holding off the dark seemed popular with the nightly barbecue crowd, but businesses found it very inconvenient trying to connect with the mainland, owing to the two-and-a-half-hour time difference with Quebec and Ontario and even more of a time gap farther west. Parents couldn't get their children to go to bed in the middle of bright daylight, and when school started in September, many were unnerved to see their kids set out for classes in the dark. Next year, the experiment was not repeated.

Queen Elizabeth's youngest son, Prince Edward, visited St. John's in the middle of the greenhouse endeavour. Eager to promote his cucumber venture, Peckford took the Prince on a tour of the hothouses, all duly filmed for television. At the time, the young prince was having a tough time back home with the British tabloids as he fended off their insinuations that he was gay.

I was appearing regularly on Peter Gzowski's *Morningside* show during that period, and he asked me about the royal visit to the Sprung cucumber operation. I replied that the cucumbers being produced were so impressive that Prince Edward didn't know whether to be delighted or alarmed when Premier Peckford advanced on him wielding a thirteen-inch cucumber. Local royalists were not amused.

Meanwhile, the humidity and heat in the greenhouses were being ineptly regulated and started to yield deformed cucumbers and blotchy tomato leaves. Moreover, everyone living around the operation—and you didn't have to be all that close—had their nights turned into day by the intensity of the grow lights. One resident suggested on *Open Line* that we could make up the financial losses by charging admission to watch professional baseball teams playing there at midnight.

Then, somehow, the "biophotic" fabric covering the greenhouses began to turn brown. Some blamed a mysterious industrial pollution for the off-colour stains, but whatever the cause, the amount of sunlight reaching the plants dropped precipitously rather than, as promised, being boosted above normal by the miracle fabric. Once more, the crop suffered.

Then, in December 1988, a special Christmas present for Premier Peckford: the whole cucumber crop upped and croaked. Nobody could fathom the reason for this seemingly spontaneous death of each and every plant. Philip Sprung himself screamed "sabotage." Some lawbreaking vandal, he alleged, had sneaked herbicides into the nutrient system. He posted a $10,000 reward for the identity of the saboteur, and he brought in "experts" to investigate.

His own people confirmed his claim that the plants had been poisoned, causing Peckford to jump on side as well. But when neither Memorial University nor the National Research Council, after analyzing samples of the plants, were able to verify the sabotage-by-herbicide scenario, the credibility of the poison allegations suffered. And the contempt and derision mushroomed.

Of course, it was a given from the beginning that opposition politicians, and much of the media, slammed the venture as a hare-brained scheme of lunatic proportions. But now, serious questioning and outright resistance were growing around Peckford's cabinet table as well. How could their government keep throwing taxpayers' hard-earned dollars at this political atrocity while essential services like schools and hospitals went begging? Finally, Agriculture minister Charlie Power, the minister most under the gun, besides the premier himself, had a New Year's epiphany.

Early in January of 1989, he resigned from the government, condemning the Sprung enterprise as a financial fiasco. When I talked to him soon afterwards, he revealed how embarrassed he was that, as a minister in 1988, he'd been sucked into this Joey Smallwood–type, quick-fix scheme from the 1950s and 1960s, promoted by outside fly-by-nighters. Both he and I wondered, as former ministers, why every government of our poor benighted province seemed to be perennially vulnerable to the predatory buccaneers slithering in here under the murky gloom of fog surrounding our shores.

A few months later, the Sprung enterprise in Newfoundland finally went under. An accounting firm took over as receiver and sold the facility to a conglomerate of Canadian, American, and other investors. For a short while, there was jubilation and a sense of redemption in the Peckford ranks as the new consortium raised production and lowered expenses. But the technology still could not prevail against our north Atlantic climate, and it failed once more.

The greenhouses that were going to provide hundreds of jobs, and export tons of cucumbers to eastern Canada and New England at a profit, and fill a historic gap—the lack of fresh, cheap vegetables in Newfoundlanders' eating habits—had achieved little but suck $20 million of taxpayers' money down a rat hole for two years. Worse, the whole preposterous thing looked profoundly wacko.

Mysteriously, in the winter of 1989, when the Sprung greenhouse had already gone belly up, the night sky of Mount Pearl was still fluorescently aglow. Apparently caretakers were leaving its lights on at a cost of $7,000 a day to try to melt the snow off the roof. Within a year or two the whole kit and caboodle was pulled apart and shipped to Montreal, and there seems to be no physical sign left that the grand greenhouse ever existed, for archaeologists to ponder over hundreds of years from now. It had entered the domain of pure fable and myth. Except for the pickle recipe booklet.

A scattered copy of that still exists as physical proof. It's entitled *Cucumber Recipes from Newfoundland Enviroponics: A Joint Venture of the Government of Newfoundland and Labrador with the Sprung Group of Companies*. It was written by a Mrs. Beverly Sprung, who must have been the wife of Phil, the misunderstood genius. It contains a foreword attributed to "A. Brian Peckford, PC, MHA, Premier." In it, he laments our lack of cucumber consumption here and touts the recipe book as designed to help tap our as yet undeveloped market. He is confident that with the new jobs, import substitution, exports, and the new technology, we are on to a good thing. And he is sure that when we taste the recipes in this book, we will agree.

In fact, the booklet contains fourteen pages of cucumber recipes of dreary sameness and banality. Only one recipe is spot on, and it has nothing to do with its taste. It's the recipe labelled: "Million Dollar Pickles."

NINE

During his reign as leader of the government, Peckford was fond of calling the whole period since 1949 "the false prosperity of the first three decades of Confederation." He was referring mainly to the province's unrelenting reliance on federal handouts in the shape of equalization and transfer payments. He struggled valiantly, but mostly in vain, for greater economic freedom from that for years. And he was also describing Joey Smallwood's industrialization schemes—the philosophy of develop or perish through rubber boot factories, and battery plants, and chocolate works, and oil refineries, and linerboard mills and phosphorous plants, and hydroelectric giveaways—irredeemable disasters, all.

Thus the saddest irony of Peckford's premiership was that despite his absolute disdain for nearly everything Smallwood stood for, his own Sprung greenhouse disaster was seen by many at the time as almost making Joey look good by comparison. The irony became especially cruel when, in the same year that Peckford's Sprung venture collapsed, the ERCO phosphorous plant at Long Harbour, a much-maligned and pilloried venture, supported by subsidies from Joey Smallwood's government, also closed down as no longer economically viable. Smallwood's ERCO and Peckford's Sprung: two putrid peas in a pod.

When Philip Sprung died at eighty-three in March of 2015, pure curiosity made me look up his obituary in the *Calgary Herald*. It made me laugh. Not that I found his death amusing. I was largely apathetic, one way or the other, regarding that event. No, what was laughable was the glowing description of the results of his "strong business acumen."

One sentence read, "In 1988, Sprung designed and completed in Calgary a massive hydroponic greenhouse operation within a space-age layout of Sprung Structures." There wasn't a word about this operation's abject failure through pollution of the ground on which the edifice had been erected. Then came the statement that, "This [Calgary] facility was later relocated to Newfoundland in a partnership with the Newfoundland Government." This was declared as if the Newfoundland–Sprung greenhouse partnership belonged on a list of Philip's admirably successful achievements instead of on a list of unmitigated lunatic disasters.

Peckford's credibility seemed irretrievably damaged by the crazy venture. The political esteem he revelled in throughout most of his days as minister and premier, chiefly through his clashes with Ottawa, began to wane drastically during the Sprung debacle and evaporated almost entirely at the end. Even some of his colleagues in government considered that he had become a severe political liability. "Oh, sure he was a leader who had dared greatly and struggled mightily" was a common refrain I heard in private encounters with them, but really, "at the end of the day," as the cliché of politicos went, he turned out to be an embarrassment.

Personally I found it amazing that, despite everything he'd done and tried to accomplish, the Sprung greenhouse flop could be used by so many to eclipse all that and utterly taint his whole career. It had become one of the most infamous projects in the province's checkered economic history. It doubtless led to Peckford's retirement from politics in 1989. He himself said at the time that he lacked the "necessary ruthlessness" to continue to lead the province. More likely he lacked the stomach and appetite—the morale—to battle mockers and scoffers for the rest of his political days.

Clyde Wells had won the leadership of the provincial Liberal Party in 1987. Peckford would say he thought Wells was a relic of the 1960s in that he possessed Joey Smallwood's narrow view of provincial government responsibilities. That was an interesting analysis of Wells, the man who had built his early political career precisely on taking on Joey's vision of politics. Peckford also suggested that a thread of rigidity ran through Wells. That was another interesting position from a man who had serious fallings-out with the likes of Frank Moores, John Crosbie, Leo Barry, Richard Cashin, Pierre Trudeau, and often Joe Clark and Brian Mulroney, as well as any media that "unfairly" criticized his policies.

Peckford's esteemed campaign organizer, John Laschinger, claimed that Peckford always trusted his nose. Every three years or so, he said, the premier would beat about the province sniffing the political breezes and then he'd phone Laschinger and tell him he was going to call an election. Laschinger would have a poll done, but "Peckford's nose was always right."

Perhaps he trusted his nose in 1989, too, as the stink of looming political defeat, rather than the sweet scent of victory, wafted in on the breeze. In any event, Peckford stayed on for only a little over a year after Wells became Liberal leader, then retired as premier in March 1989.

When Peckford resigned, John Laschinger has stated, he had no money, no job, and no home. Therefore, supporters put together a dinner to pass the hat and raise some funds for him. Prime Minister Brian Mulroney was guest speaker, with Mila, and John and Jane Crosbie, in attendance, so the effort was able to gather in about $100,000. Now Peckford could at least put a roof over his head. "But the fundraising effort was criticized," wrote Laschinger in his book, "as a backdoor way of financing the retirement of a political leader."

I personally had no problem with a politician, who had left power after many years, openly receiving a thank you and goodbye gift of money from a broad spectrum of admirers. But also I wondered why anyone would be surprised if there was some criticism. After seventeen years as an MHA, most of them as minister and premier, Peckford would have retired with a pension—enviable in amount to most people.

And I believe his pension became available, as a retiring premier, when his years of service and his age totalled to fifty-five years. So, it would have been collectible immediately upon his retirement at the age of forty-seven, when he still had many productive years ahead of him. Some wage-slaves might not join in on shedding tears with Laschinger for poor penniless, homeless, jobless Brian.

Peckford's reputation over the greenhouse failure did not improve in the immediate future. The new Liberal government of Clyde Wells, in July 1990, appointed a Royal Commission headed by Justice Seamus O'Regan to investigate the involvement of Peckford's government in the fiasco. O'Regan's report, two years later, found that the Peckford administration had not conducted a proper investigation of the technology employed, or the project's economic viability, and that it had neglected to consult with experts on the project's operation.

The commission concluded that although the provincial government and Sprung were joint partners, "the financial risk of the project was almost entirely with the government without justification." Whereas Sprung invested $4 million in the project, and the government had originally agreed to put in $11.4 million, the project in fact cost the government $22.2 million. Justice O'Regan found that the government acted in an "improper fashion" by not subjecting the loan guarantees to debate in the House of Assembly: all future government ventures should be assessed by independent experts, and any financial commitments should be fully debated in the House. O'Regan concluded that Peckford and his government had unnecessarily caused considerable loss of public money.

I couldn't find any reference to the greenhouses in Peckford's memoirs, *Some Day the Sun Will Shine and Have Not Will Be No More*, and you will search in vain for the word "Sprung" in its index. Understandably, Philip Sprung seems to have been turned into a non-person in Brian's own personal history.

The words "hydroponic," "greenhouse," and "cucumbers" are similarly absent. I do hope, though, that one of these days Brian will tackle the subject head-on in another written work, to give readers the benefit of his thought processes as he and his colleagues were considering and supporting the proposal. There may be an object lesson there for other leaders who may be inclined to strive too hard and unwisely in their zeal to do their best for their people. And at the purely human level, many people, myself included, would like to know what it felt like to grow so desperate as a leader, watching impotently as your province slid toward a financial black hole, that you'd entangle yourself and your government in a project like this.

On the other side, an argument could be made that Peckford's hydroponic project was a brilliant concept but that he was simply too far ahead of his time in fostering it. The National Aeronautics and Space Administration (NASA) has reportedly done extensive hydroponic research for its Controlled Ecological Life Support System, which is a self-sustaining life-support system for space stations and space colonies. Perhaps NASA heard Clyde Wells talking about putting greenhouses on the dark side of the moon, because the hydroponics planned for the planet Mars are said to be far advanced.

In 1993, Peckford and his wife, Carol, and their son moved to Qualicum Beach, British Columbia. One of his colleagues from the Frank Moores days said to me then, "It breaks my heart to think that, when Brian came in as premier so full of ideas and expectations after Frank, he'd also have to leave his own province when he was finished. After everything he tried to do, he didn't deserve that."

Following ten years of all-out toiling as premier, added to several years of the same as a minister in Moores's government, what did Peckford have to show, upon his retirement from politics in 1989, for that huge effort?

Well, as a province, that year we still had the highest per capita debt and the highest unemployment in Canada, and the jobs here yielded among the lowest average income in the federation. As part of one of the world's most prosperous nations, this province was next thing to a third-world country.

Many would have agreed with that assessment at the time. And a full generation would pass before Peckford's jubilant prediction, back in the mid-1980s, "One day the sun will shine, and 'have not' will be no more!" changed from mere political rhetoric to economic fact. But not everybody, even before our "have" status was achieved, took such a dim view of Peckford's legacy. In 2000, the Newfoundland Ocean Industries Association recognized Peckford for his outstanding contributions. I think they saw the reality of his impact.

Since returning to private life, Peckford appears to have been active in business and public service. He set himself up as a business consultant and has sat on various boards of directors, including the board of the Canadian Broadcasting Corporation. Some found that appointment a little ironic, since he had boycotted the St. John's CBC in exasperation, as premier, at some point during the 1980s.

His intelligence, energy, and experience have been in demand in British Columbia. In 1998, he was asked to conduct a one-man inquiry into the decline of Fraser River salmon stocks and into fishery management. In 2008, the Harper government appointed him chair of a panel to study federal chronic disease policy, especially diabetes, and to submit a report to the federal Health minister.

Meanwhile, he has also acted as an adviser to the woebegone British Columbia Conservative Party. In the 2005 provincial election there, the party had received just one half of one per cent of the votes cast. Six years later, in 2011, a year or so after Peckford joined the advisory committee, the party was regularly polling, according to the surveys, more than ten per cent and has gone as high as twenty-three per cent. I don't know if that was attributable to Peckford's contribution or not, but he seemed to be doing something right.

In the BC election of 2013, the Conservative Party received less than five per cent of the popular vote. But that was still more than double the percentage received in the 2009 election, and the highest percentage return since 1979. It seems to be just the sort of near-impossible challenge that Brian Peckford used to relish taking on in Newfoundland and Labrador, sometimes even meeting with triumph.

My own assessment of Peckford, as premier, is similar to that of the political opponent in dire straits, whom he had helped years ago without question: "Brian Peckford is a good man." He attempted many things that went nowhere. But they were positive endeavours, not negative, and they were far from futile. Peckford laid to rest many of our tribal myths about the fishery, the offshore oil, and the Upper Churchill project. He tried, affirmatively, to turn them to our advantage, and he certainly discovered what didn't work. But without trying them, he might not have found what did work: his never-say-die endeavours on the province's role in the offshore produced the 1985 Atlantic Accord.

Long after the Sprung nonsense has faded into relative insignificance in our history, his Accord, plus his social policies on equity and on our arts and culture, will be lauded and extolled.

A good man? Yes. A good premier? I believe Brian Peckford will be seen in the perspective of history as one of our best.

TEN

Clyde Kirby Wells's final year and my first year at Memorial University overlapped, but I have no real memory of him there. Unlike my recollection of other senior male students, like Patrick O'Flaherty, Peter Neary, George Ivany, Graham Skanes, Bill Rompkey, and similar luminaries whom we freshmen looked up to in admiration and awe, I can only recall Clyde, if at all, as from a haze. Yet when he graduated in 1959, he received the John Lewis Paton Society Award for outstanding contribution to student life. I can only assume that his contributions, then as later, were of the more serious kind and that he was not the type to be carrying on in the common room having a laugh or playing poker with the b'ys.

The first time I formed an impression of Clyde Wells was during the winter of 1964–65, when I was studying law in England. In a letter I got from my father, who was in Premier Joey Smallwood's cabinet, he made an amused mention of how irked Joey was over an insurrection in the ranks by a young Corner Brook lawyer. Joey had wanted to give his Liberal Party a more youthful sheen, since he himself was only a year or so away from drawing down his old-age pension. So, that fall of 1964, he called a convention in Grand Falls to set up a Young Liberals Association.

Leaving nothing to chance, he had lurking in the wings his handpicked candidate ready to "run" for president of the association. But out of the west rode a modern young Lochinvar determined to save democracy. This little-known knight in shining armour ran for the presidency and won against the premier's own anointed man. Well, to hear Joey ranting behind closed doors, it was a *coup d'etat*, a *bloodless* coup, perhaps, but a goddamned coup nonetheless. Who the hell did this—what's his name? Clyde Wells!—think he was?

Long afterwards I asked Joey why, feeling the way he did about Clyde at the time, he would include him among the other Young Turks he recruited to run for the Liberal Party in the provincial election a couple of years later, in September 1966. Joey answered with a quote from President Lyndon Johnson: "I'd rather have him inside the tent pissing out than outside the tent pissing in." But then Joey added his own rueful kicker: "What I didn't expect, once I'd dragged him body and bones inside the tent, was that he'd straight away start pissing on me."

Joey not only dragged Clyde, in his late twenties, inside his tent, he sat him right down at the big boys' table. He had him sworn in as a cabinet minister during the summer of 1966 even before he had a seat in the House of Assembly. The word floating around among us other aspirants was that, for the Government House ceremony, Joey arranged to have Clyde and his wife, Eleanor, flown like royalty from Deer Lake Airport to St. John's in the Lundrigans Inc. private jet.

The Honourable Charlie Ballam, one of Joey's longest-serving cabinet ministers, became dead wood as a result of Clyde's ascendancy, and Joey dumped him. Charlie had been a prominent labour leader before getting elected to the National Convention in the late 1940s to help decide Newfoundland's fate. Thereafter, for seventeen years following Confederation he was a Corner Brook Member of the House of Assembly and Minister of Labour in Smallwood's cabinet. That summer of 1966, Charlie heard on the radio an announcement by the premier that Minister Ballam had retired. It was his first inkling of it.

I can well imagine how hurt he was when Joey jettisoned him like that. Two or three years before, while working as a student in Corner

Brook for the summer, I'd driven Ballam and some other bigwigs out to the Deer Lake Airport. Before setting out he said to me gravely from the back seat, "Drive carefully, young man. You are carrying a very valuable cargo here." And he pointed at himself. Anyone with such a highly developed sense of self-worth had to be devastated by the callousness Joey showed him, his old comrade-in-arms. Joey tried, inadequately, to soothe Charlie's ego by appointing him to the board of the Newfoundland Power Commission.

Mr. Ballam's feelings were not the only ones Joey wounded before that September 1966 election. Ed Roberts was poisoned by his treatment as well. He was Joey's executive assistant and slated to run in White Bay North as part of Joey's gang of new and relatively young candidates. They included Deputy Mayor of St. John's John Crosbie, prominent lawyer Alex Hickman, prominent broadcaster John Nolan, prominent journalist Bill Callahan, prominent insider Ed Roberts, and twenty-four-year-old me. In addition to Wells, Joey appointed Crosbie and Hickman to his cabinet before the election. Ed was left out and understandably aggrieved, especially by the pre-eminence accorded to the upstart Clyde Wells.

Also resentful was Steve Neary. He was already an elected Member of the House from Bell Island and a highly regarded former union leader, having been president of the Newfoundland Federation of Labour. He couldn't believe it when Joey picked Clyde Wells to be minister of Labour over him. Nor apparently could the Newfoundland Federation of Labour. They promptly passed a resolution asking Joey to appoint someone who was at least known to the workers of the province.

Early in Clyde Kirby Wells's political career, before he became the hero of Meech Lake, many observers would wonder why he found it so difficult to get himself elected personally. Perhaps a column by Roger Simmons in the Corner Brook *Western Star* newspaper during the campaign leading up to the September 1966 election gives us a clue.

According to Simmons, who was at this campaign meeting, Wells explained to the Corner Brook audience his reasons for running. It was not because of what he planned to do for the district of Humber East if elected, but why the job of cabinet minister and MHA would be good for *him* right now.

In case that didn't cause enough buzz and snickers in the second city's bars and malls, Simmons then hired a cartoonist to depict Minister of Labour Wells in the newspaper as a little boy in short pants, looking up at Joey and asking, "Daddy, what is a strike?"

Next, an editorial in the *Western Star*, also published during Simmons's same guest editorship of the paper that summer, predicted that Clyde Wells would hold his cabinet portfolio for the shortest period of time in history. Simmons's forecast not only turned out to be wrong, but ironically enough—perhaps proof of the existence of karma in the universe—Simmons himself, years later, would go on to achieve that record himself.

He would become a minister in Pierre Trudeau's federal cabinet for just ten days in 1983 before being forced to resign under charges of income tax evasion. And there'd be more—call it karma with a vengeance: Revenue Canada would hire Clyde Wells as their prosecutor in the case. And he would vigorously prosecute Simmons, hammer and tongs, against two hotshot defence lawyers, one local and one from Toronto, but so effectively that Simmons was convicted of wilfully failing to pay income tax of several thousand dollars, and fined.

But back to the election of September 1966: Wells was up against Progressive Conservative candidate Noel Murphy, a well-known Corner Brook medical doctor and businessman. Murphy was also the sitting MHA in Humber East and Leader of the PC Opposition. A lot of people I knew in Corner Brook thought Clyde, despite the personal credentials of Murphy, should have wiped him out. Clyde had everything going for him: Joey himself was running in the adjoining district of Humber West, and campaigned on Clyde's behalf, and poured money into the district; plus, the Liberal Party enjoyed overriding popularity throughout the province and would win all but three seats, mostly overwhelmingly. Even those three that Joey lost in the Tory St. John's area were missed by only a handful of votes. Yet in spite of all those advantages, Wells managed to beat Noel Murphy by fewer than 400 votes.

When I first saw Clyde after the election, as we were all being sworn in as MHAs in the House of Assembly, the main thing I noticed about him was his bearing. He was stocky and not tall, but he carried himself with an erect military posture; his movements were grave and deliberate. I was not surprised to learn that he had helped pay for his education by joining the Canadian Officer Training Corps at Memorial under Dean Mose Morgan's guidance.

After graduation from law school he'd been a lawyer in the Canadian Army, Judge Advocate General's Office, from 1962 to 1964, with the rank of captain. Some of Clyde's later success in life probably derived from the contribution his military days had made to his physical deportment. Added to his persuasive reasoning ability, he always looked solidly impressive.

I found Wells's maiden speech in the House of Assembly in December of 1966 to be noteworthy. Joey himself appeared to appreciate most of it, although the part he seemed to like best was where Clyde frankly acknowledged that he'd been elected because of the tremendous admiration the voters had for the premier.

When Clyde turned to praising Bowater paper mill in Corner Brook as Newfoundland's greatest industry and started pointing out the shortcomings of Newfoundland's legal system, including the need for a Supreme Court judge in Corner Brook, Steve Neary leaned over and whispered a rhetorical question to me: "Are you supposed to use the House of Assembly to do PR work for your clients and lobby for services that will benefit your law practice?" Steve, throughout his highly successful political career, and later as a valued commentator, never really liked the cut of Clyde's jib and nearly always suspected his motives.

In his maiden speech, Clyde also criticized the province's denominational school system—the fracturing and duplication of facilities, the waste of money, the inadequate education. He instanced in negative terms his own experience growing up in Stephenville Crossing, where he'd had to attend a one-room denominational school. I saw Joey stiffen a little during this onslaught. He depended significantly on the political goodwill of many Catholic and Pentecostal leaders, who were the main champions of the continuation of the system.

My father, Fred Rowe, an educator and extensive writer on Newfoundland education and history, said to me after Clyde's speech that he must have an exceedingly good brain to have survived his schooling: the statistics showed that a student whose childhood education was gained in a one-room school in those days had about one chance in 900 of graduating with high school matriculation.

ELEVEN

Clyde was first tested seriously as Labour minister early in 1967 when a strike by hospital workers occurred in Grand Falls. There had been job action among health care workers leading up to the election, but the challenge of that, if I remember correctly, was largely handled by Joey, with his withering media attacks against those who would dare threaten to strike against the sick, and the halt, and the dying.

Wells seemed to enjoy handling this continuation of the labour struggle, and he took it on with alacrity. After a few days, he brought in legislation to end the walkout. Introducing the bill, he surprised no one by placing himself on the side of law and order and four-square against anarchy. He found it inconceivable, echoing Joey, that a union would go on strike against the sick and the dying. His legislation outlawed hospital strikes under any circumstances on pain of heavy fines and even decertification.

Joey backed him up, not sparing the labour movement the memory of the IWA strike in 1959, and that union's extermination in this province less than a decade before. Where was the IWA now? he wondered in the House. And he contrasted its future, after he'd decertified it, to his own Liberal Party, which was still in government and elected in even greater numbers. Indeed, the premier and the minister seemed to be heart-to-heart in the conviction that the whole notion of strikes in the civil service was contrary to the public good.

Even as they spoke, though, the legal possibility of such strikes was becoming a reality in the federal civil service and would soon become the norm in the provinces. Meanwhile, facing severe criticism from organized labour for destroying the rights of workers, which had been gained over a century of bloody battles against reactionary employers like him, Wells responded that he hadn't taken away any rights from the union, merely the *unlawful* right to strike.

This would set the stage for Wells's perceived extremely conservative stance regarding unions over the years to come. One labour leader would suggest that, in his legal practice, nobody could find even one instance where Wells had acted for a union in a labour dispute, as against always acting for the employer. Even much later, in his second general election as premier in 1993, he would ask the electorate who they wanted to govern the province, the duly elected government or the public service unions. And he would win handily.

A year or two after he was first appointed to the cabinet and elected in Humber East in 1966, the stress on Wells from his law firm, and from his family, had become too great to bear. Family and firm were in Corner Brook, and he was spending most of his time away from them in St. John's, attending to his department, the cabinet, and the House of Assembly. He told me several times he was finding the separation and the conflicting burdens absolutely frustrating and frankly intolerable. He was looking for a young lawyer who could shoulder some of the load back at his law office.

Not long after I was admitted to the Bar as a practising lawyer in 1967, Clyde asked me if he could get together with me, when the House adjourned that day, for a chat. I invited him and his friend, Gerry Myrden, the MHA for St. Barbe South, and married to my cousin, back to my house for a drink. There, without beating about the bush, Clyde asked me to join his law firm in Corner Brook for $13,000 a year. The measure of his desperation was that he was prepared to offer that amount of money (probably $90,000 in 2016 dollars) to a rank legal novice. I admired Clyde and I was flattered by his invitation. But I'd just gotten married a few months before, and moved into our new home, and recently joined the great St. John's law firm of Halley, Hickman, Hunt and Steele. Hence, it was impossible.

Around this time, Clyde gave Joey his resignation as minister of Labour but stayed in the cabinet as minister without portfolio. Later, Joey would characterize his early experience with Clyde Wells to me along these lines: "Typical Wells the opportunist—he wanted to have his cake and eat it, too. He wasn't prepared to do the work but wanted the title and prestige of being an honourable minister. He never could stick to anything. He joined the army, milked it for all it was worth, and then after a couple of years, he bought his way out for greener pastures. I pitchforked him into cabinet, at the price of considerable disgruntlement to worthier candidates, and in the election I dragged him by the heels into the House. He could have said no, if he couldn't handle it all, but of course he didn't say no—he wanted the glory of it all. But then after a few months, he got sick of his ministerial responsibilities and wanted to go back to minting money practising law."

During this period, Steve Neary launched his scathing public attack on lawyers' real estate fees. They were way too high, he claimed, a complete con job, and it was all because the Law Society, which he called the "Lawyers' Union," had a monopoly and could charge whatever legal fees they felt like, without the consumer having the benefit of any competition. Even worse, he asserted, the Lawyers' Union had a secret scale of fees for every transaction, and no lawyer could deviate from it by charging lower fees without incurring discipline from the Lawyers' Union.

Neary's onslaught hit a resonant chord with the public, and the issue took off in the media. At one point there was a debate on television between Neary and the president of the Law Society, who was entitled "Treasurer" in those days. The title of treasurer for the top position was all the proof you needed, said Neary, of where lawyers' true interests lay: money and lots of it. The treasurer tried to justify the fees on the basis of professional responsibility and liability for each of those large transactions. That was met with a jaded, "Yeah right," from Neary and many of the public.

When it became clear that Neary had made mincemeat of the treasurer in the eyes of the populace, many lawyers feared that this was getting out of hand. A special meeting of the Law Society was convened to deal with the crisis, which I attended. Wells was not there, but he floored most of the other lawyers present: he sent in a telex from Corner Brook agreeing with Neary.

Now, Wells already had a well-deserved reputation for charging high legal fees. So, other lawyers practically gave themselves hernias trying to figure out his rationale on this issue. But his reasoning was simple, really. If you wanted the very best legal representation, which would be Clyde, on a difficult legal matter, then you had to be prepared to pay him top dollar for it. But that didn't apply to purely clerkish matters like routine real estate transactions, most of which were performed by the lawyer's secretary, anyway.

Steve Neary's initiative led to a Commission of Inquiry into the issue, with the result that lawyers' advertising and competition on legal fees were thereafter loosened up considerably. What I found amusing was that Steve Neary, who never, to my knowledge, sided with Clyde Wells on anything, had an ally in Clyde regarding his legal fees initiative. True, Steve would journey to Corner Brook a couple of times in the 1980s to feel out Wells on running for the leadership of the Liberal Party. But several of the savvy politicos, including Steve himself, at our monthly poker table at the time, "kidded" that he was doing it not to encourage Clyde but to ascertain if he was going to run, so that Steve could decide on his own future ambitions.

* * * * *

In the late 1960s, Joey created a cabinet committee to deal with John Shaheen and his proposed Come By Chance oil refinery. The committee consisted of three of the several lawyers in the cabinet, John Crosbie, Alex Hickman, and Clyde Wells. Before long, there was hell to pay between the committee and the premier. Not the least of the problems was that Joey normally sided with Shaheen against his own cabinet colleagues on vital issues, especially when it came to providing more government money or financial commitments to the refinery. I wasn't on the inside during that period, but judging by what Ed Roberts and I would in fact go through from 1968 to 1971, playing a similar role, the three committee members experienced an absolute nightmare.

In those days, John Crosbie told me, he appreciated Clyde Wells in cabinet and on the committee and even liked him. He was intelligent and alert to everything, didn't kowtow to Joey—certainly never brown-nosed him. Just like John himself, in other words. Well, that attitude, up against Joey's personality and position on the refinery, was not going to work for long. And sure enough, the time came when Crosbie and Wells could not take it for one second longer. Hickman was prepared to weather the situation out, but the other two found it insufferable and planned to abandon ship.

The excuse they found was the extra $5 million in interim or "bridge" financing that Shaheen was now demanding in order to keep the refinery deal from collapsing and which Joey wanted the cabinet to okay. Small as the amount was in the overall financial picture, Crosbie and Wells claimed it was the straw that broke the camel's back. On May 14, 1968, the pair went to see Joey in his office, intending to resign.

They had their letters of resignation in hand. But Joey was too nimble for them: before Crosbie could even start, Joey passed him an elaborate letter firing him and detailing his many heinous reasons for doing so. Crosbie bellowed, "Like fuck you are!" and banged his letter of resignation down on his premier's desk. "I resign." Joey had no letter firing Wells, who simply passed over his letter of resignation.

Joey held an immediate news conference in which he slandered Crosbie and his business uncles and brother. He accused John of sundry conflicts of interest and of attempting to shake down the government to benefit his ravenous family's businesses and alleged untold rip-offs of the government by his rapacious relatives.

Joey must have forgotten that he wasn't in the House of Assembly, where he would be immune from prosecution for defamation, when he issued his accusations, because after John's family members announced they were suing the premier for slander and libel, Joey backed down. He withdrew his allegations and broadcast an apology. Meanwhile, I don't recall hearing Joey make any mention of Clyde Wells. It was as if he was a non-entity in the piece, or at most a mere devil's apprentice to John Crosbie, the great Satan.

Joey mostly tended to belittle Clyde. He married up, he'd say, referring to Wells's wife, Eleanor: he married the girl who lived in the big house on the hill, and ever since then he's been striving to meet his wife's approval. He used to say the same thing about Alex Hickman's need for spousal approval, too.

In our caucus, Joey scoffed at the very idea that either Crosbie or Wells had resigned because of the "bridge" financing for Shaheen. In Crosbie's case, in addition to the voracious family greed, he said, it was simply a matter of vaulting ambition, pure and simple—raw, unadulterated, overweening ambition. He had entered cabinet and the House of Assembly with one objective and one only: take over the Liberal Party by hook or by crook and become premier. The man was a pathological case of overbearing gluttony for power, declared our premier of nearly twenty years.

Now, as for young Clyde: he had resigned solely because the premier had kept asking him, reasonably and sensibly, whether he was going to continue to treat his cabinet position as a mere hobby, while he concentrated on practising law, or whether he was going to become, finally and at last and once and for all, a full-fledged cabinet minister. Clyde only attended about one in twelve cabinet meetings on the province's business, Joey said, because he was too busy building up a big law practice for himself.

Wells responded that that was untrue. As I recall it, though, Wells himself made it clear in the House that he had resigned over more than the oil refinery. There was also, he said, the important matter of his Corner Brook law practice. This frankness over his selfish reason for resigning, at that particularly inopportune time, undermined Clyde's appeal to many hardcore Liberals, at least in the short run. It added to the blame heaped on him and Crosbie for resigning right in the middle of the federal election campaign and causing, it was alleged, the dismal showing of the Liberal candidates here in the election results of June 25, 1968.

Trudeaumania was then rampant across much of Canada, resulting in new Liberal leader Pierre Trudeau's majority government victory. But this province elected six Tories out of our seven MPs. (The "Noisy Six," who would become the bane of Trudeau's existence.) Only one Liberal, Don Jamieson, won, with a much-reduced vote.

Joey was mortified. He'd led the charge in getting Trudeau elected Liberal leader in Ottawa that spring, and now our much-vaunted Father of Confederation had failed abysmally in delivering the votes of his province to his chosen man. He never forgave Crosbie and Wells for his humiliation and heaped blame and denunciation on their heads. His reproaches for their desertion may have been much deserved because of their horrible timing, but blaming them for the poor Liberal showing in this province seemed unwarranted: the election turned out as bad or worse for Trudeau and the Liberals in Nova Scotia and PEI; our two local villains had nothing to do with that.

The results were probably more a matter of Trudeau's perceived effeminacy at the time, his lapel rose, his scarlet cape, his floppy hat, plus his apparently confirmed mid-life bachelorhood—wink wink, nudge nudge—traits which weren't appreciated so much east of effete Quebec and Ontario, here in the Atlantic Provinces where men were still men.

Still, you had to wonder why Crosbie and Wells, rather than waiting out the election, would have chosen their inopportune time to make their dramatic move, knowing that at the very least it could not have helped the Liberal cause. Their disgruntlement had been known in cabinet for weeks, and my father told me at the time that, when he felt out

Crosbie and Wells about their rumoured resignations, both cabinet colleagues assured him that, if they in fact were to resign, it would certainly not take place until after the June federal election. Who knows? Could it be, perhaps, that egotism, or hubris, or self-interest, sometimes trumps altruism in politics?

TWELVE

After Crosbie and Wells resigned from cabinet, Joey had their seats in the House of Assembly moved across the aisle to the Opposition side. When they protested and insisted that they had only resigned from cabinet and not from the Liberal caucus, Joey wouldn't listen. He ordered their seats and desks to be bolted to the floor over there.

In other words, true to form, after suffering a perceived threat to his dignity and authority, Joey acted in perhaps the worst possible manner against his own self-interest. If they'd been relegated to the backbenches of the government side, Crosbie and Wells would only have been a nuisance; but they became, after he'd forced them to be fixtures on the Opposition side, the most effective and nasty opponents in the House that Joey had ever faced.

The media came to be particularly enamoured of Wells, especially the way he, with Crosbie, took on the shortcomings of the Come By Chance refinery deal. A friend of mine from university days, who'd become a House of Assembly reporter for CBC, told me that he and others in the press gallery thought that Clyde Wells was the best debater—and Joey-baiter—they'd ever seen in the chamber. Years later, Rex Murphy would tell me he believed that much of Clyde's political reputation was media-generated.

Joey now announced he wanted to *re*organize the Liberal Party, although in truth the party had never been organized in the first place. He called a big Liberal meeting for September 1968 at the stadium in Grand Falls, all the while proclaiming that he intended to leave the party in good shape for his successor when he resigned as leader before the next election. As later events would show, he was, in reality, already making plans to be kept on as leader by overwhelming and irresistible public demand. Moreover, he wanted to smoke out John Crosbie and his burning ambition to topple him.

Crosbie, in order to get back in the party as a member in good standing, was prepared to sign a declaration of support for the Liberal Party and its principles. By doing so, he'd clear the way for his run in the leadership race that Joey was proclaiming for 1969. Joey accepted Crosbie's letter, but Clyde Wells, according to the premier, refused point-blank to sign one like it. Wells disputed that. His letter, he said, was the same as Crosbie's. Joey wouldn't relent. And as a result, Wells garnered as much news coverage as Joey's big meeting did, when he appeared outside the building, barred from entry, but sporting a lapel button declaring, "I am a Liberal."

To Joey it was not so much a matter of Wells proclaiming himself a Liberal but rather the kind of Liberal he might turn out to be. Joey had memories from four years before, in this very town, when his orderly organizing of a Young Liberals Association had been derailed by Clyde's insurrection. To buttress his decision to keep Clyde out now he publicly asked, "Who wants that kind of a Liberal in the party, anyway?" He himself, he continued, had dragged Mr. Wells into the House of Assembly by the heels in the first place. I recall that not everybody found all this strictly rational.

Meanwhile, Joey had to fill the voids left by the resignations of Crosbie and Wells and by the vacancies formed by some long-time ministers who were informed by Joey on the radio news that their health was forcing them to retire from cabinet. Then he bumped a number of us up. The new ministers included Steve Neary, Bill Callahan, John Nolan, Ed Roberts, and me. At barely twenty-six years old, I was not that long out of short pants.

Joey set the big Liberal leadership convention to begin on Halloween, 1969. John Crosbie announced at once that he was running. Smallwood waited until June of that year, when he was halfway around the world, to make his definitive intentions known. I was in Hong Kong with him and his son, Bill, when he paced the floor of the hotel suite at three o'clock in the morning, agonizing, he told us, over his gruelling decision.

Then he boarded a plane and flew back home without even stopping at a hotel—from Hong Kong, to Hawaii, Los Angeles, Toronto, and St. John's—to declare that he was forced by his conscience, in the best interests of the entire province, to keep the great Liberal Party from falling into "the wrong hands." Those defiled hands, he revealed, belonged to one John Crosbie.

The duel between Smallwood and Crosbie was not long becoming a metaphorical bloodbath. John called Joey a ludicrous tyrant who'd be considered a joke if he wasn't so dangerous. Joey said he had buried John's father, Ches, six feet under during the Confederation battle; now he would bury his son, not six, not twelve, but *eighteen* feet under. Both camps would end up spending a million dollars each (well over $6 million in 2016 dollars).

Clyde Wells became Crosbie's leadership campaign manager for the west coast. I don't know how well he did on electing delegates for his candidate there, but several Crosbie organizers told me later that Clyde was more impressive describing how the constitution of the party, and the whole process, were defective, than he was in dragging out support for Crosbie delegates. Then he was reported missing in action.

Highly regarded Stephenville lawyer Fred Stagg, whom I'd known at Memorial and who'd articled under Wells, was a staunch Crosbie supporter. He told me later that everyone was flabbergasted when Wells suddenly disappeared for the ten days immediately leading up to the convention. They discovered he'd gone moose hunting.

Fred Stagg would later leave the Liberal Party and become a PC. He would get elected to the House in 1971 as MHA from Port au Port District. There he would tell me of his gut-wrenching disillusionment with Wells, especially when Wells bailed out of the legislature a year or so after the leadership convention. The man abandoned politics, Stagg said, when he was needed most.

Back to the October 31, 1969, leadership convention itself: it was so bloated with delegates and observers that it had to be held at Memorial Stadium in St. John's. Wells announced that he was going to attend the convention, whatever Joey might say. What Joey said was that he was not a Liberal and he was not going to be allowed in. The credentials committee was clear: he would be barred at the door. Ed Roberts and I conferred with each other. This had all the elements of an asinine standoff of moronic proportions.

Ed and I didn't directly ask Joey, "What are you—nuts?" but the question was inherent in our arguments. By keeping Clyde out, we told him, he would be turning the man into a hero and a martyr—a big story now and hereafter. Let him in and the whole foofaraw would become a non-story in the media. But Joey didn't like the idea of possibly being portrayed by the press as having caved in to the likes of Clyde. And he couldn't see what the incurable shit disturber would actually do if security barred him at the door, except leave.

We told Joey that there was no telling what he might do. First of all, he would make it look as if Joey was afraid of him. You could say what you wanted about Clyde Wells, but you couldn't deny that he'd proved himself to have the courage of his convictions, and that was the angle that would be picked up on by the media—the man possessed tremendous moral courage.

Joey didn't like it when we said that. He made it clear that he would have liked it better if we'd said that Clyde Wells was only a self-serving prick. So I told him that Clyde coming into the convention would be only like a fart in the elevator—unpleasant at that moment, but soon dispersed when the door opened. Joey seemed to like the image, and yielded. Clyde entered, with a short flurry of attention by the press that was quickly superseded by events.

When the results of the voting were announced, the words that would be used by many were that Joey Smallwood had "demolished," "crushed," or "obliterated" John Crosbie. But I was frankly surprised that Crosbie had received so many votes, considering that Smallwood had had the vast majority of Members of the House out in their districts for weeks, working on electing his slates of delegates. Joey won by 1,007 votes to Crosbie's 440. It was, in effect, a foreshadowing of the fallout to come for Joey and his party.

But Crosbie supporters there weren't pleased in any way; they must have thought beforehand that he was actually going to win, because they were absolutely devastated by Joey's re-election. Chaos ensued on the convention floor for many minutes. Some young Crosbie-ites wept tears of bitterness, burned their Liberal membership cards, shouted Sieg Heil and Heil Hitler at Joey, over and over, and gave him the Nazi salute.

Karl Wells, a highly popular CBC personality, restaurant reviewer, and award-winning writer, told me later in the CBC cafeteria that he was at the convention as an observer, and he was near the Crosbie platform when Joey asked Crosbie over the mic, through the racket, to come up on stage and join him there. Clyde, Karl said, was beside himself with anger, grabbed Crosbie by the arm, and shouted: "No, John, don't give the old bastard the satisfaction." Crosbie had to tug his arm loose to get away and go up.

After the convention, Wells and Crosbie announced that they were still Liberals, albeit of the independent ilk. They were joined now by disgruntled Liberal MHAs Beaton Abbott and Gerald Myrden, and, I think, Tom Burgess, and they continued the Liberal Reform Party in the House of Assembly. There the pair presented, along with other former Liberal ministers who had crossed the House to the official Tory Opposition, the most formidable challenge to Joey's control of the legislature he had ever faced.

On one occasion, for example, Joey got the bright idea to bring John Shaheen and Homer White, the top brass of the Come By Chance oil refinery project, onto the floor of the House to explain to the population in televised sessions just how good the refinery really was. Crosbie and Wells, in their best cross-examining pit-bull lawyer style, made mincemeat out of them. Wells especially, who seemed to be a natural in front of the camera, became a bit of a local TV celebrity.

THIRTEEN

Late in 1970, Wells resigned from the House and left active politics altogether. He announced that he wouldn't join Crosbie and others who were officially disavowing Liberalism and joining the Tory Party. He was standing on principle, he declared: he was a Liberal, and you either believed what you've said about the Liberal Party, and your position in it, or you didn't. And he himself believed what he'd said. So much so that when new PC leader Frank Moores, who was about to run in Joey's own district of Humber West, sat in Clyde's house in Corner Brook to destroy a bottle of Scotch and try to persuade him to become a Tory candidate, Wells disclosed to a reporter that he told Frank no. He couldn't see how he could proclaim the virtues of the Liberal Party one day and then turn around on his convictions the next day.

But within the year, during the election Joey called for the fall of 1971, when I was in my district of White Bay South going door to door, Steve Neary reached me and said that Clyde Wells had made a radio commercial supporting the PC Party. Furthermore, Steve told me in disgust, the self-proclaimed great white hope of the Liberal Party was actively helping Tory candidate Tom Farrell win Wells's own former seat of Humber East.

That 1971 election turned out to be a virtual tie in seats between Smallwood's Liberals and Frank Moores's Progressive Conservatives, although the PCs had handily won the popular vote. In January of the new year, after the mind-boggling machinations detailed in my book *The Premiers Joey and Frank,* Joey resigned the government in Moores's favour. A few weeks later, the pragmatic Mr. Moores had his friend, the neighbouring Liberal MHA, bribed to the tune of at least $100,000 not to turn up at the House of Assembly. At the same time, Frank had the Liberal MHA sign a letter of resignation that gave him a majority and allowed the Queen's representative to accede to Frank's request, as premier, for a fresh election.

Ed Roberts, who'd become the new leader of the Liberal Party after Smallwood resigned, told me during this March 1982 election that Clyde Wells was back on side. And he had undertaken to ensure that every west coast district had a Liberal candidate, supposing he had to run in one himself. I was shocked, therefore, as I plodded through White Bay South, to learn that on nomination day there was no Liberal candidate in Frank Moores's district of Humber West and that the PC leader had won the seat by acclamation.

On top of everything else, this default cut the guts out of our campaign and our morale sank into our boots, or, as my own campaign manager mused to me, "The arse is effin gone out of 'er!" Whichever of those mixed metaphors was worst for us applied to our situation. On election night the Liberal Party dropped from twenty seats to nine and the Tories ended up with thirty-three Members in the House of Assembly, and the first of substantial majority governments for years to come.

During most of those years of the 1970s, Clyde concentrated on what he told me was always his greatest love outside of family, the practice of law. And he thrived, acting for big, high-paying clients in Corner Brook and St. John's. I ran into him occasionally in connection with my own practice.

When I was meeting with clients or attending hearings in Corner Brook, I'd often stay at the Glynmill Inn. Sometimes, during breakfast in the dining room, I'd see Clyde appear at the door and cast his eye around the room. Then he'd enter with brisk dignity and make his rounds of some of the tables, shaking hands convivially. Perhaps he was simply greeting his visiting clients, in the course of which he'd also say hello to anyone else he knew. But his demeanour always struck me as if he was the Lord Mayor ascertaining who was sojourning in the city and welcoming those of note to his domain.

Once when I met with him at his office on legal business, I noticed that the cord to his telephone receiver was in poor shape and nearly worn through. He explained that he had given up smoking, a pernicious habit he'd somehow acquired in Stephenville Crossing as an eight-year-old boy. In the course of fighting the powerful, insidious addiction, he would fiddle with the telephone cord with his fingers whenever he was on the phone until it became frayed right down to the wires. His sad motivation for quitting once and for all, I believe he told me then, was the tragic death of a family member, at a relatively young age, from cancer.

It was on that occasion that we finished our meeting in his office arguing on behalf of our respective clients by way of a stand-up shouting match which determined nothing. It was a highly unusual experience for me with another lawyer, and I remember feeling afterwards that perhaps nicotine withdrawal was partly to blame, although that couldn't have been my own excuse for participating.

Then, a few weeks later, we met in my office in St. John's, and this time the discussion terminated with both of us on our feet, toe to toe, shouting louder into each other's faces. As Clyde stomped out of my office and hustled through our premises and down the stairs, glancing neither left nor right, I noticed that a pall of silent astonishment had descended on the secretaries and other lawyers. I was half at fault, since I did half the shouting, but we all agreed that we'd never heard the like of that before, and speaking for myself, I had never before, and never again, found myself taking part in a similar phenomenon with any other lawyer.

In any case, I was glad to learn from him in months to come that he was successful in his struggle against tobacco. When I decided to give up smoking myself, I recall thinking that my own addiction could not be as powerful as Clyde's, since I had not started till the relatively old age of fourteen or fifteen—a marketing flaw on the part of the cigarette companies—and if he was able to overcome the horrors of withdrawal, I could too. And I did, although I don't think I ever got around to thanking Clyde for his example.

During the 1970s, Lynn Verge was one of the few female lawyers, if not the only one, in Corner Brook. She had articled at Clyde Wells's law firm, but he disappointed and discouraged her afterwards by telling her there was no place for her at the firm (I think he meant as a partner) because she might have babies. Wells would rationalize this later by saying he was in no way being misogynistic; he was merely pointing out the obvious, that in a law firm everyone had to carry his or her own weight continuously, and no lawyer could expect partners to carry him or her during a leave of absence. Right, and no doubt his edict applied to men who might have babies, as well.

Lynn would go on to a stellar career in politics, and although I'm sure vengeance would have been the last thing in the mind of this no-nonsense and thoroughly decent woman, Wells would get his comeuppance at her hands a decade or so in the future.

Clyde's expanding professional achievements afforded him all the accoutrements, paraphernalia, and trappings of success. He was reputed to be reaching the status of the highest-income lawyer on the west coast, if not the entire province. He bombed around Corner Brook in the big Lincoln, lived in the big house in the best neighbourhood, and hung and chilled with family and friends at his extremely nice country estate on a lovely lake a few minutes out of town. There, though a very moderate drinker, he sipped on high-end Appleton Estate rum. Later, he would also enjoy his thirty-eight-foot luxury sailboat moored at a marina in Conception Bay.

Some lawyers I talked to in Corner Brook called him, good-naturedly, a yuppie. Clyde sometimes got a bit prickly over insinuations that he was wealthy and privileged. He reminded people that he'd gone to a one-room school, that he was one of nine children, and that his father had worked in the freight shed for the railway.

I recall a statement that Cabot Martin made to the *Globe and Mail* at some point during this period about Wells. Martin was a highly regarded lawyer and a top adviser on oil and gas to Premier Brian Peckford. He was asked, I believe, about the mystique and aura of mystery that seemed to envelope Clyde, especially because he'd taken on the indomitable Joey Smallwood so frontally and helped play a part in his downfall.

Martin, a native of Port aux Basques and steeped in west coast values and behaviours, replied point-blank that Wells was not mysterious. He was in fact very ordinary. Like many others who strived and succeeded professionally, he was simply a petit bourgeois whose measure of success was having a house next to W. J. Lundrigan, the founder of the west coast's biggest construction company. Martin said he was not making this point as a criticism—there were lots like Wells—but only so that people did not delude themselves in inflating the essence of Wells, the man.

Maybe so. But very few professional strivers I've known have so dominated whatever they've touched. And sometimes, for Wells, that included matters entirely outside of law and politics. Wells had always complained in the House that the west coast of Newfoundland, and his own Corner Brook in particular, perennially received short shrift compared to the capital, St. John's. He felt, evidently, that this applied as well to the religious denomination of which he was an adherent, the Anglican Church. Hence, of course, he lobbied hard for changes.

One Tory MHA, an Anglican himself, told me that he was frankly astonished at the role Wells played at the 1976 meeting of the Anglican Synod in St. John's. Wells took the bit in his teeth and, almost single-handedly, dominated the proceedings with marshalled arguments and persuaded the attendees to agree to a major restructuring: they voted to split the St. John's–centred, single Newfoundland diocese into three parts. Wells would become the chancellor of the Diocese of Western

Newfoundland. And an added bonus for him—if not everybody's cup of tea—was that he got to write the constitution of the new diocese.

My Tory MHA informant, even as a political opponent of Wells, could only shake his head in admiration. He did concede, though, that some others seemed perplexed at all Clyde's time and effort and dogged determination to achieve success in a church matter that not everyone considered overriding in importance to begin with.

Concerning this single-minded character trait of his, one of Clyde's good acquaintances said to me, chuckling, in a deliberate understatement: "It's almost as if Clyde gets a little too serious about things." However, Nancy Riche, a labour leader both in Newfoundland and nationally, had a different take on him. Years later, when she and I were waiting to go on a *Here and Now* panel on CBC Television, we reminisced about Clyde's perceived anti-union stance as premier. She stated, "They all said how serious he was. Well, he wasn't that fucking serious. I'm guessing he had a bit of fun on that fancy yacht of his while he was rolling back workers' wages in collective agreements he'd already signed."

Amongst lawyers I knew, Wells did have somewhat of a reputation for inflexibility on disputed matters and for being very difficult to negotiate settlements with. Differences that should have been settled by compromise, some said, often ended up needlessly in court. One story that made the rounds concerned a case that went to trial and which the chief justice ruled should never have been brought to court in the first place; he awarded all costs against Wells.

One Corner Brook lawyer described him as a dog with a bone, even after an issue had been decided at trial. If a court didn't agree with him, the court was wrong. Appeal, appeal, appeal was Clyde's watchword. Go to a higher court. That seemed to be mainly an opposing lawyer's complaint, though. Some actual clients I talked with, or heard about, thought the man was a marvellous lawyer in court and out. A case in point, which showed both sides of opinion on Wells, involved a minister in Frank Moores's cabinet, Dr. Tom Farrell.

FOURTEEN

On April 25, 1978, in the middle of the night, a fire broke out in Farrell's apartment in Elizabeth Towers, causing serious damage and forcing the evacuation of all the residents, many of them elderly. My own aging parents lived there. Farrell was under considerable stress during this period, from accusations against him in the House of wrongdoing as minister. The Royal Newfoundland Constabulary investigated the fire and a couple of months later turned their reports in to the Department of Justice. No public action was taken by the department, but in August, Farrell resigned from cabinet.

In September, the police reports, in which the investigators accused Farrell of arson, came into my hands as Leader of the Opposition. At least one of the investigators believed that a cover-up was happening, similar to the combined police and Department of Justice cover-up of criminal child abuse at Mount Cashel Orphanage, which would later become an international scandal. I studied the documents, and believing that a miscarriage of justice was being perpetrated, I had them delivered to some media. The next day, a headline in the St. John's *Telegram* said: "Report concludes blaze deliberately set by Farrell."

On October 30, Farrell was arrested and charged with arson. He retained Clyde Wells to conduct his defence. A preliminary inquiry was held and, on December 21, Judge Joseph Leclair dismissed the charges on grounds of insufficient evidence. I read the transcript of the inquiry and concluded that Wells's representation of Farrell was exceedingly clever and ingenious and articulate. I was not alone. A senior criminal lawyer who studied the case as well said to me, "If I was accused of murder I'd want Clyde to defend me—especially if I was guilty." Later, another Judge, A. S. Legrow, was appointed to investigate the cause of fire. On December 4, 1981, he concluded that "by accident or design the flame was applied by Dr. Farrell."

Meanwhile, Farrell had retained Wells to sue the *Evening Telegram* and CBC for defamation. These media were now in the impossible position of having to prove the truth of the allegations of arson in the police reports, which allegations had already been dismissed by provincial court judge Leclair. Both media were found liable for defamation. Judge John Mahoney presided. Ten years earlier, Mahoney had been attacked by John Crosbie for being in a shocking conflict of interest as Liberal Attorney General, when he was accused of negotiating on behalf of the government with his own law partner, who was representing buccaneer promoters John C. Doyle and John Shaheen.

Mahoney now awarded Tom Farrell $150,000 in damages. This was an inordinately large amount, the highest in Canada for libel up till then. One lawyer said to me that, judging by that huge award, Mahoney was making sure he was not going to be accused of bias against a former PC minister.

I didn't think any such idea had entered Mahoney's mind, and I gave him the benefit of the doubt. I'd sat in cabinet with him, and he'd even been part of my regular monthly poker game, and I found him to be a straight shooter. But I did think that, regarding the amount of his defamation award, Mahoney was wrong—in fact, completely out to lunch. And so did Clyde Wells. But for opposite reasons.

Wells appealed Mahoney's decision, claiming that the award of damages was too low. The Court of Appeal decided that the original amount awarded by Judge Mahoney was, in fact, far too high, and reduced the amount to $35,000. Wells was reportedly flabbergasted by the Appeal Court's "wrong" decision, and he sought leave to appeal again, this time to the highest court in the nation. But the Supreme Court of Canada refused to even hear the matter, and leave to appeal was denied.

According to Farrell's own report, he didn't see much, if any, of the money he was awarded: it went to pay Wells's legal fees. But Farrell has said that Clyde, knowing he was broke, didn't charge him for his appeal. (That was the appeal led by Wells that had cut Farrell's award down to less than one quarter.) On hearing that Wells hadn't charged for the lost appeal, a former legal associate of his said to me, "But of course. With Clyde it's never about the money; it's always about the principle of the thing."

Wells was sometimes criticized for taking on cases against his own province's interest. One example occurred when Premier Brian Peckford had the House of Assembly enact the 1980 Upper Churchill Water Rights Reversion Act, which basically expropriated on behalf of the province the Churchill Falls (Labrador) Corporation's interest in the Upper Churchill project.

When the issue went to the Newfoundland and Labrador Court of Appeal, Wells acted as lawyer for Royal Trust, a corporation which had put upwards of half a billion dollars into the Upper Churchill development, and he argued strenuously against the provincial government's position. Ultimately, the Supreme Court of Canada, partly as a result of Wells's reasoning and contentions, ruled unanimously that Newfoundland and Labrador did not have the right to break the Upper Churchill deal.

Another important case Peckford put before court involved his assertion that the province, not Ottawa, owned and controlled the offshore resources on the continental shelf. Wells was among several lawyers who acted for the federal government and argued against Newfoundland and Labrador's position. In the end, the Supreme Court of

Canada ruled that the federal government, not the province, owned and had jurisdiction over the offshore.

In both these cases, denigrators maintained that Wells was somehow an unpatriotic Newfoundlander to represent "enemies of the province" like that. I always considered such an argument to be exceedingly obtuse. Our rule of law wouldn't prevail very long if lawyers failed to represent clients because of the unpopularity of the clients or their positions. Everyone was entitled to legal representation from a lawyer—if possible a lawyer of their own choosing—whether accused pedophiles or murderers or federal governments. And lawyers have a professional duty to represent them, barring overriding considerations like conflict of interest. So, to my mind, Wells was acting correctly as a lawyer and in no way improperly.

Again, there have been criticisms of Wells for representing the federal government in their prosecution of his fellow Liberal partisan, Roger Simmons, for tax evasion. Apparently it was one of the smallest tax evasion court cases in Canadian history, totalling some $5,000. Simmons had resigned from the federal cabinet under that cloud, and Wells prosecuted Simmons vigorously, culminating with the argument that the evidence against him was overwhelming and only a confession could be more conclusive. Simmons was convicted and fined.

I had a beer with some lawyer friends at the Ship Inn at the time and there was a fair amount of head-shaking. One lawyer, a Liberal activist, knew the case well and wondered about a lawyer prosecuting his fellow Liberal and his own former client—apparently Wells had acted for Roger in the 1960s on a routine real estate matter. He thought that even if there was no strict conflict of interest, many other lawyers in that position would have removed themselves because of the perception, and the client would have understood their difficulty. But obviously Wells didn't want to. When I replied to the other lawyer that, in his criticism of Wells, his own political partisanship was overriding his professional responsibility, he said it wasn't a matter of professional responsibility, it was a matter of whether someone had class or not.

I told him I hesitated to even contemplate what he thought of me in that case: when Brian Davies, the founder of IFAW, the International Fund for Animal Welfare, was charged in the 1970s with interfering with the seal hunt, he and his mainland lawyer contacted me to represent him in court here. Despite my own strong pro–seal hunt position, and the animosity of most of my fellow Newfoundlanders toward Davies and IFAW, I agreed to do so. As a lawyer I didn't have to love the man, I only had to give him my professional lawyer's best. And, irony of ironies, I said to my lawyer friend who was criticizing Wells, the person prosecuting Davies on behalf of the federal government was none other than Clyde Wells himself.

So, on that basis, I claimed, my friend should elevate Clyde high in his esteem for prosecuting the unpopular anti–seal hunt enemy, and he should drop me into his category of unclassy louts for defending him. My friend laughed that he didn't know about the first part of my argument about Wells, but he certainly agreed with the second part about me.

In 1981, Wells left Corner Brook, the city he'd championed so persistently and vociferously over the years, and moved his family and his law practice to St. John's. Joey Smallwood had said to me and others, years before, that every time he heard Wells "bawling and whining" about his concern for Corner Brook, he always knew that when he felt important enough, and that there was more money to be made, the velocity of his desertion of the paper town for the capital would make your head spin.

I recall malicious tongues in Corner Brook opining that, because Bowater was Wells's law firm's major client, he knew beforehand that the paper mill was on the verge of announcing possible closure, with devastating consequences to the city, and that was why Wells moved out. But Wells himself gave the simplest, most plausible explanation: the great bulk of his practice was now in St. John's and, as a result, it had taken him away from his family in Corner Brook far too much.

By all accounts, Clyde's law practice in St. John's continued to flourish magnificently. He represented some of the biggest names in business in the province. In 1985, he became chairman of the board of Newfoundland Light and Power, the utility company that enjoyed the monopoly to distribute electricity to the bulk of homes and businesses in the province at prices set by the Public Utilities Board.

A former partner of Wells in Corner Brook told me he figured Clyde in St. John's was making twice as much as a judge of the Newfoundland Supreme Court. Wells would conclusively state in years to come that, of all the important occupations he filled—politics, practising lawyer, corporate director, judge—the one he liked best and derived greatest satisfaction from was the practice of law. It is perhaps surprising then that he would leave that delight in 1987 to re-enter politics.

FIFTEEN

Wells sometimes sounded as if his running for office was a moral duty rather than plain ambition on his part. Or maybe he simply responded to the opportunity—what some might call opportunism.

I had learned that, after I'd developed difficulties with my own caucus back in 1979 and called a Liberal leadership convention for that summer, Wells was getting ready to run for leader of the party. He obviously thought that my weakened position, plus the negative legacy the PC Party inherited from Frank Moores, gave him a good chance of becoming leader and beating the upstart new premier, Brian Peckford. It was only when Don Jamieson returned as Liberal leader that Wells put his plans on hold.

Then nothing was heard from him for some eight years regarding leadership, despite urgent pleas from Liberals imploring him to take over. That period happened to coincide with Peckford's highest popularity, when the task of bringing the Liberal Party back into power constituted a serious challenge. Liberal leader Leo Barry did create an admirable resurgence in the 1985 election by dramatically increasing Liberal seats, from eight in the previous election under Len Stirling to fifteen. But in 1987, Barry also encountered difficulties and dissent in his caucus and called a leadership convention. This, plus the fact that

Peckford was heading into the serious decline in popularity that would cause him to resign just two years later, appeared to be the signal for Wells to contemplate a run for the leadership once more.

At first, though, when asked by the *Telegram* if he might reconsider an earlier refusal to run, he told them, “Not bloody likely.” His problem, reasonably enough, was income. The Liberal Party was broke and burdened with a heavy debt at the time. Steve Neary, who had been an interim Liberal leader, earlier, told me that there was certainly no money—the party was at least a half-million dollars in debt and had no capacity to borrow from a bank to pay a leader’s salary. Clyde was not a Member of the House and, hence, could not even draw a fraction of his accustomed income that a combined MHAs and Leader of the Opposition’s salary would have provided. No wonder he initially declined all entreaties to go for it.

Within a couple of weeks, though, he did announce he would run for the Liberal leadership. The mind-changer was that a group of wealthy businessmen got together to solve the money problem. One of them, whom I’d always considered a good Tory, told me later that he’d sized up the situation and decided that he and the whole province would be completely crazy to pass up an opportunity, for the sake of a few dollars, to have someone of Clyde’s calibre as premier, whatever his political stripe.

Wells denied that certain businessmen were contributing money to him as a salary. And evidently that was technically true. A trust fund was established that contributed to the Liberal Party, whereupon the treasurer of the party was to issue a cheque, as salary, to the leader. Wells said he didn’t know who was contributing the money to the party. He may have been alone in his blissful ignorance. Everyone else with a modicum of savvy knew that some of the most eminent businessmen in the province, including Harry Steele, Harold Lundrigan, Tom Hickman, and Mel Woodward, were backing the cause, with esteemed senior lawyer Jim Chalker acting as chair of the trust fund.

Immediately after he’d won the leadership with ease in June 1987, Wells came on my *Open Line* show as a guest to take calls. During our conversations off the air, he asked me how much of an income I thought might be reasonable in his circumstances. I told him I figured that $100,000 to

$125,000, the approximate income of a reasonably successful St. John's lawyer at the time, might be appropriate. I heard later that he would draw down from the party as salary, before he became Leader of the Opposition and entitled to a cabinet minister's salary, the amount of $125,000.

Premier Peckford criticized Wells for taking his party salary. That seriously annoyed Wells, since Peckford himself was drawing $7,000 at the time from the PC Party while he was being paid from the public purse as premier and MHA. Liberals thought Peckford then added insult to injury with his crass tactic already referred to: he delayed the by-election in the empty district of Windsor–Buchans for six months, until just before Christmas, which kept Wells uncomfortably on the party payroll longer than he or the party had expected.

Prominent labour leader Dave Curtis, as a president of the large Newfoundland and Labrador Association of Public Employees, and a president of the Newfoundland Federation of Labour, decried Wells's lack of transparency. He declared scornfully that if any other politician in Canada was getting money from unknown sources, it would be a scandal. But because Wells *announced* he was doing it, he became a man of integrity. One lawyer acquaintance laughed that it was akin to a defendant defusing an issue with the old legal technique of "confess and avoid."

For his part, Wells replied to all criticism that if the party salary bothered people, they should turf him out in the next election. After his by-election on December 17, a big Liberal said to me that Clyde should be more careful about tempting people like that, because they might take him at his word. He pointed out that, with the Tory Party on the decline and the Liberals on the ascendant, the knight-in-shining-armour leader was still only able to win the by-election in that basically Liberal seat by 428 votes.

Wells provided his usual effective opposition during Peckford's last days, especially over the Sprung greenhouse boondoggle. He also repeated his intention of repealing the province's legislative endorsement of the Meech Lake Accord, although few people cared, or even knew at the time, about the constitutional pact that would become the hallmark of his premiership.

After he became premier, I asked him more or less rhetorically how he liked being premier of the province. "Well, it's a hell of a lot better," he said gravely, "than being Leader of the Opposition." I could see his point. I'd been Leader of the Opposition and considered it to be the worst, most thankless job in the world. But I didn't get the idea that Wells was according high praise to his new job of premier, either. I remember concluding that this man actually *does* think he's martyring himself and his personal contentment to politics and government, out of a sense of moral duty!

The president of the Fish, Food and Allied Workers Union, Rick Cashin, was one of many who seemed bemused by Wells's attitude on that and other things. Especially with regard to his lack of light wit or sense of humour, Rick sometimes said, "He's not of this place." Once on *Open Line* himself, Rick recounted over the air in amazement that he'd been listening to the show when I said something offbeat to Wells, without eliciting a glimmer of reaction from him. But when I'd revealed to Clyde that I was joking, said Rick, "*Then* he laughed." Rick also used to call him the "Anglican Archbishop."

Wells always said it wasn't true that he was humourless. It was just that he didn't make jokes about serious subjects. To that point, some acquaintances have remarked that, well, he certainly seemed to find everything pretty serious. One told me that he didn't really like music, and that he must have been the only person in the world who was in his teens and early twenties during the late 1950s and early 1960s who couldn't stand rock and roll.

Some have found his grave and orderly traits endearing. His wife, Eleanor, was reported somewhere to have chuckled over Clyde's propensity, whenever he was planting flowers, to arrange them all in straight, neat rows like marching soldiers.

I'm not so sure that Wells entirely lacked the light touch. I recall people's reaction when the Peckford government said there was no reason you couldn't grow cucumbers in greenhouses in Newfoundland,

and Wells replied that there was no reason you couldn't grow cucumbers on the dark side of the moon, either, if you were prepared to spend the money. Judging by the people I heard chortling and repeating his response to each other, they found it kind of humorous.

After the Sprung flop had squeezed the ruthlessness out of Premier Peckford, he called a PC leadership convention for March 11, 1989. A minister, Tom Rideout, was elected on the third ballot, defeating highly regarded Len Simms, former Speaker and minister, by twenty-six votes.

The ink was barely dry on Rideout's appointment as premier when he called an election for April 20. Finally, Wells's big chance had arrived. But a poll by Decima Research taken during the last week of March showed Rideout's Tories ahead of Wells's Liberals by twenty points: about fifty per cent favouring the PCs to about thirty per cent for the Liberals. When the poll "leaked out," no seasoned politico I talked to could believe the numbers. Even Rideout's top advisers told him to be wary. But based on his presumed big lead, Rideout went for it.

Then, another poll, taken halfway through the campaign, showed that Rideout must have been a political genius to defy all those warnings: the popularity of the PC Party had actually gone up to fifty-six per cent. Still, Rideout's savvy professional strategist from his successful leadership race, John Laschinger, told me when he was on my show a couple of years later, that he had continued to warn Rideout because he'd seen this phenomenon several times before.

When John Turner took over the leadership of the federal Liberal Party from Trudeau in 1984, the polls showed him, as the new prime minister, miles ahead of Brian Mulroney and the Tories. Turner called an election. But then, under the spotlight he was seen not as new at all but as a clone of Trudeau and a continuation of the discredited old government. This came out with blinding clarity when Mulroney nailed him in their debate for rewarding so many Trudeau cronies: "You had a choice, sir. You could have said no." Turner lost the government, and Mulroney won one of the biggest victories in Canada's history.

The lesson for Rideout should have been that to sustain his lead in the polls, he had to distance himself from the tired and discredited Peckford government. He had to become an agent of change with an entirely new vision, completely different from the old ways. But Rideout couldn't or wouldn't confront the Peckford legacy, oppose it, and portray himself as an instrument of transformation from the previous PC government.

If he'd done that, as other parties in BC and Nova Scotia had also done successfully before him, the analysts said, he would have won the election. But the more he was perceived as an apostle of Peckford, the more he dropped in the polls. Brian Peckford himself had distanced himself from Moores on being elected leader, had criticized Moores, and portrayed himself an agent for change who was leading a different party and government; this had most likely allowed him to overcome the initial popularity of Don Jamieson.

Leading up to election day, the *Telegram* and the *Sunday Express* published professional polls showing the Tories still substantially ahead of the Liberals, by six per cent and eleven per cent. Still, the drop in popularity from the other two polls was significant and should have been a scary indicator to the PCs.

An event that must have been the dead giveaway that Rideout was starting to be considered only a hangover from the same old Peckford bunch occurred during a debate between Rideout and Wells at Memorial University. From the outset, a student told me later, Rideout was more than holding his own, and he had the audience with him by describing Wells as yesterday's man and a man of the 1960s. Then a group in the audience started shouting at Rideout, "Mr. Cucumber, Mr. Cucumber." Whether this was a claque set up by Wells's organizers or a spontaneous outburst, it knocked the wind out of Rideout's presentation, and it made him, instead of Wells, look like the "same old, same old."

The most notable element of Wells's own campaign occurred about halfway through, when he was speaking about the forced outward migration of so many young people from Newfoundland to find work. He blamed this departure of thousands to the mainland on the failed policies of seventeen years of Tory government. And then, as if struck by a thunderbolt, he underwent a miraculous transformation from stiff and tediously rational to emotional and compassionate. He now started to orate passionately about bringing "every mother's son home."

For a man who disliked talking much in public about his own personal or family matters, he surprised a lot of observers by detailing his gut-wrenching and heartbreaking experience when his own son had to leave the province, taking Clyde's beloved grandson with him, because there was no work here. Now, the fact that his son's move was a deliberate, willing choice, in order to do the particular job he wanted to do, Clyde did not emphasize. Thus, his "bring every mother's son home" speech was extremely effective, as he lumped himself in with listeners and viewers who were also suffering from the forced absence of their loved ones. Wherever he emitted that speech during the campaign, it brought the audience to tears.

There was one small incident when Tom Rideout was a guest on my *Open Line* show which, according to some political observers, may have had an impact on the election and influenced its outcome. It concerned religion. I liked to think that the religion of a candidate or a party leader was irrelevant in this province by the time of the Wells-Rideout faceoff. But I may have been wrong.

I'd known Rideout for many years, having first met him and his family in the largely Roman Catholic community of Fleur de Lys, in the early 1960s. He'd been a young teenager then, when he told me that one of these days he was going to be premier.

Now he was premier, and I mentioned to him on the air that all three previous premiers since Confederation had been Protestant, and he must be proud to be the first Catholic premier of Newfoundland, since we joined Canada. He acknowledged that he was proud of that, and we moved on to other issues.

I was surprised to hear from some people later that they hadn't realized Tom was Catholic. The name Rideout was to them an English Protestant name in Protestant communities in the province. They thought the revelation on *Open Line* might have had a negative impact on some of the Protestant voters, who formed a majority in Newfoundland and Labrador. I replied that if such prejudices were still alive here, it was just as likely that the revelation would have been a positive influence on Catholic voters. They didn't think so. Catholic voters would have known already that Tom was Catholic. The popular vote was so close, and the margin of Liberal victory so small in some districts, that any negatively influenced Protestant voters could easily have made the difference.

I couldn't prove their argument false, with certainty, in the case of Tom Rideout. I could only say later that the Catholic origins of Brian Tobin and Danny Williams didn't seem to make any difference among Protestants in their future big victories.

A greater influence on the voters may have been a poll dreamed up and fabricated by the Liberals a few days before the election. According to informed writers on the subject I talked to, including Claire Hoy and John Laschinger, Liberal campaign strategists panicked over the two legitimate polls in the newspapers showing the PCs ahead, and they decided to simply invent their own poll. The made-up poll was then leaked to the media and very cunningly showed not a big lead by the Grits, but a narrow, more credible lead of 3.5 per cent over the PCs.

Wells denied knowing about any such fake poll. If he didn't know of at least the possibility of its phony, Liberal origin, he was the only politically perceptive person in the province who didn't. The question of its genuineness was the talk of the town in St. John's leading up to election day, with barstool politicos fervently debating the poll's merits and whether, in fact, it was legit or counterfeit.

The irony was that this bogus poll was closer to predicting the actual results of the election than the professional polls were. The question was whether there was a cause and effect between the Liberal poll and the election outcome. There were strong arguments both ways over whether the close correspondence between poll numbers and election result was purely coincidental, or whether the underhanded chicanery actually helped bring about the closeness of the vote and the victorious outcome for the Liberals.

Whatever the case, the popular vote between the PCs and the Liberals was neck and neck. In fact, the PCs actually won. Their candidates received just under forty-eight per cent of the total votes, as against just over forty-seven per cent for the Liberals, a difference of less than one per cent. Astonishingly, in view of the PCs' tarnished image, in contrast with the Liberals' leader in shining armour, more voters in the province wanted Tom Rideout and the Tories in government than wanted Clyde Wells and the Liberals.

But because of a lucky split in the votes, district by district, the Wells Liberals won thirty-one seats in the House and the Rideout PCs won twenty-one. The NDP lost the one seat they had. Because of labour-government animosities during the Peckford years, much of the leadership of the public sector unions had supported Wells, not because they loved him, but because he seemed to be, at the time, the lesser of two evils. There was talk that he had almost succeeded in recruiting NAPE president Fraser March to run for the Liberals. But that mutual admiration would soon change.

Steve Neary, who spent a lot of time with Joey Smallwood in his last years, told me that Joey could die happy after that election. Joey didn't like Clyde very much, but he had voted for his Liberal candidate and was delighted on election night when, after seventeen years, the Liberal Party finally went back in power. A small smile also came to his ravaged face at the news that Clyde, who'd run in his former home district of Humber East, personally lost his own election there to Lynn Verge, who beat him by 138 votes. Not that Joey was being mean or vindictive, of course, said Neary, but he did seem content that the election results seemed to have balanced things out nicely.

Joey was partially paralyzed and unable to speak because of a stroke he'd suffered, but Neary told me his enjoyment was really obvious when one of his guests, watching the election returns, turned to him and said, "Skipper, too bad you didn't go over and run in Humber West and haul poor Clyde in by the heels again."

SIXTEEN

At the big victory celebration at west coast headquarters on election night, one of his former legal associates later told me, Wells faked it pretty well. He swallowed down his disappointment and put on a "shit-eating grin," calling his personal defeat merely a minor detail. He would ask one of his elected colleagues to step down immediately to open up a by-election, he said, so that this time he'd get elected and, as premier, be able to sit in the House of Assembly. Everyone in the audience, my informant said, secretly crossed their fingers. Wells never seemed to be the easiest candidate to get elected. A former partner of his was reported as voicing the opinion that the better you got to know Clyde, the less inclined you were to vote for him.

An old saw in elective politics is that oppositions don't win; governments lose. Author and commentator Rex Murphy applied that to this 1989 election. He'd been a senior adviser to Liberal leader Leo Barry, and fleetingly to Wells, too, and saw first-hand the advances Barry had made against Peckford's weakening Tories in the previous election. He told writer Claire Hoy after the 1989 election that anyone who thought the Wells Liberals won was wrong; the PCs lost. "They strangled themselves. . . . Tom Rideout had the intuition of a beach rock. . . . There was no way barring a mass rape on the beach that the Liberals were going to lose."

Yet what was intriguing to many of us observers was that the Tories, after several years of decline, almost *didn't* lose against Wells. Why? Perhaps it was just as Rex Murphy had said about the early Clyde Wells: he had an excessive reputation for standing up to Joey, and thereafter, as long as the prince was in exile, his stock increased. His reputation, Rex concluded, was press-developed and press-fed. Throw into that mix the cruel—and who can say how accurate?—remark of Wells's former partner regarding the relationship between knowing him and not voting for him, and perhaps an answer emerges.

But meanwhile, in 1989, he was a premier-in-waiting with no seat in the House. Thereupon, another member of his caucus, this time Eddie Joyce of Bay of Islands, resigned to cause a by-election. Fortunately for any anxiety-prone Liberals, the PCs and NDP fielded no candidates. I haven't seen it documented anywhere, and it might be apocryphal, but there were oral reports that when Wells was acclaimed as the new Member for the district without having to actually run, the entire Liberal caucus dropped spontaneously to their knees and hove up a huge prayer of thanks. It had the ring of truth.

Mr. Joyce, who'd go on in years to come to be a successful Member of the House, in opposition and government, was lodged in the interim in a position in the premier's Corner Brook office.

Early in the election campaign, Tom Rideout and Justice minister Lynn Verge took time out of the hustings to perform a noteworthy and thoroughly commendable act. On April 4, the government appointed a Royal Commission of Inquiry into the justice system's handling of child-abuse allegations at Mount Cashel during the 1970s. Samuel Hughes, a retired Ontario Supreme Court judge, was made chair. A few weeks after the election, in June, the Wells government reappointed the Hughes Commission and enlarged its mandate.

*****

Within a couple of years after that 1989 election, the Meech Lake Accord and events following it would determine that Clyde Wells would never again be hard to elect anywhere in the province. And very likely he would have been easy to elect anywhere in English-speaking Canada, possibly even as prime minister.

The crisis about to be perpetrated by Wells had its friendly beginnings on April 30, 1987. While he was campaigning to become Newfoundland Liberal leader far away in remote coastal outports, Prime Minister Mulroney and ten agreeable premiers met behind closed doors in pleasant surroundings at the government conference centre on Meech Lake in the Gatineau Hills. There, with no media present, and without any public consultation, they arrived at a harmonious deal, and all the first ministers agreed to amend Canada's constitution to incorporate it. Thus was the Meech Lake Accord cozily spawned.

This was in keeping with Progressive Conservative leader Brian Mulroney's pledge when he was running for prime minister in 1984. He'd promised to reopen talks with the Quebec Government to amend, to their liking, the constitution of 1982. That was the epoch-making document which the Quebec Government had refused to sign with Prime Minister Trudeau and all the other premiers. But now this Meech Lake Accord was more to Quebec's taste, not surprisingly, since it was based on a document which the Quebec minister of Intergovernmental Affairs had drafted the year before, containing his province's requirements and conditions. Quebec's premier, Robert Bourassa, was therefore able to sign Meech with alacrity in 1987.

Shortly after the meeting, I saw a caricature of Premier Bourassa in the *Montreal Gazette* by cartoonist Aislin, alias Terry Mosher, which captured the hidden agenda of the comfy arrangement. It showed the Quebec leader saying, "I promise that with Meech Lake in place there would be no more threats of separation. . . . We wouldn't have to bother." Truly, Quebec had achieved, and perhaps rightly so, everything the province could want, pushing right up against the boundary of outright sovereignty.

Aislin also captured the misgivings that some others felt about the Accord, with a cartoon of Brian Mulroney over the label "Meech Lake

Monster." One of those with misgivings greater than most people was Clyde Wells. He'd taken the time from his leadership campaign to study the document as soon as it became public. And he didn't like it. And perhaps he didn't like Brian Mulroney, either.

Reportedly, Wells and Mulroney were together a year at Dalhousie Law School in Halifax. Mulroney had a "big man on campus" reputation at Dal, and I doubt that his style was Wells's cup of tea. In any event, owing to Mulroney's preoccupation with politics and a spate of bad health, he flunked out his first year. He then moved to Laval University in Quebec City, where he began first-year law again. After graduating, Mulroney was able to associate with one of the biggest law firms in the Commonwealth in Montreal, apparently because of his charm and contacts, despite failing his bar entrance exams twice.

Former prime minister Pierre Trudeau, who knew Mulroney early from politics and law in Quebec, didn't seem to like him very much, either. Right from the beginning of Meech, he assumed the role of opponent in chief. In a newspaper interview and a speech, Trudeau suggested that Mulroney was spineless and referred to his Accord with contempt: he was a pusillanimous prime minister, Trudeau stated, who was giving the country away to the provinces.

The Meech Lake Accord recognized Quebec as a "distinct society" within Canada. It restricted federal spending powers in areas of provincial jurisdiction; any province could opt out of those federal programs and still receive federal funding for its comparable provincial program. Existing agreements between the provinces and Ottawa on immigration became entrenched.

A provincial government would nominate people to fill its vacancies in the senate, and the federal government would have to choose appointees from the list. The provinces would nominate persons to be appointed by the federal government to the Supreme Court of Canada, and a minimum of three of the nine judges had to come from Quebec. Each province, and Parliament, had a veto over future constitutional amendments regarding central institutions, the establishment of new provinces, and the use of the English and French languages.

No wonder Premier Bourassa and his colleagues were tripping over each other in their eagerness to get that document signed by every first minister. I remember thinking, when I first read the thing, that it was as if Quebec had separated from Canada and then rejoined the country again, but this time on precisely its own terms. But I didn't regard that as necessarily a bad result. I'd always had great sympathy for the French fact in Canada, realizing the sensitivity of their history as a nation defeated by the English, their insecurities as a small minority surrounded by an ever-growing sea of anglophones, and their wholly understandable aspirations to render their language and culture safe and assured. If that took a little asymmetrical federalism to accomplish, then so bloody be it!

On the other hand, I could see as well the consternation of federalism purists like Clyde Wells, who recognized a true federal system as the best protection for a small and powerless and utterly vulnerable province like Newfoundland and Labrador. The impossible clash between Quebec's bottom-line demands for its own rights and powers, versus a true-believer federalist's demands for the equality of all provinces—the hopelessness of squaring that circle—created the elements of political havoc, and heartbreak, in the future.

Pierre Trudeau reasoned from the start that the Accord's distinct-society clause would weaken Canadian unity and bring forces into play that could cause the breakup of Canada. Others in Quebec argued the contrary: not bringing Quebec into the constitution in a way that recognized the francophone majority could lead to the breakup of Canada. The latter argument would prove, in a few years, to be closer to reality.

SEVENTEEN

The legal deadline for Parliament and all the provincial legislatures to approve the Meech Lake Accord was June 23, 1990, more than three years from its signing. That looked like plenty of time. But Premier Brian Peckford didn't wait. He had the House of Assembly debate the deal early in July of 1987. His support, he explained, was mainly based on loosening federal control over offshore resources and allowing Newfoundland and Labrador more jurisdiction over management of the fisheries. The House ratified the Accord.

Clyde Wells made it clear throughout—when he was running for the Liberal leadership, when he became leader, and when he got elected to the House and led the Opposition—that he thoroughly opposed the Meech Lake Accord. If all provincial legislatures had not approved it by the time he got elected premier, he vowed, he would have the House of Assembly rescind the Peckford-driven ratification.

True to his word, right after the Liberals won the government in April of 1989, Wells included in his May 25, 1989, Throne Speech an item that the government would request Members of the House to annul its adoption of Meech Lake. Not that it was a big deal in people's minds at the time. I don't remember the Accord even being discussed as an important issue during the election campaign. But anyone who would actually listen to Wells's major concerns with it, instead of merely wringing their hands over his prospective destruction of Canada, would see that his anxieties were clear, substantial, and strong.

The clause granting a veto to Parliament and each province over future amendments to the constitution, he feared, was a catastrophe in the making. It would, for all practical purposes, preclude the possibility of any changes to the constitution forever, including necessary reforms to the Canadian senate.

Wells wanted to change the current senate to a Triple-E Senate, meaning "equal, elected, and effective." That would call for senators to be elected in equal numbers from each province to exercise powers that could allow the smaller provinces, especially the poorer, "have not" provinces, to effectively counterbalance the overpowering clout of Ontario and Quebec in the House of Commons. The veto clause in Meech meant that Newfoundland could kiss goodbye all hope of ever rising to that fair and just political status.

John Crosbie called Wells's notion of a Triple-E Senate a disaster. Far from being a protection for poorer, less powerful provinces, it was simply a prescription for absolute deadlock between the two houses of Parliament. But what I personally found incomprehensible at the time was how divorced from reality Wells's fears about the provincial veto was. It wasn't the fact that every province would have a veto that would prevent the creation of a Triple-E Senate in the future. It was the certainty that, veto or no veto, Quebec would never, in a million years, consent to changes in the senate that deprived that province of any of its power in confederation. The absence of a veto would not bring Wells's hope of a Triple-E Senate one inch closer to realization. A Triple-E Senate was simply never going to happen, at least not as long as Quebec stayed in Canada.

Some observers figured that that was what Wells had in mind when he dug in his heels on the Meech Lake Accord: encourage Quebec to leave Canada. He would tell a newspaper, perhaps in reaction to insults thrown at him and his province during the great Meech controversy, that if Quebec separated from Canada there'd be more federal money for Newfoundland and Labrador, since Quebec got more on a per capita basis than other provinces.

John Crosbie had to write a letter to the editor contradicting Wells on that. All the provinces except BC and Alberta, he said, received more money from the feds per capita than Quebec did. But Wells's point hit a resonant chord among many in English-speaking Canada: we could well be better off if a discontent Quebec, instead of forever being the tail wagging the dog with threats of separation, simply separated amicably, and then perhaps entered into a mutually beneficial arrangement with the rest of us.

I recall even saying on the air at the time that I was topping up my oral French so that I could personally go to Quebec and argue in favour of its separation. I was only *half* joking. Because, really, how long could the rest of Canada put up with a province that endlessly hijacked the national agenda with demands that were never satisfied?

Other elements in the Meech Lake Accord bothered Wells. Being a believer in a strong central Canadian government that would use its powers to aid the more disadvantaged provinces, he could not agree with the proposed restrictions or constraints on federal spending.

But worst of all for him was the "distinct society" clause. The special designation whereby Quebec "constitutes within Canada a distinct society," right in the body of the Accord, would confer on that province a special legislative, legal, and constitutional status not enjoyed by the other provinces and might undercut the Charter of Rights and Freedoms.

At the beginning, Wells was not alone among the premiers in his disagreement with Meech. Premier Frank McKenna of New Brunswick, who had been elected in 1987 with every single seat in his legislature, very early expressed his opposition and still had not ratified the Accord by the time Wells became premier. Similarly, Premier Gary Filmon of Manitoba had not yet sought legislative approval. Part of Filmon's problem was that he presided over a minority government. One member elected to the legislature there was a First Nations member of the NDP named Elijah Harper.

But Wells emerged as the leading critic. On April 6, 1990, two and a half months before the Accord's cut-off date, his House of Assembly formally voted to withdraw its support for the Meech Lake Accord. National newscasts and public affairs programs vied with each other to interview this eloquent, knowledgeable, and zealous politician from the sticks who had the temerity to take on the fluent, bilingual prime minister of Canada and frequently get the better of him.

Somewhat unnerved by the setback, Mulroney intoned one time that Newfoundland should be thankful for the way it was welcomed into Canada in 1949—I think there was even mention of Newfoundland receiving a "hand up" from the rest of Canada. Now, in return, he said, Newfoundland should welcome Quebec. Wells labelled Mulroney's statement historically incorrect and "paternalistic tripe" that didn't even warrant a response.

John Crosbie early on saw the risks. He knew what Clyde was like from the old days and advised his colleagues in the Mulroney cabinet that he was a dangerous opponent. On television, Wells always came across as someone extremely well informed and right on top of this constitution business. Even citizens who at first greeted Meech Lake with a yawn and glazed-over eyes had to sit up and notice when they saw this fresh-faced underdog with steely blue irises—Wells reportedly hated it when reporters referred to his steely blue peepers—taking on powerful Quebec and Ottawa. He was able to bring the constitutional clash right down to earth on the TV set. He would do whatever he had to do, he made clear—*whatever* was necessary—to protect the interests of Canada and his province: "We're not talking about cabbage, or kilowatts of power, or barrels of oil, here," he said with barely subdued passion. "We're talking about the *constitution* of this country for the next century."

A lot of people in the RoC, "the Rest of Canada," i.e. Canada outside of Quebec, loved what Wells was saying. Although a majority in English-speaking Canada might have been in favour of the Accord back in 1987, the polls showed that, now in 1990, a majority opposed it.

* * * * *

As the deadline approached in June, Mulroney warned that the failure of Meech Lake would feed Quebec's separatist movement, to the point of breaking up Canada. Mulroney's friend, the separatist Lucien Bouchard, whom Mulroney had recruited into his cabinet as his most powerful minister from Quebec, joined in on that species of fear-mongering. Wells rebuffed it as a mere tactic to bully the Accord's adversaries into endorsing the deal against their rational judgment. On the contrary, he informed the media, "No federation is likely to survive for very long if one of its supposedly equal provinces has a legislative jurisdiction in excess of that of the other provinces." He was sounding a bit like Pierre Trudeau.

Communications of support were pouring in from across the country. Some of it was from the lunatic fringe and from loutish bigoted yahoos who saw in Wells their champion to nail Quebec and "Stick it to the Frogs." Bitter reproaches over this low-life attitude that supported Wells flowed from the Quebec Government, and many in the Quebec public, joining the federal government and the premiers who backed the Accord. Some of the criticism of Wells from Meech supporters implied that he was anti-Quebec, and even racist.

Wells always said he was appalled at any bigoted support for his Meech Lake position. He repudiated the anti-Quebec sentiments contained in some of the messages of endorsement, and he fervently denied that his constitutional arguments were a rejection of Quebec language and culture. Even John Crosbie, while horribly embarrassed by his Newfoundland compatriot's attempt to destroy his boss's vision and legacy, would later defend Wells, in all honesty, against accusations of prejudice.

People thought Wells was hostile to Quebec and Quebecers, Crosbie said, but that wasn't it at all. He had a fanatical idea of how, under the constitution, every province was absolutely equal to every other province and should therefore have exactly the same powers. He said Wells was simply not prepared to compromise on that: "Politicians who are too principled," he lamented, "are a real bloody menace."

Wells always claimed he was never against the idea of Quebec being a distinct society. Quebec's distinctness was an obvious fact, he said. His objection was to placing the term in the body of the Accord instead of in its preamble. Perhaps this was an example of what eminent columnist and writer Jeffrey Simpson had in mind when he called Wells "the nitpicking premier of Newfoundland."

Wells maintained that no one province, i.e. Quebec, should be able to impose constitutional amendments on everyone else. When reporters would suggest that this was exactly what he was now doing himself—imposing his views about the constitution on everyone else—he escaped from the trap by calling for a national referendum on the Accord.

Constitutional *process* was always a big issue in Wells's mind. Instead of just having eleven men hidden away in a closet, amending the people's constitution, and presenting the nation with a *fait accompli,* he dared Mulroney to call a countrywide referendum and let ordinary Canadians vote yea or nay on the Accord. Mulroney, visualizing a country-wrecking gang-up against French-speaking Quebec in English-speaking Canada, rejected the idea.

Aislin, in a cartoon called *Clyde and Brian* in the *Montreal Gazette*, drew a caricature of Wells saying to Mulroney, "But if Meech was as important as you always said it was, why didn't you let Canadians vote on the matter?" His caricature of Mulroney replied, "Because Clyde, it was far too important."

Instead, the prime minister called a first ministers' conference for June 3, 1990, to let saner heads prevail, end this ridiculous tussle, and put Meech Lake to bed once and for all. He would later say he "rolled the dice" with his timing of the meeting, a statement that would come to destroy his credibility. He meant that, with a cynical view to manipulating Clyde Wells, he deliberately made the period of time before the deadline unnecessarily tight. No normal man, he figured, could withstand the united arguments and appeals and urgings of his peers for long in such a crisis situation. Wells would capitulate, he thought, because Wells was a normal man. (That was Mulroney's first mistake.)

The conference lasted a full week, day and night, from June 3 to 10 June, and then ended in a dubious final "agreement" that would blow up in everyone's face.

Having argued across Canada that the original closed-door Meech Lake process was wrong, Wells now agreed, strangely, to attend this closed-door meeting in June 1990. Perhaps the reaction by many in the anglophone media, that Wells's opposition to the Accord jeopardized the very existence of Canada, was getting to him. Perhaps he felt that if he had the chance to rationally explain to the prime minister and premiers, away from the media hoopla, how his arguments in favour of altering Meech were correct, they would see the light. Surely these intelligent men would comprehend how wrong and futile it was for Ottawa and the anglophone provinces to resort to stupid, even self-destructive measures to keep Quebec in Canada at all costs.

One gets an idea of the kind of hard, unyielding advice Wells was receiving when one realizes who his constitutional advisers were. Newfoundlander Eugene Forsey, renowned globally for his constitutional knowledge, was Wells's main adviser. He was so firm in his views against Meech that when he got the idea that Wells might be even *contemplating* compromise under all the pressure, he quit.

Deborah Coyne had become Wells's senior adviser on the constitution soon after his election. She was brilliant and highly educated, with a degree in economics from Queen's University, a law degree from Osgoode Hall where she was gold medalist, and a Master of Philosophy from Oxford in international relations. For years she was good friends with Pierre Trudeau, so much so that, in May 1991, she would give birth to a baby girl in St. John's and list Trudeau as the father. Evil-minded folk said that Wells's key constitutional advice came by way of Trudeau's pillow talk.

Frank Moores saw a Trudeau conspiracy in Coyne's appointment. One of his friends told me Frank found it passing strange that, of all the constitutional lawyers in Canada, the fact that Clyde picked the one closest to Trudeau couldn't have been accidental.

The start of the conference was not auspicious. Reporters accosted Wells on his way to dinner with the first ministers and told him that Bourassa was refusing to even consider opening up the Meech Lake Accord. Wells replied that if compromise was in fact on the agenda, then you couldn't have a compromise on just Quebec's terms. That wouldn't be compromise, but blackmail. With that, the premier of Ontario, David Peterson, in the arrogant manner that would be his trademark throughout the conference, accused Wells of poisoning the well.

From the start, I personally wondered what Wells hoped to achieve at these meetings. He knew that Bourassa was constantly portraying himself to be as much of a Quebec nationalist as the Parti Québécois—just without the separatism. Once, at an annual meeting of eastern premiers at Montebello in Quebec, and chaired by Bourassa, the Quebec police stopped Wells at the door and wouldn't let him in because he didn't have on the special lapel pin that allowed participants entry. Wells wouldn't wear the pin because there was a map of Quebec on it which included Labrador within Quebec's boundaries.

Now, how he could expect to make progress with anyone who, at a supposedly co-operative get-together, was that insensitive in the cause of Quebec nationalism defies reason. Besides that, could the intelligent and experienced Wells have been actually naive enough to think that Bourassa would be able, in any way, to backtrack on the original Meech document without being figuratively massacred by the jingoistic Quebec media and the hyper-defensive francophone populous? When Bourassa at one point did feebly suggest some miniscule compromise on the senate and made it public, he was immediately met by a bombardment from the Quebec media for selling Quebec out. Consent from Bourassa to changes in Meech was just not in the cards, and it was not going to happen.

EIGHTEEN

In the course of trying to make the impossible happen, though, Wells was treated to a barrage of criticism, some of it personal insults. From the time he announced his opposition to Meech Lake, right up to the end of the June 1990 conference and beyond, the federal side and some premiers and some media accorded him what must have been one of the fiercest verbal batterings on record.

When Wells insisted he was not rejecting Quebec but rejecting a system that perpetuated a Class A province, i.e. Quebec, and a Class B province, i.e. Ontario, and eight class C provinces, i.e. all the others, the media and the premiers piled on him. It was as if he were the nefarious leader of a fifth column with a clandestine mission to do everything in his power to wreck the best country in the whole wide world. Their attitude was that if an anglophone premier took firm exception to a constitutional question, he was pigheaded; if a Quebec premier did so, he was standing on principle.

John Crosbie, privately and publicly, said Wells was displaying an appalling degree of fanaticism, called him "a bloody fanatic," and claimed he had lost his senses.

While Wells was making his points at one session, Bourassa stood in his place, gathered up his papers in a huff, and stomped out of the room without so much as a "*Je m'excuse*." Later, he insisted he had left in such fashion not as a discourtesy or an insult but because he had to prepare for something else.

Even Governor General Jeanne Sauvé had joined the fray. In her retirement speech around Christmas, 1989, she counselled the parties to "ratify their pact" as a warning about the failure of the Meech Lake Accord, and she supported the concept of a distinct society. Wells had to respond to the Queen's representative that it was inappropriate for the Crown to intrude in political affairs like that. I don't know if he had reacted in a similar way to the Queen of England, way back in October of 1987. Evidently overcome by her fervour to save Canada, Queen Elizabeth II had publicly championed the Accord herself.

Retired senior statesmen of great respect, like Robert Stanfield and Jack Pickersgill and others, emerged to accuse Wells not only of breaking up the country but of instigating increased financial hardship in Atlantic Canada by his position. On a couple of occasions, I even had visits on *Open Line* from some retired politicians and senators from the mainland to make these same accusations.

Wells had to respond how offensive he found it that they would expect the poorer provinces to embrace Meech for fear of losing their handouts from Ottawa. He also found it passing strange that the pro side of the Meech Lake debate never defended the Accord on its merits.

Senator Lowell Murray, Mulroney's henchman in dealing with Wells, joined the eleven leaders for the dinner discussion at the Museum of Civilization on June 3, 1990. All along Murray had been giving Wells the impression there was room for dialogue, when in fact, with Bourassa's attitude, there was no room at all.

The next morning, at the beginning of the meeting in the conference centre, Wells threw on the table some papers containing earlier negotiating proposals, including possibilities on the distinct-society clause which Murray had given him, and asked what had happened to them. Bourassa was surprised by the documents and said he'd never laid eyes on them before, and furthermore, he would not discuss the distinct-society clause. Senator Murray, caught red-handed in his manipulations, excused himself by asserting that talking to Wells was like talking to the cardinal in Rome who has the last word on dogma.

Wells reiterated that he could not agree with a Quebec veto on reform of the senate, and there would be no solution to the impasse unless Bourassa would compromise on that. But Bourassa waved the thought off with disdain: it was not up to Quebec to compromise.

One Quebec Tory MP, the assistant deputy speaker in the House of Commons, called Wells a mental case. Then he extended his diagnosis to the rest of the province. Newfoundland had a mentality different from the rest of Canada, he said. Most of them were unemployed and forty-four per cent couldn't read or write. He was forced later to apologize and resign as assistant deputy speaker.

At the same time, Wells's idea of possibly subjecting the Accord to a referendum in his own province was reportedly derided behind closed doors in Ottawa. Some politicians and advisers sneered at the very notion of Newfoundland and Labrador's semi-literate population having a referendum, with more than forty per cent of them unable to read the question.

A few Tory MPs from Quebec announced that, as a result of Wells's attitude, they were giving up on Canada and forming their own group in Parliament. Among those who later joined this separatist Bloc Québécois was Lucien Bouchard, who would become its leader.

A Tory MP from Ontario concluded that, "We would be better off if we towed Newfoundland out to sea and sank it." Quebec's Intergovernmental Affairs minister shed no tears over that prospect: "Canada can survive without Newfoundland," he concluded.

Bourassa seemed to find Wells's uppity stance on Meech hard to credit. Didn't Ontario and Quebec pay for sixty-eight per cent of the financial support of Newfoundland? Wells reacted that he didn't want Newfoundland and Labrador to be doomed to accept that situation, either the handouts or the patronizing attitude, forever.

Wells believed the opposition to him on Meech Lake was really saying that you people in Newfoundland are lesser-quality Canadians: "You can't express your conscientiously held views on constitutional development because you're dependent on handouts from Ottawa. That is unacceptable." He claimed that Newfoundland and Labrador was blackmailed into accepting the Upper Churchill Falls deal back in the 1960s; accepting Meech Lake would make the province vulnerable to such blackmail again.

Some premiers wondered where Wells got off, regarding himself as such a constitutional expert. I knew that he'd been named years before by the national Canadian Bar Association as his province's representative on their constitution committee. I recalled running into Professor Gerard La Forest, who'd been the director of research for the constitution committee, and he mentioned Clyde Wells. La Forest had been one of my professors at law school, whom I liked and admired immensely, and after a remarkable academic and government career in the law, he would be appointed as a justice of the Supreme Court of Canada. He told me he thought that Clyde had a decidedly superior, analytical, legal mind.

Premier Joe Ghiz of Prince Edward Island had also been on that constitution committee with Wells. Mulroney and some of the premiers alleged that Ghiz possessed, as a graduate of Harvard with a Master degree in Law, far greater academic credentials on constitutional matters than Wells did. Ghiz drew on his superior constitutional knowledge during the conference to characterize Wells as "a fucking prick."

Someone there claimed Wells was fuelled by vanity and megalomania. They said that if he was confronted on a point of law by someone who knew more than him, like Joe Ghiz, he'd wave around some of the thousands of letters and telegrams he'd received and bray: "Do you know how much support I've got?"

When Wells said he wanted a "Canada clause," which would include Canadian values beside Quebec's distinct society, and a declaration from all first ministers protecting the Charter of Rights from the distinct-society clause, Bourassa impressed the others with his command of the subtleties of the English language: "If that's the way you feel, fuck you."

* * * * *

Toward the end of the conference, with Premier Peterson screaming tirades at him, and former Edmonton Eskimos quarterback Premier Don Getty tackling him to prevent him from leaving the room (denied by Getty), Wells was reported to have broken into tears several times. Although he admitted that he had taken a terrible browbeating from the others, still he couldn't forgive himself for becoming emotional and losing his self-restraint.

Some among the feds whispered that he was suffering a nervous breakdown and had become psychologically unreliable. The English-language CBC, which carried on throughout like a federalist cheerleader, described him as emotionally distraught, and CBC's French-language counterpart, Radio Canada, which carried on throughout like a separatist cheerleader, said the same thing in French.

A senior aid to Premier Peterson of Ontario drafted up a strategy paper on how to discredit Wells and any other premiers not in favour of Meech: plant doubts with CBC about their personal stability. When that stratagem leaked out, Peterson pretended that he didn't know a thing about this project concocted by his trusted adviser. Peterson's disavowal didn't stop his underlings from muttering cryptically to the media about poor Clyde's unbalance. Unaccountably, some subordinates of McKenna, who'd been an earlier target of the slander, joined in.

On the subject of unbalance, Frank McKenna of New Brunswick was the worst. Like many observers of his career path, I took notice of him after he was first elected with all the seats in his legislature. My interest went up when I read that he attributed his best traits to his Newfoundland grandmother. But her genes must have become recessive at the conference; following his performance there I never could understand why so many people had a continuing love affair with the guy.

He had started out, after his election as premier in 1987, questioning some provisions in Meech Lake, leading the charge against it, and demanding changes. I don't know how badly Wells may have been misled into thinking that he had in McKenna a strong and reliable partner in their objections to the Accord. I gather Wells was counting on a united front involving himself, McKenna, and Gary Doer of Manitoba. But at the June conference, McKenna moved from hard to soft criticism, with some bizarre notion of a "parallel accord."

Then, at one point, he surprised everyone by suddenly rushing out of the dark to stand in front of the nightly television cameras to say he was now totally on side with the feds and the other premiers. But not satisfied with having knuckled under to big boys Mulroney, Peterson, and Getty, he now described Wells, with whom he'd recently been an anti-Meech collaborator, as "radical and extreme."

Meanwhile, Jean Chrétien's leadership tacticians were also pestering Wells to make a deal. The federal Liberal leadership convention, in which Chrétien was the top candidate, was soon coming up, and he wanted this cursed Accord put to bed and out of the news. Everyone in Quebec knew that, like his mentor Trudeau, he was against the Accord, but Chrétien didn't need Quebec delegates to be constantly reminded of it by the daily headlines from the conference. With Paul Martin and Sheila Copps running against him, he wanted to avoid any risk of losing another leadership convention.

I would have been surprised if Wells had not been a little emotional and distraught, enduring the trench warfare of that week, virtually alone. One of his aides told me that the absence of his wife, Eleanor, was a serious gap in Clyde's life during the week's activities. As bad luck would have it, she was ill at home in St. John's. I didn't know her well, having met her only a couple of times, once at a cocktail party at their nice house on Glenridge Crescent, but by all accounts she was humorous, easygoing, level-headed and solid, and enjoyed a bit of fun. When I saw a behind-the-scenes TV documentary of the Meech Lake conference, showing Clyde saying good night to each of his entourage every night, and being left in his hotel room to agonize alone, I could well imagine his need for what Napoleon called two-o'clock-in-the-morning courage, to face the next day. He could have used some of Eleanor's company and strong traits.

After a nightmarish, marathon week of record-breaking squabbling, a final draft of a document was produced. In it, Wells had gained nothing except some vague "guarantee" that senate reform, Aboriginal issues, and the veto clause would be considered again when the first ministers convened in the future. Wells's abhorred distinct-society clause had stayed the same as the day he arrived. Everybody signed the document, but in Wells's case, he affixed an asterisk next to his signature which, he insisted, meant he did not agree with the contents but indicated that he was merely agreeing to submit the thing, like premiers McKenna and Doer, to his legislature before the June 23 deadline.

Mulroney and the pro-Meech crowd, however, certainly tried to give the impression that they had all arrived at a deal. Wells's claim that he was still adamant in his disapproval of the Accord, and that he was simply giving the House of Assembly the right to decide the issue by free vote, seemed to be a subtlety that was largely lost on many in the hubbub. And as it would turn out, he had placed himself a trap where he could be characterized as deceitful for reneging on his covenant, whatever it was.

Why hadn't Wells just walked away from the Ottawa quagmire at some point during the week, when he must have seen that it was hopeless? In fact, I believe he said later that, if he had his time back, he would have walked out of that dinner of the first ministers in Hull, the night before the conference. Perhaps his statement at the end of the conference explained his failure.

He said he had found himself under constant pressure to agree, out of fear that the collapse of Meech would do irremediable damage to Canada, and he certainly wanted no responsibility—either on himself or his province—for causing that. If such was his motive, he must have had some tense moments a few years later when, as a direct result of the Meech Lake Accord debacle, the country would come within a hair's breadth of breaking up.

NINETEEN

On Sunday, June 10, the day after the Meech conference, Wells flew home. At St. John's Airport, a crowd numbering in the hundreds met him with cheers of support. Wells stood there bawling his eyes out. Anyone who knew him was flabbergasted. They'd never seen him display emotion before, except for perhaps a "touch" of anger or exasperation. But now, here stood this stocky man with the military bearing, right in front of them, with big tears rolling unashamedly down his face.

The messages of support continued to stream in. No doubt many were captivated by the image of this sturdy man of principle, who contrasted markedly with the cynical Mulroney, the slippery dice roller who had intentionally timed the negotiations to generate a false crisis situation. People seemed to forget that the whole Meech Lake process was a well-intentioned effort to make Quebec feel more at home in the federation. To many in English-speaking Canada, the entire debacle seemed to stink merely of Mulroney's slick style, which undermined to a nullity the good concept and its well-meaning content.

Some observers, though, were disturbed at Wells's sophistry in his use of the messages of support, and of the large percentage of polled Canadians who backed him. On the one hand, he decried the substantial proportion of bigoted louts who, in their praise of his position, expressed their prejudice against Quebec and Quebecers. On the other hand, when members of the media asked him how it felt to be all alone in his opposition to the Accord, he'd reply that the seventy per cent of Canadians polled who'd indicated they supported him (which included a lot of bigoted louts) showed that he wasn't alone.

Frank McKenna and David Peterson, and Brian Mulroney himself, each spoke in support of the Accord to the MHAs in the House of Assembly. During his visit, Mulroney and a minion or two had dinner at Wells's home. They afterwards swore that, there that night, Clyde remained firm in his solemn undertaking to hold a free vote on the Accord in the House.

But unexpectedly, the approval process started to fall apart elsewhere. A soft-spoken Cree named Elijah Harper, from his seat in the Manitoba Legislative Assembly, raised his eagle feather and said no. It was only a procedural point, but an important one. The Manitoba Assembly apparently required public consultations in matters like the Accord. There wasn't time for that before the June 23 deadline, so unanimous consent from the Members of the Legislative Assembly was needed to dispense with it. Elijah Harper noted that Aboriginal groups had not been involved at all in negotiating the Accord in the first place, and so he would not consent to bypassing public consultations.

Mulroney proposed that the courts be asked to grant Manitoba a three-month extension if the Newfoundland and Labrador House of Assembly endorsed the Accord by the June 23 cut-off. This did not please Wells. He was well and truly sick of the resumption of pressure on him from Ottawa at every turn, and he denounced the feds for trying to manipulate and bully his province yet again. Besides, here was one more example of another province receiving some benefit that was not being accorded to Newfoundland. If Manitoba was going to get an extension, he declared, then Newfoundland and Labrador insisted on having one, too. Ottawa balked at what they apparently considered this kindergarten-level me-too sulk and said no.

Meanwhile, the New Brunswick legislature ratified the Accord, and now it was supposed to be up to the Newfoundland House of Assembly to say yea or nay. The resolution was in fact being debated in the legislature when Wells had the debate adjourned and would not allow it to come to a vote. His reason for doing so seemed to be based on his calculation that a majority of the MHAs were going to vote "no," and since the Accord was already dead in Manitoba, he wanted to save Newfoundland from any blame for defeating the Accord.

Pro-Meech politicos and media went nuts. Mulroney couldn't believe that a premier would go back on his solemn word like that. He said to *Maclean's* magazine: "Mr. Wells signed a formal constitutional instrument before the people of Canada committing his province to either hold a referendum on Meech or a vote in the House of Assembly. He did not attach conditions to it: the commitment was unequivocal. He cancelled the vote—he dishonoured his signature. He'll have to live with the consequences." The prime minister was reported elsewhere as muttering that the next time he went to see Clyde he'd think about bringing a gun.

John Crosbie said that Wells had promised to hold a vote in the House and he didn't: "A pretty scurvy piece of work."

Others pointed out that he had signed something he didn't believe in, and whatever weasel words he might use afterwards, he broke his word on putting the question to a vote. The Halifax *Chronicle Herald*'s Jim Meek said: "He's a guy who lied to the nation. He's got the 'God syndrome' real bad."

The spring after Meech, I was a guest speaker at a large convention of business persons and professionals in Victoria, BC, and discovered that delegates there from across Canada were still interested in discussing it. Many I talked to, both pro and con regarding the Accord, were still surprised at Wells's final action. Even those who agreed with his position on the Accord itself couldn't quite comprehend why Wells had reneged on his public undertaking and didn't allow a vote on it in the House. "He claimed he wanted to spare his legislature the blame?" one journalist there questioned. "He really must think he *is* a messiah, to take upon himself the sins of others like that."

* * * * *

At the time of the Meech Lake failure, I didn't hear any pro-Meech advocates attacking Elijah Harper for his position. They wouldn't dare accuse him, or the Aboriginal chiefs who supported him, of obstruction. Mulroney hadn't even bothered to send Jake Epp, a heavyweight federal minister from Manitoba, to Winnipeg to try to persuade Harper. Ottawa and supporters of Meech Lake attacked Wells almost exclusively. He had made himself practically the sole lightning rod for both denunciation and praise, for all time.

I recall that a couple of days after the Meech Lake conference ended in Ottawa, an Angus Reid poll asked people if they approved or disapproved of their leaders' actions during the week of negotiations. Wells received the highest approval rating: nearly seventy per cent in Canada outside of Quebec. In that province, though, where the mother tongue of nearly eighty per cent of the population is French, only twenty-five per cent of the respondents approved of his actions.

There would be reports in the future that Wells was diligently learning French. This was the clear giveaway to many that he was preparing to go for the prime ministership down the road. His low numbers in Quebec polls were nothing, some said; his numbers were high enough in the rest of Canada that he didn't even need Quebec. When I suggested to callers on the air that perhaps he simply wanted to become bilingual, since he was, after all, a premier in a bilingual country, I was told not to be so foolish. He wanted to know French, one of his supporters replied, so that he could understand better what Quebec was plotting against the rest of us.

Meanwhile, a real federal Liberal leadership convention was held on June 23 at the Olympic Saddledome in Calgary. Wells attended, and anglophone delegates hailed him with roars of approval and shouts of praise. Pro-Wells T-shirts and buttons were evident, and there were indeed calls for Clyde Wells to be prime minister the next time around. The Quebec benches mainly booed.

Leadership front-runner Jean Chrétien embraced Wells and thanked him for his help. The Quebec media reported that Chrétien's thanks had nothing to do with the leadership but were for his help in defeating the

Meech Lake Accord. The three-amigos conspiracy theory was boosted further when Wells and Trudeau greeted each other at the convention like long-lost buddies. They enthusiastically shook hands and thumped each other on the back, as if after a great victory, and then Wells sat with Trudeau in his private box. Chrétien received nearly fifty-seven per cent of the votes on the first ballot.

A few years later, some Quebec analysts would credit that coziness of the three at the leadership convention for the big boost in the separatist vote, under Prime Minister Chrétien's watch, in the 1995 Quebec referendum.

Certainly the pathetic failure of the Meech Lake Accord, after the months of rancorous debate, did send the fortunes of the separatist movement in Quebec soaring. Brian Mulroney's buddy, Lucien Bouchard, who'd been a prime catch for the Conservatives in the 1988 election, even though he had worked for the "Yes" side in the 1980 referendum, reverted back to separatism once more, but this time to emerge later as the terrifyingly effective leader of the cause.

After Meech, a last-ditch constitutional effort was attempted. Canada's first ministers cobbled together something called the Charlottetown Accord. It was largely a clone of Meech but with enough "improvements," including senate reform, Aboriginal self-government, and a Canada clause, to allow Wells to acquiesce in saying nationally that he supported it.

A referendum was held on the Charlottetown Accord in October 1992, and the new document received the support of a majority in Newfoundland and Labrador, the highest in Canada with sixty-three per cent, after Prince Edward Island. But several other provinces voted against it, including Quebec, with fifty-four per cent there voting no. The toxic notion of amending the Canadian constitution was now dead in the whole country, except for Quebec. In that province, the idea of the big final constitutional change was alive and well: the idea of getting out of Canada.

The Bloc Québécois was originally a tiny splinter party of protest in the House of Commons. But in the 1993 federal election which made Chrétien prime minister, the Bloc won fifty-four of Quebec's seventy-five seats, and Lucien Bouchard became Leader of the Opposition. Meech Lake had led to the ludicrous spectacle of a party restricted to just one province, and interested only in its separation from Canada, becoming the Loyal Opposition in Canada's national parliament.

In 1995, a referendum on Quebec's separation was defeated by a hair, 50.58 per cent to 49.42 per cent. That minuscule margin of victory for federalism was probably engineered, as we shall see, by the actions of fellow Newfoundlander, and federal cabinet minister, Brian Tobin. A colleague of Wells in the House of Assembly said to me the day after the referendum: "Clyde must have fallen to his knees, when he saw the one per cent against separation, and thanked God and Tobin that he escaped the fate of going down in history as the man who destroyed Canada."

A decade later in 2006, Conservative prime minister Stephen Harper would get the jump on the Bloc Québécois by tabling a motion in the House of Commons. It didn't say that Quebec was anything as wussy as a "distinct society," the term that had caused Wells such grief. It said straight out that this House recognizes "that the Québécois form a *nation* within a united Canada." At first the Bloc Québécois said they wouldn't vote for it, but the next day they came on side, and the motion was passed by an overwhelming majority of MPs.

A few Trudeau-ite Liberal hangovers in the House held out, but elsewhere there was scarcely a whimper of serious dissent in the land. I don't know how Clyde Wells would have voted had he been there. But by then he was ensconced in the Supreme Court of Newfoundland, having been appointed chief justice of the province by Trudeau's disciple as prime minister, Jean Chrétien. As such he was unable to speak out on the motion. But I think we can make a shrewd guess what he might have said, had he not been muzzled.

TWENTY

Strange as it may sound, the Meech Lake interlude must have almost been a pleasant diversion from the other challenges facing Wells as premier in the early 1990s. Underlining everything else, he had to cope with some of the worst economic and financial times in the province's history. Unemployment was hovering around twenty per cent, and thousands of jobs in the fishery were being lost even before the coming collapse of the cod stocks.

There seemed to be a lot of wheel spinning by the federal and provincial governments leading up to that catastrophic cod failure of 1992. The Total Allowable Catch was constantly being lowered, with reports from knowledgeable observers that the conservation measures were far too little, way too late. Federal and provincial programs of the dismal make-work type were inaugurated to help displaced fishermen, and sometimes to keep fish plants open that had no fish to process.

The frustration and exasperation of fishermen could be seen in their infuriated rampages in a federal fisheries office, and even at an office of their own union, the Fish, Food and Allied Workers.

There was much sabre-rattling regarding foreign overfishing on the Nose and Tail of the Grand Banks, just outside the 200-mile limit.

Populist politician John Efford formed a group called the United Fishermen of Newfoundland and Labrador and brought officials and participants from Iceland to the province to tell us how they had kicked British trawlers out of their waters during their famous Cod Wars. The Icelanders appeared on my *Open Line* show and described their ruthless tactics, led by the country's own coast guard, in cutting the nets of the UK vessels. Little Iceland had won its Cod Wars against the mighty Great Britain. I myself had to say on air that, by comparison, Canada was nothing but a wimp.

The Atlantic premiers, led by Clyde Wells, demanded that the Canadian navy be used to put a stop to the foreign overfishing. Just a couple of years before that, when MPs George Baker and Brian Tobin had suggested a similar tactic, Wells described such proposals as highly irresponsible. Now it was Prime Minister Mulroney who was rejecting out of hand Wells's own notion of resorting to gunboat diplomacy.

Richard Cashin, head of the fishermen's union, the FFAW, began announcing plans for a flotilla of fishermen to go out and confront the Spanish and Portuguese fishing vessels just outside the 200-mile limit. In 1992, Cashin sent out some trawlers to encounter them and to urge them to cut back.

Premier Wells and Fishery Products International president Vic Young flew to New York with pleas to the United Nations to halt the overfishing. The premier called the European fishing fleets international pirates. And he was right, or at least some reputable UK journalists agreed with him. I recall reading an article in the UK paper the *Guardian* a few years after our cod collapse here. It was headlined, "EU fishing fleets devastate third world." After helping scoop up all the cod on the Grand Banks, they moved on to use their skills elsewhere, undaunted.

According to a United Nations report, overfishing by foreign fleets, including those from Europe, caused alarming reductions in fish stocks off West Africa and South America. Poor country after poor country had been plundered by first-world foreign fleets, which then sailed on and redeployed their forces in new seas.

For example, the European Union paid a third-world government hundreds of millions of pounds sterling to fish in its waters for a few years, even though the stocks were already badly depleted. "Developing" countries were forfeiting the future survival of their fish stocks for paltry short-term gains. The fish stocks in the waters of many advanced countries had already been severely depleted because too many heavily subsidized fleets had chased too few fish. As a result, the foreign fleets were continuously looking elsewhere for stocks to despoil. I remember saying on *Open Line* at the time that such destruction was okay for the advanced, civilized European Union, though, because they saved the seals off Newfoundland, didn't they?

In the early 1990s, Wells had gone directly to European capitals with our plight, and the Europeans did announce a temporary moratorium on northern cod. But there were comments in this province and elsewhere that when the Europeans pulled out of here, it wasn't because they were such wonderful environmentalists, but only because they could no longer find any fish out on the Nose and Tail: we've done all the good we can in these parts, they were basically saying. Righto, then, off to Africa.

On July 2, 1992, the Canadian Fisheries department noticed themselves that there were no codfish off the coasts of Newfoundland and Labrador. Minister of Fisheries John Crosbie had to shut down the northern cod fishery completely. The moratorium was to last for just two years, he said. Suddenly, the province was faced with an annual billion-dollar loss to its economy and tens of thousands of fisherfolk and plant workers were out of work. Premier Wells compared the blow to the effect of nearly half a million auto workers in Ontario losing their jobs overnight.

Apparently Ottawa never consulted Wells on the close-down of the cod fishery or any compensation plan. This lack of communication was attributed to the fallout from Meech Lake and, in particular, Crosbie's continuing rage at his bullheaded compatriot. When the feds came up with a support "package" for displaced fishermen and plant workers, it was so inadequate that it could only be deemed a punishment of Wells. The word I was getting from Ottawa was that, although Crosbie did in fact press hard for more money, Quebec ministers dug in their heels and muttered around the cabinet table: no, let's nail that little bastard.

What nailing Wells might have to do with the past decades of federal mismanagement of the fishery, and the resulting loss of 30,000 or 40,000 jobs in Newfoundland and Labrador, mystified everyone whose brain was not boggled by spite and rancour. Crosbie, who had reason to dislike Wells as much as anyone, nevertheless put it across to his colleagues that he was going to resign in protest over the meagre financial support. Within a week or two, the "package" from Ottawa was enhanced by hundreds of millions of dollars.

There were complaints from workers, who were not directly employed in the fishery but who had nonetheless lost their jobs because of the close-down of the fishery, that they received nothing. Wells, who had never been brought in on any of the planning and called the packages too little too late, was reported to want deductions from the federal package for income that fishermen received from other work they might do. Regarding that, Fish Union president Richard Cashin called Wells and his government righteous and so conservative as to be to the political right of southern Alberta.

Crosbie said that in provincial dealings with Ottawa, Wells was the worst premier in Newfoundland's history. He also brought attention to a poll by the *Telegram* on the biggest newsmaker of the year, in which Crosbie had received five times as many votes as Wells. But local commentators at the time didn't view it as much of a popularity contest. Remarks included, "Shut down a five-hundred-year-old fishery? Yeah, that'll make you newsmaker of the year every time."

The fishery was only part of Wells's problems. From the start of his premiership he had to deal with the province's dire financial straits. There were some galling items: in his first budget in June 1989, for example, he had to meet $14 million in commitments by Peckford for the project Wells had always condemned, the Sprung greenhouse. And there were some mildly embarrassing items: the next year he closed down the quarter-million-dollar ombudsman's office, which he had so vigorously advocated twenty years before. He rationalized the cut by declaring that my *Open Line* show was already doing the job at no cost, which was flattering but scarcely an accurate comparison of the two activities.

And a few years later, he would implement a cost-cutting measure which Brian Peckford, when faced with similarly desperate deficits, had pledged never to do no matter how bad the province's financial situation became: Wells dismantled or sold off a couple dozen provincial parks. A lot of people considered the loss or privatization of those public parks to be an act of official vandalism. Smallwood and my own father, as minister responsible for their creation, had intended those provincial treasures to be preserved under public ownership for all future generations.

It must have pained Wells greatly, though, to have taken that measure. I recalled a time, years before, when he and I were on opposite sides in a court case, and we had to fly together in a small plane up the Great Northern Peninsula to the courthouse in St. Anthony. All the way up, he waxed enthusiastic about the passing scene below—the developing Gros Morne National Park, and the coastal plain and the magnificent Long Range Mountains beyond—and it was clear to me that he dearly loved it all.

Apparently feeling the need for a legal kindred spirit in his cabinet, Premier Wells inveigled Ed Roberts back into politics. I heard grumblings that some passed-over private members felt slighted, snubbed, and affronted. But an opportunity, not to be missed, to counter an embarrassment, had to be taken advantage of. A by-election was opening up in the district of Naskaupi in Labrador as a result of the troubles of MHA Jim Kelland. He was a minister in Wells's cabinet when allegations of sexual assault of a woman surfaced against him.

People were aghast when it turned out that the police report on Kelland had been lost or misfiled by the police. Lynn Verge, who, to the satisfaction of many, played the role of Wells's recurring nemesis, accused the government of political interference to delay the investigation. As usual, when there was the least hint of his being associated with even a whiff of impropriety, Wells went off the head. He raged that for Verge to raise unproven allegations like that was nothing short of despicable. But remaining undeterred, Verge came back with the reasonable suggestion that there had to be something drastically wrong when a police report on a cabinet minister had been lost for a year.

Wells demanded why she hadn't taken up the issue with newly appointed Minister of Justice Ed Roberts. Verge replied sensibly that Roberts was considering running in Kelland's vacated district and that there might be—let's see, now—an appearance of a conflict of interest, perhaps? Judging by conversations I had, the clear winner in the court of public opinion on that one was Verge. Or perhaps many observers just dearly loved to see Lynn Verge taking on Clyde Wells and dressing him down, and reducing him to sputtering, "That's despicable," or his even more mocked mantra, "That's just silly."

She'd had to do it notably after he refused to allow a minute of silence in the House of Assembly to pay tribute to the fourteen women murdered in December 1989 at the École Polytechnique de Montréal by Marc Lépine. She reported that he gave as his reason for rejecting it that everyone had to be treated equally in the House. I heard people express their amazement: how many occasions equal to that atrocity were there going to be, requiring a tribute? And in any event, he was talking about *one minute*.

Ombudsmen, provincial parks—important as they were, those cuts were minor in their impact on people compared to the other shattering financial decisions that confronted him. Faced by a provincial debt that was over $5 billion in 1990, probably the highest per capita debts of all the provinces, he swung the machete. And many people described his actions as a policy of "slash and burn."

In his spring budget of 1991, he chopped a couple thousand civil servant jobs, eliminated vacant positions, and laid off ten per cent of management. Dave Curtis, the president of the Newfoundland and Labrador Federation of Labour, said that Wells had a medieval view of workers and possessed a classic master-servant view of the workforce.

When the government unilaterally rolled back wage increases in collective agreements already negotiated and signed, the public service unions erupted in fury. They claimed that he had actually allowed some agreements to be concluded after he'd already decided to put into effect his rollbacks and wage freezes. CUPE, the Canadian Union of Public Employees, pointed to a three-year deal giving their members a 22.9 per cent increase, which was signed by the government the very same day the budget, containing provisions for the wage freezes and rollbacks, was being printed.

Wells claimed the unions knew of government plans beforehand because they had been told. Fraser March of NAPE said that was nonsense: Wells couldn't tell them he was going to do it, because of budget secrecy.

Thus began the infamous "Clyde Lied" campaign.

TWENTY-ONE

Everywhere Wells ventured in the province, he was dogged by posters and buttons containing cartoon pictures of him with his fingers crossed, containing the caption, "Clyde Lied." Leaving his office in the Sir Richard Squires Building in Corner Brook one day, he was surrounded by angry union members who blocked his car. Together with chants of "Clyde Lied," they exchanged heated words with him. An observer told me later that it looked like an extremely volatile situation, and she wouldn't have been surprised if there had been violence. Television has a way of intensifying hostility, but that scene and others like it certainly looked menacing.

Back in St. John's, nine union members stood up in the gallery of the House of Assembly, with Wells looking on, and opened their jackets to flash the T-shirts they were wearing, each containing one letter and spelling out, C-L-Y-D-E L-I-E-D. Wells protested what he described as "the dishonest representation" of the public sector unions, in particular NAPE. I'm not sure, however, that his words of protest were as effective as the other side's "Clyde Lied."

This attack on his honesty must have been gut-wrenching to a man who so valued his integrity that, when an overpayment of equalization to the province of over $70 million was belatedly discovered, Wells insisted on paying it all back to the feds. This astonished many in a province where, instead of opening new hospital beds as promised in his campaign, Wells said he was forced by necessity to close down hundreds.

A more pragmatic premier might have tried to negotiate a reduction or cancellation of this equalization payback to rich Ottawa from his nearly bankrupt province. The money had already been long spent, from coffers now empty, on desperately needed public essentials. After all, this was a province where government money became so tight in 1992 that the libraries had to close down for two weeks.

Wells was starting to gain the reputation for being the most fiscally conservative politician in Canada. Preston Manning, leader of the Reform Party of Canada, didn't even seem to resent, in his admiration, being ousted from that position. Manning appeared on *Open Line* some months before the federal election of 1993, in which his party would win fifty-two seats in the House of Commons. I told him that someone in the national media had said to me that Clyde Wells was making Preston Manning look like Karl Marx, the founder of communism. Manning laughed and allowed that the comparison might have been a slight exaggeration, but there was certainly a prominent place for Clyde in the Reform Party. Western Canada, he said, loved Clyde's stand on Meech Lake. When I queried innocently whether that love might include Clyde leading the Reform Party to government, with Clyde himself as prime minister, Manning responded happily that such a scenario was certainly not out of the question.

Leaving the possibility of bright federal glory, though, and moving back to Newfoundland's fiscal black hole, Wells almost appeared to go out of his way to impose a pall of gloom over our revenue side. That included the offshore oil industry. Amidst the ups and downs in the Hibernia development, Wells proclaimed himself very skeptical about the future of oil revenues: Hibernia was not the saviour that Peckford had always painted it, he said: the jobs generated by it would be the size of two fish plants, and royalties would only be of the order of about $8 million a year.

The day after he'd signed an oil agreement on Hibernia with the federal government in 1990, he'd come on *Open Line* and said that if he'd had his own way—if the agreement wasn't already a done deal—he would never have signed it. Newfoundland and Labrador, he claimed, had made one hell of a lot of concessions in it.

To the great consternation and embarrassment of our federal minister, John Crosbie, these kinds of negative remarks led media commentators across Canada, especially in Calgary, to ask loudly why, if Premier Wells was right in his doom and gloom, the federal government was putting over $3 billion into the offshore oil project. Crosbie, who always had to battle skeptics in his own Ottawa Government and in other provinces, complained about now having to take on the premier of his own province as well. Wells, he claimed, had become as dictatorial in his opinions and positions after one year as Joey Smallwood had after twenty-three years.

I recall a discussion in 1992 with the thoughtful and extremely well-informed vice-president of VOCM radio, Elmer Harris, before he was to go on air with a commentary on Hibernia. He stated that John Crosbie should receive all the credit for getting Hibernia up and running again after one of its many stumbles; if it weren't for Crosbie's dedication, the Hibernia project would be in limbo, if not dead. The oil industry owed its existence to Crosbie. In the past year, Elmer added, Crosbie had twice saved the Newfoundland and Labrador economy from collapse—the fisheries package and the Hibernia development. But details on Wells's role in saving the economy, as the great Mike Critch of VOCM news might have added, were scanty.

Eminent Memorial University economist Dr. Wade Locke very early zeroed in on one of the basic dismal truths about our oil industry: with the equalization clawback by the federal government, this province would only make a paltry few million a year from Hibernia. That was where our crucial problem lay. Nearly a decade would go by after Wells had vacated the scene before a premier emerged to tackle that problem effectively.

Clyde Wells's change in perspective on the oil industry over the years since he left the premiership has been remarkable. I was particularly struck by an article in the July–August 2014 edition of *National Magazine*, the official periodical of the Canadian Bar Association, in which Michael Dempster interviewed Wells about his role as premier nearly two decades after he'd retired.

"Then, after years of 'have-not status,' Newfoundland and Labrador underwent a sea change," the article states. "Wells negotiated agreements to start development in the Hibernia offshore oil field, the beginning of the province's economic turnaround." Huh? Where could Dempster have possible gotten that bizarrely inaccurate idea? Far from negotiating it, Wells, as mentioned, expressly stated back in 1990 that he would not have signed the agreement, if it had not already been negotiated by others beyond the point of no return.

"Wells was also premier when the province's economic landscape changed," the article continued. "Construction on the massive production platform in the offshore Hibernia oil field would begin in the early 1990s. While Wells signed the agreements, he credits his predecessors, particularly former Progressive Conservative premier Brian Peckford, for laying the groundwork." Gosh, that was nice of Mr. Wells. Especially since it was Peckford and John Crosbie who laid the groundwork, and later Brian Tobin and Danny Williams who then built upon it, after Wells had bemoaned Hibernia's worth as the equal of two fish plants.

The article went on: "Hibernia, followed by the Terra Nova and White Rose offshore oil fields and significant contributions from nickel and iron ore operations, helped Newfoundland become an economic leader in the country. 'There's a good deal of pride in it,' Wells says. 'Speaking personally, I'm delighted to be in a position where the province is contributing back to the great country of Canada some of the tremendous financial support that Canada contributed to Newfoundland when it was in need. That's the way a federation should work and it's marvellous. It's working beautifully.'"

Did anyone else find it bizarre the way Wells seemed to insinuate himself into deserving to take personal pride in Newfoundland's "have" status based on the offshore oil and nickel resources? Some would see Wells's negative actions, rather than any positive ones, as his best contribution. It's not mentioned in the article, but one thing he really could merit a good deal of credit and pride for—a bunch of negative actions, paradoxically—was the way he uncompromisingly got the province back on the financial rails, with cuts and rollbacks.

Newfoundland's "have not" status during Wells's premiership, plus the fishery collapse, the inadequate federal compensation program, and the lack of work in rural areas, made people leave in droves for bigger towns and cities or migrate out of the province altogether. Instead of realizing his promised hope of bringing every mother's son home, Wells had to watch the rural population, according to Statistics Canada, plummeting by nearly 50,000 during the 1990s.

To try to kick-start and diversify rural development, he set up the Economic Recovery Commission. The members of the commission were some of the brightest minds in the province, led by Doug House, who'd been the chair of the earlier Royal Commission on Employment and Unemployment.

The Economic Recovery Commission was designed to help create small businesses in all regions of the province. But the bleak economic times and financial restraints, plus resistance from the "Old Guard" bureaucracy, and lack of support from Wells himself, as House described it, doomed the poor commission to failure. With half-hearted backing, if that, from Wells, and hence little public support and few results, Premier Brian Tobin couldn't send the commission packing fast enough when he came to take over from Wells in 1996.

A laudable initiative to save money and provide better services occurred when Wells decided to tackle the prickly, tangly issue of amalgamation of municipalities. In the St. John's area, as an example, his government suggested that the municipalities of Mount Pearl, Goulds, and Wedgewood Park should merge with the capital city. All three places opposed the idea vehemently. But the smaller two towns were forced by legislation in 1991 into joining St. John's, while the City of Mount Pearl was permitted to maintain its independent status. However correct the amalgamation policy might have been, regarding financial savings and efficiency, the citizens of the swallowed-up towns screamed dictatorial tactics.

There was a similar reaction by administrators and workers affected when he took the sensible decision to abolish the unfair, inefficient, taxation-without-representation school tax system and the school tax authorities.

In both amalgamation and school tax abolition, most objective, thinking people agreed with his policies, but even some of them decried the arrogant and authoritarian method in which his government executed them. Some people claimed he was a hypocrite. Hadn't he bailed out on Joey Smallwood for being a dictator? And here was the proof that he was now being a far worse bully than Joey ever was. He had clobbered the two powerless little towns, Goulds and Wedgewood Park, into submission, some claimed, but he backed off Mount Pearl, just like a true bully, because the stronger municipality had taken him on and called his bluff.

On this question of dictatorship, even Wells would say later that he had come to see the merits of Smallwood's strong leadership in government: you couldn't have fifteen or twenty departments and scores of agencies going off in all directions.

In his second election, in 1993, Wells launched his campaign by asking who was going to govern the province, the public service unions or the government elected by the people. On election day, he increased his majority by four seats to thirty-five, while the Tories under Len Simms dropped five seats to sixteen, and Jack Harris, leader of the NDP, picked up a seat in Signal Hill–Quidi Vidi. Wells's Liberals received forty-nine per cent of the popular vote to the Tories' forty-two per cent.

He took the results as a sound mandate to continue his public service job cuts and to reduce amounts going to virtually all government services. By 1995 he was able to proudly preside over a balanced provincial budget. At the start of his premiership, just five or six years before, many had deemed it an impossible feat.

Wells's zeal to save the government money by rationalizing government activities got him into trouble the year after his second election. In 1994, he took it into his head to privatize the Crown corporation Newfoundland and Labrador Hydro. On the face of it, the proposition made all the sense in the world. By far, most of the electricity in the province was produced by the publicly owned Hydro, and that electricity was virtually all distributed by Newfoundland Power, a utility company owned by Fortis Inc. Therefore, bringing both corporations together was a rational move in and of itself; plus the sale of Hydro to Newfoundland Power would cut the province's debt by well over $1 billion.

Wells explained the idea clearly in news conferences and made speeches to the board of trade and similar groups pointing out its manifold benefits. But from the start, many in the public didn't like the scheme. And the rate of approval did not increase as time went on. He called *Open Line* several times to justify it, but the calls opposing the privatization only increased. Although he made it clear that the sale price would be arrived at objectively, at arm's length, and for a market value determined by impartial experts, an increasing number of opponents questioned his prior close connection to the purchaser. For years he'd been on the board of Newfoundland Power as a director, and right before he became leader of the Liberal Party, he was board chairman. A common refrain became, "The whole thing stinks to high heaven."

Still, Wells continued to assert his determination to follow through with the privatization, come hell or high water, and stated adamantly that he would never surrender in his objective.

Opponents argued that Hydro had made profits for the government for years and that Wells's deal would cause electricity rates to go up. But in addition to that, the Crown corporation, up to now an unglamorous utility outfit, started somehow to take on the characteristics of a beloved provincial icon. Well-known activists and commentators Greg Malone and Sue Kelland-Dyer, among others, were especially effective in making the privatization proposal look like an unpatriotic act. Calls to radio and television, protest demonstrations, letters to newspapers, petitions—some opponents even compared the proposal to the financially disastrous Churchill Falls deal, which, they contended, Wells had sung the praises of so loudly back in the late 1960s.

The premier was caught in the toils of a largely irrational public opinion monster *against* him now, similar to the monster comprising the tens of thousands who had *supported* him on the Meech Lake controversy. A privatization opponent gleefully, if somewhat irrelevantly, quoted from Hosea: "For they have sown the wind, and they shall reap the whirlwind . . ."

One of his own Liberal caucus, Wally Noel, knocked Wells for failing to hold public hearings on the issue. Noel contrasted his handling of Hydro with his behaviour on Meech Lake, where he had built his national and provincial reputation because he had listened to what people said.

Noel was on to something: polls showed that Wells's approval rating among voters had dropped substantially from Meech Lake to the Hydro controversy. In April 1991, it had been seventy-one per cent; in November 1994, it was fifty-two per cent. That latter number was by no means shabby in the circumstances, by any political measure. Most premiers would have been happy to have it. But the drop must have shocked Wells. By the end of the year, he decided to suspend the privatization plan he'd vowed never to withdraw, and the next year he gave up on it altogether.

Looking back to his idea from the vantage point of the Muskrat Falls multi-billion dollar project, undertaken by the Crown corporation Nalcor, saddling it and the government with looming backbreaking debt, a beleaguered taxpayer has to wonder today if Clyde Wells was not absolutely right.

In 1995, Wells turned to a matter that had bothered him all his life, the denominational education system. Determined, no doubt, to leave a legacy of reform in education, he started a process intended to replace the old religious school system with a more secular and efficient one. Following a Royal Commission on Education in Newfoundland, *Our Children Our Future*, conducted by Dr. Leonard Williams and published in 1992, Wells held a referendum in September 1995. Over 54.4 per cent of the voters were in favour of amending the Terms of Union to create a single inter-denominational education system.

But the legislation introduced in the House of Assembly early in 1996 would have established a hodgepodge, hybrid system. The proposals would reduce the number of school boards from twenty-seven denominational ones to ten fully-elected "inter-denominational" boards. Each board would contain ten denominational representatives and five persons of no declared denominational affiliation. Most schools would become inter-denominational, but where there was demand, and numbers warranted, schools for specific denominations or denominational groups could continue to exist. A registration process would be conducted by school boards to determine the demand for inter-denominational and "uni-denominational" schools.

The main impact on teachers would be that, except for uni-denominational schools, teachers would no longer be hired or dismissed on denominational grounds. School boards would also be required to attempt to place in other schools teachers who were dismissed from a uni-denominational school for denominational reasons. The Denominational Education Councils would be replaced by a single inter-denominational body with primary responsibility for religious education.

Good God! It was akin to legislating how many angels could dance on the head of a pin. The new scheme, if anyone could be bothered to understand it, seemed to preserve or make worse some of the sorriest aspects of the old system.

Some good reforms were, in fact, proposed on the periphery, such as a School Construction Board with responsibility for approving proposals for school construction, based on province-wide priorities; the formation of school councils giving parents more say in education; the performance of schools to be reviewed by an external assessment body reporting to the public; and the establishment of francophone and Aboriginal schools. But the reality is that it was, at its core, a timid, half-hearted, confusing halfway measure, and it was doomed to dismal failure.

Push-back from some churches and citizens would culminate in 1997 with the Roman Catholic Church, the Pentecostal Assemblies, and twenty-nine parents challenging the "re-designation" process in the Supreme Court of Newfoundland and winning their case. Premier Wells's pathetic education reforms were dead. Within a year, the removal of the denominations' stranglehold on education would be tackled forthrightly and properly by a new premier.

TWENTY-TWO

In December 1995, Wells announced he was resigning as premier and called a leadership convention for early in the new year to replace him as Liberal leader. Brian Tobin announced his candidacy and resigned from the federal cabinet on January 7, 1996. When no one ran against him, he was elected leader by acclamation on January 17, 1996.

Wells had made no secret of the fact that he didn't like politics very much. So he was not sad to be leaving the "top" job for his first love, the practice of law. Still, the way he was forced to leave at the very end must have hurt his dignity. If he expected a little breathing space and a gracious transfer of power from himself to Tobin, he didn't get it. Tobin couldn't hustle him out the door fast enough. A Liberal organizer close to both of them at the time told me, "Brian gave poor Clyde the bum's rush."

As soon as Tobin had won the leadership, the intense pressure was applied by his entourage on Wells's entourage to vacate the premises. *Now*! "It was a wonder," said the organizer, "that Clyde didn't find his coat and briefcase and files strewn about the steps of Confederation Building after being flung out of the premier's eighth-floor window." On January 26, a little over a week after becoming leader, Tobin was sworn in as premier and almost immediately called an election.

Wells put the best face on it. Stressing to interviewers that anonymity was a wonderful thing, this man who never shunned the spotlight, and whose legal cases were often on the news, said he welcomed a return to the anonymity of the practice of law. He didn't labour in the legal salt mines for long, though. Two years later, the man who, like Trudeau, so admired Wells's stance on Meech Lake, Prime Minister Jean Chrétien appointed him to the Court of Appeal of the Supreme Court of Newfoundland, and shortly after, in 1999, as chief justice of the province. It was the culmination of a brilliant personal career.

But apart from achieving dazzling personal success throughout life in acquiring the high positions he sought, what did Wells actually accomplish for the public good?

He took on Joey Smallwood and no doubt played a strong role in loosening his grip on Newfoundland politics. But then, as Fred Stagg pointed out, he abandoned that fight when Newfoundland needed him most.

He took on the prime minister and all the other premiers of Canada in a principled stand regarding Meech Lake. But then he slipped out from under it in a very dubious way at the end and left a residue of discontent and resentment in Quebec which came close to ending the Canadian federation.

He took on education reform in a way that was doomed to failure.

He was going to save the province over a billion dollars by privatizing Newfoundland Hydro. But he had to retreat from his vowed undertaking in complete disarray.

He fought tooth and nail against the creeping bankruptcy of the province and succeeded, but in a way that allowed the entire labour movement to declare that "Clyde Lied," with an arguable claim to plausibility.

And then there were the millions of dollars in court damages and settlements, as a consequence of alleged violations, under his watch, of the Public Tendering Act.

* * * * *

When Wells began his premiership, his governing trademark throughout his term was going to be honesty and integrity. I remember, early on, a good friend of mine complaining to me and others that he and some big supporters of the Liberal Party could not get a look-in when it came to government contracts. Wells had left them all out in the cold, twisting in the wind.

They even sought a special audience with the premier to lay out their case for a taste of patronage. After that meeting, my friend didn't get the idea they'd made much headway with Wells. Clyde seemed very self-righteous, he said. Apparently, though, somewhere along the line, they must have advanced their position more than they'd thought.

Before Wells left office, there were several alleged violations by the government of the Public Tendering Act. One involved a $24 million deal comprising three contracts for the construction of hospitals awarded to Trans City Holdings Limited. Principals of that company were known Liberal supporters. Two unsuccessful bidders sued in the Supreme Court of the province, alleging violations, and in 1996 they received damages of $1.5 million and $1 million, together with court costs.

Then, in 1999, the Wells government had to negotiate an out-of-court settlement with another unsuccessful bidder concerning the same hospital contracts. The settlement was reported to be in the area of $750,000.

Meanwhile, Frank Ryan, a prominent St. John's businessman who'd played a large role in Brian Peckford's campaigns, was confronted by a breach of contract on the part of the Wells government to renew a lease in the Murray Premises. As a result, he lost the ownership of the building and sued the government. He and the government ultimately settled in 1998, and he received between $4 million and $5 million compensation from the provincial treasury. One lawyer, close to the scene, described the breach to me as a pure case of political vindictiveness on the part of Liberal government decision makers.

* * * * *

Clyde Wells, whatever his other unsuccessful or dubious initiatives, and alleged breaches, did put the province's finances in order. He balanced the budget. Wells himself considered this to be his greatest achievement. And it was indeed an impressive feat. He may even have saved the province from insolvency.

But considering all that he tried to do, and achieved decidedly mixed results at, that one worthy but rather prosaic achievement didn't require much vision. It reminded me a little of Orson Welles's speech in Graham Greene's film *The Third Man*: "In Italy for thirty years under the Borgias they had warfare, terror, murder, and bloodshed, but they produced Michelangelo, Leonardo da Vinci, and the Renaissance. In Switzerland they had brotherly love—they had 500 years of democracy and peace, and what did that produce? The cuckoo clock."

But that's just an idle thought of mine; I don't think many would regard Wells's financial achievements for the province as a cuckoo clock. A lot of people I talk to about the province's premiers still revere him for dragging the province back onto the financial rails.

I myself have mostly admired Clyde Wells, from my first encounters with him in the House of Assembly in the late 1960s to when I ran for election under his leadership in 1993, wanting to be part of what he was trying to achieve, financially and economically. Regrettably, the seat turned out to be impossible to win.

In 1994, he agreed with compassion and graciousness to deliver the eulogy at the funeral service in George Street Church for my father, with whom he had sat in cabinet nearly thirty years before. And in the years after that, our brief personal encounters have been pleasant and stimulating, and his views thought-provoking.

A couple of lawyers with whom I've discussed Wells's contribution to the province nursed the idea that, no matter what he tried to achieve for the province, it was peanuts compared to how he so skilfully navigated and executed his own brilliant career. No man in Newfoundland's history has done it better, they said, apparently in admiration. You could call it "enlightened self-interest," or even "opportunism at the genius level." No good opportunity escaped him, and no inopportune situation was so skilfully avoided.

The analysis has him seizing the opportunity to become a cabinet minister in his twenties but abandoning politics when it became inconvenient. He stayed away from the Liberal leadership when obtaining it and the premiership was a difficult challenge, but jumped into the leadership when the then Liberal leader and the PC government seemed vulnerable. He got out of politics while his anti–Meech Lake buddy was still prime minister, and accepted at his hands an appointment to the Newfoundland Court of Appeal and chief justiceship of Newfoundland. His enlightened self-interest worked brilliantly, even in spite of his political tin ear that often made it such a challenge, early on, for him to get personally elected.

Critics of Wells, many of them his fellow legal professionals and former political opponents, point out what they consider his narrow, tunnel vision in both his ideas and his career trajectory. To me they often sound as if they're jealous and resentful. I'd rather cast his personal success in terms of the fact that, all Wells's life, many intelligent people have wanted or needed to avail themselves of his talents and have actively pursued him. They did that in his law practice, seeking what they believed he could contribute to their well-being, and being willing to pay him his healthy concept of what he was worth. And they did it with a view to placing him in political leadership, where they knew he'd strive to do his best, with his considerable ability, for his partisan team and for his province.

TWENTY-THREE

I saw twenty-three-year-old Brian Vincent Tobin on CJON television, in 1977, giving Geoff Stirling a hand with solving the world's more pressing problems. His job at CJON was to help present the evening news with director Randy Simms. But Stirling, the station's brilliantly unconventional owner, liked to get together with him on the air to discuss and resolve tangly public issues. He already sounded articulate and savvy, and Geoff told me at the time that young Tobin had a golden future ahead of him in national television.

Geoff's impression of Brian's golden future was a little different from what I heard at VOCM Radio. Brian had briefly worked there before CJON, and according to inside reports, he was so awkward and clumsy with the equipment that his fellow employees dubbed him "T'umbs Tobin." (As in "all thumbs.") They joked years later that it was a fine thing Brian didn't have a clue in the control room because, if he'd been any good he'd still be in there and would've missed out on being federal minister and premier.

After I was elected leader of the Liberal Party in 1977, I advertised for applications from people who wanted to be executive assistant to the Leader of the Opposition. Half a dozen of the men and women who applied were first-rate. Among them was Tobin. But before the interviews, a fellow Member of the House and I encountered a law student who'd known Brian when he was an undergraduate student at Memorial University. The aspiring lawyer told us that, wherever Tobin happened to be on campus, there always seemed to be, purely by coincidence, of course, a toke or two of pot there, too. He laughed and said that, according to his legal training, though, nobody could be deemed guilty by association. Hearing this, my MHA colleague, who knew we'd be interviewing Brian, said, "We'll have to watch that—the last thing we need is some flaky space cadet around the place."

Several senior caucus members and I interviewed the candidates for EA, who included, incidentally, a highly regarded former deputy minister. It was clear from their answers that the youngest of them, Tobin, was miles ahead of the others in his feel for politics and public affairs. We asked each to turn around and look at a map of Newfoundland and Labrador on the wall behind them, coloured entirely in red and blue: what was wrong with the map?

Some of them zeroed in on the idea that the red represented Liberal districts, while the blue was Tory. But they were mystified by the total Tory blue area being way smaller than the red. Weren't there far more PC Members in the House than Liberals? Tobin didn't hesitate, though. He said there was too much Tory blue and not enough Liberal red. In the last election, the Tories had won nearly all the smaller-in-area urban seats, while the Liberal Party had been mostly relegated to the geographically larger rural districts. If the Liberals were ever going to win back the government instead of remaining just a coastal fringe party, we had to elect a lot more members in that small blue area.

After the interviews, my colleague, who'd encountered the law student with me, said, "I take it all back. The young fella's no flaky space cadet." By unanimous decision, Tobin got the job.

Executive assistant to the Leader of the Opposition was a nice little position. It was not as glamorous as being in the office of the premier or a cabinet minister, where policy was being formulated and important decisions made. But it was okay, especially for a young guy in his early twenties. So I expected Tobin to be somewhat pleased to get it. I had no idea.

When I called his station to tell him he'd won the competition and to offer him the post, he put his hand over the mouthpiece to muffle the sound. But his hand didn't deaden it quite enough. The roar of delight that came out of him could be heard from my receiver by the other people across my office. I've known no other person so eager and enthusiastic about getting involved in politics and so open in displaying his fascination and zeal.

Tobin was a good executive assistant. My rough-and-tumble travels around the province were much more pleasant because of his good-humoured company. He was attentive to questions and requests for help that came into my office and very clued in about what was going on in his generation. And he was perceptive about the media in all respects. Once, when we sat down in Toronto with a public relations group to bone up on the fine political arts of spin-doctoring, image management, and media manipulation, Tobin found it hard to keep quiet. Our main PR guru there was torn between being very annoyed and very impressed. How could he not be, on both counts? Many of Brian's gratuitous opinions were better than his.

Tobin's later well-known, seize-the-bull-by-the-horns shtick was evident early. We were at a Liberal convention in Ottawa around 1978, when Prime Minister Pierre Trudeau presented himself at an accountability session. From the stage in a hall at the Hôtel Château Laurier, he gave a speech and answered questions from the audience of delegates.

I'd had dinner with Trudeau and other provincial Liberal leaders the night before for a freewheeling discussion, including how he should publicly handle the media frenzy over his recent separation from wife, Margaret. Someone at the table even made a cringe-worthy comment about her partying at Studio 54 sans knickers, and her liaisons with the Rolling Stones, Ted Kennedy, Jack Nicholson, and so on. But we did cover numerous federal-provincial issues as well, so there was no need, for purposes of information, that I ask him a question now at this public event. However, Brian and I thought, for reasons of visibility—we'd learned some deep stuff from our PR session—that I should make a comment on an issue of the day affecting Newfoundland and ask Trudeau for his reaction.

I joined one of the lineups at the microphones just in time to hear the facilitator on the stage say that the prime minister would only be able to take one more question. As I started to go back to my seat, I saw Tobin quietly creeping up the steps leading to the side of the stage, approach the woman, and whisper into her ear. Thereupon she whispered into Trudeau's ear, and he scanned the audience, with his hand above his eyes to cut out the glare, and mentioned that the new Liberal leader from Newfoundland had been attempting to ask a very important question on behalf of his province—"Mr. Rowe?"

I was forced to jump the queue to the mic, which was not to the delight of everybody else who'd been waiting there. Now, to make this turn of events as significant as it had been labelled, I could no longer lob at Trudeau the softball question I'd intended. I had to comment more severely and ask Trudeau pointedly what he intended to do about it, as if I was asking a question of the government in the House of Assembly.

I strongly implied to the PM that the feds were screwing Newfoundland on the offshore oil and asked him why his government was doing such a reprehensible thing. The momentary grimace on Trudeau's face indicated he didn't like my premise. How the hell, he was thinking, did Newfoundland's minister of Energy, Brian Peckford, get in here? But he answered in a polite if hard-nosed way. Later, our delegation, with one or two exceptions, said they thought my question was great; I'd said something that had to be said. I wasn't so sure. I had the uncomfortable feeling I'd needlessly ambushed my federal colleague.

Tobin was delighted, though. If you were going to do something in politics, "go for it." Execute it for maximum public effect, not in a passive, wishy-washy way.

One of Tobin's problems as executive assistant was that he was smarter and more articulate and more creative in his thinking than many of the elected MHAs in my caucus. I held daily caucus meetings when the House was in session. There we discussed our strategy on government policy, and we decided on the questions, the more embarrassing the better, that we would throw at the premier and ministers in the House that day. The discussion around the table was restricted to MHAs, unless a staff member was invited to respond. Tobin was at every meeting, and he could not resist sometimes chiming in spontaneously with his own original suggestion or his take on a particular topic.

I could see some MHAs exchanging looks of irritation when that happened. My difficulty was that Tobin made far more sense and expressed it better than most of the others. Still, the nature of political egos was such that a delegation of MHAs came into my office to petition along these lines: "Whereas we MHAs are elected, and whereas staffers are not elected, now therefore please tell Tobin in caucus to shut the fuck up." I did curtail him a little, but I noticed that the MHAs who'd seemed most offended were now spending more time in Tobin's office digging up and talking over with him their questions and remarks for the House.

But, despite being politically savvy beyond his years, Brian was sometimes a delayed adolescent in one respect. A couple of mornings, on road trips, in order for me to make it to a planned meeting on time, I had to leave him behind in our motel because he had overslept and wasn't ready to go with me in the car. I was amused, one time, when I glanced out the window of a Society of United Fishermen hall to see him scrambling out of a pickup truck he'd flagged down twenty miles back to arrive in time for the meeting.

People in my district of Twillingate liked Brian a lot. The president of the Liberal Association there suggested to me that if I ever decided to run in another district, we should get Brian to run in this one.

TWENTY-FOUR

After the provincial Liberal Party under Don Jamieson had lost to the Peckford Tories in 1979, Tobin became executive assistant to Don as the new Leader of the Opposition. Then, in December of the same year, came the downfall of Joe Clark's government. It was defeated on John Crosbie's "short-term pain for long-term gain" budget, and a fresh federal election was called early in 1980. Jamieson asked Tobin to go out to the west coast of Newfoundland, since he'd been born and spent his childhood in Stephenville, and try to recruit a Liberal candidate for the federal riding of Humber–Port au Port–St. Barbe.

Brian and I talked about it and went over a few names. The seat was not an attractive prospect for the Liberals. Jack Marshall had been a highly popular PC Member of Parliament there for years, having wrestled it away from domination by the Liberal Party since Confederation. In 1977, I had recommended to Pierre Trudeau that Marshall, who was Jewish, be appointed to the senate. Trudeau agreed, not to get rid of a very effective and popular Tory in the riding, as some surmised, but simply to recognize the man's accomplishments and background, whatever his party stripe might have been.

It was by no means the first time Trudeau had reached outside the

Liberal Party to make a good appointment. If he had in fact done it to try to win the seat back for the Liberals, the ploy, as was eminently foreseeable, backfired. The seat was captured in a 1978 by-election by Fonse Faour, a lawyer in his late twenties, the first New Democrat MP in the history of the province. And he was re-elected in the general election of 1979.

After the 1980 election campaign was under way, Tobin came back from his mission to the west coast with bad news for Jamieson. No one wanted to run for the Liberal Party there. That was not entirely surprising. Fonse Faour seemed extremely popular. People affectionately referred to him as the Fonz or, because of his nattily dressed look, Fancy Faour. And nationally, the Liberal Party appeared to be in disarray.

Pierre Trudeau had previously announced his retirement as leader, and pundits touted the PC Party as being in the same situation now as in 1958–59. That was when Diefenbaker, after first winning a minority government, then came back from the next election with the biggest majority of seats in the history of Canada. To many, Clark appeared to be poised to pull off a similar victory.

Tobin wondered if he should become the Liberal candidate by default, just to fill the hole. Jamieson couldn't care less, one way or the other. He had his heart set on retiring as Liberal leader soon and only wanted to make sure each district had a Liberal candidate in this election, even if the person was mere cannon fodder.

Brian and I talked about the pros and cons, short term and long term, of his running. We concluded that, in the circumstances, he had no hope of winning the election. Not only was he up against the Fonz, but the Tory candidate was also well known and respected in the area. Brian didn't stand a chance. But if he did throw his hat in now, it would be a good experience, and he'd be back in his office in Confederation Building in a few weeks. That was the short term taken care of. In the longer term, we surmised that his campaign might make enough of an impact in the riding to allow him to carve out a promising provincial seat to run in, next election.

Talking to him, I could see that, at twenty-five, he could not resist taking advantage of this opportunity to be the Liberal candidate, however dismal his prospects. He decided to go for it.

The next day, as he left the Opposition office, carrying his suitcase, he poked his head in my door and said, "Well, here goes nothin." We laughed, but he did look more than a little forlorn walking out of the warm building all alone, heading for the airport and the frigid, nearly eight-week winter campaign.

Tobin's talents as a communicator, organizer, and effective campaigner came out during the next few weeks, as did his good judgment in marrying, a couple of years before, his sweetheart from their teenaged years, Jodean Smith. I didn't know Jodean well, but I'd met her enough times, and heard enough about her and her family from Brian, to realize she was a person of high intelligence and progressive ideas, to go with her open, vivacious attractiveness.

I learned that Jodean played a significant role in the outcome of Brian's election. She spent time campaigning door to door in harsh winter conditions. My mother was from the west coast, and I knew from her all about the blizzards, winds, and temperatures there in February: her hometown of Woody Point, she told me, held the record for average annual snowfall on the Island. So I can only imagine the impression on the good hearts of men and women on the St. Barbe coast of a young slip of a wife with her parka hood up, knocking on doors, asking for votes for her husband.

But there was something even more important about her that contributed significantly to Brian's good decisions in the election, and which would come out patently in several of his noteworthy actions in the future. One example, during this first election campaign of theirs, occurred when Brian appeared with the two other candidates at a session of debating and questions at a Knights of Columbus Hall. All three candidates were Roman Catholic, and the inevitable question came up concerning their positions on abortions.

No doubt the audience figured the question and answers on that topic, considering religion and place, would be purely formal. And sure enough, the NDP and PC candidates answered to applause that they were against abortion. But Tobin flabbergasted and gobsmacked everyone there, especially his own supporters, by responding that he was Catholic like the others, but he wasn't running to represent just Catholics. He was running to represent everyone in the riding, and he was pro-choice.

One of Tobin's main organizers, whom I knew well, Jack McCarthy from Corner Brook, told me later, when we happened to sit together on a plane from St. John's to Deer Lake, that he went up to Brian at the end of that meeting and said, "We might as well give this up right now: you just lost the election."

That seemed to be the general sentiment, I replied to Jack: a Liberal lawyer from Corner Brook, who'd been at the meeting, told me that he'd turned to his friend next to him and muttered, "If there's a God, we're fucked."

But over the next few days, Jack continued, he started to notice that Tobin's profile was going up. His pro-choice statement in the Knights of Columbus Hall, of all places, had shot through the entire district. Men were saying, "One thing about that fella Tobin—he's all guts." Plus, I said to Jack, I could only imagine the positive reaction of many of the women in the riding. He nodded thoughtfully: it was one of those times when a genuinely truthful but risky response by a politician who "inadvisedly" spurned the easy route and showed some backbone and integrity paid off.

Tobin's political instincts, speaking ability, and personality overcame what appeared to be some other strong, opposing elements. He had to take on frontally, for example, the allegation that he had deliberately smeared the reputation of a one-time favourite west coast son, Dr. Tom Farrell, by distributing police reports accusing Farrell of arson. A fire had started in his apartment in the Elizabeth Towers that had forced the evacuation, in the middle of the night, of mostly senior citizens.

I had already stated publicly, and an inquiry had found, that Tobin was in no way responsible. And in any event, a judge would formally declare, what already seemed clear to all, that, on the evidence, "by accident or design" Farrell had caused the fire. So the allegation against

Tobin found no traction, leaving his opponents sputtering only that he was slick and slippery. Teflon Tobin, they called him.

And he had to run without the support of the Corner Brook Liberal premier-in-waiting, Clyde Wells, who snubbed him and his candidacy. He wouldn't give Brian any support. But that was in fact a blessing in disguise, because Wells's popularity was such among those who knew him best that he found it a challenge to get himself elected personally. It forced Tobin to become entirely his own man and to build up his own base of support.

Nationally, the Joe Clark of 1980 turned out to be no John Diefenbaker of 1958. Trudeau, redrafted as Liberal leader, fought a feisty campaign and led his party back to government. Included in the national victory was Tobin's riding, where he beat the Fonz by over 3,600 votes. Overnight, Brian had gone from obscure backroom boy for an ineffectual leader of a dispirited provincial Liberal Party to Member of Parliament supporting a regenerated majority government in a House of Commons headed by a prime minister with a zealous four-year mission. Luck? Of course. More than a little. But, as I said to Brian, rather inelegantly, when he came back to the Opposition office to collect his stuff and say farewell: luck can be described as brazenly seizing an unpromising opportunity by the balls, and stretching your abilities to the utmost, and working your arse off, all to create that lucky break.

There would be more of them to come.

I don't recall much about Brian Tobin's activities in Ottawa from 1980 to 1984, during Pierre Trudeau's last kick at the can as PM. Bill Rompkey had already been let go from the cabinet. But when Roger Simmons had to resign as minister in 1983, for income tax evasion, I remember being surprised that neither George Baker, nor even Tobin, young though he was, was immediately appointed in Simmons's place. A newsman in Ottawa told me that Trudeau, when asked off the record why he didn't fill the Newfoundland gap around the cabinet table, for some reason muttered in disgust that the entire Newfoundland caucus could go fuddle duddle themselves.

Once, when I was in Ottawa on business during this period, Brian invited me to lunch in the parliamentary restaurant. He was as upbeat as ever and was able to joke about how we were seated at the least propitious table in the place, right next to an area overactive with rushing waiters and clanging utensils. I didn't have the idea that he was gaining much opportunity to shine during those years, sitting in the backbenches of an administration dominated by a prime minister preoccupied with his own legacy.

I had lost much of my own interest in active politics, federally and provincially, before this. I was now more engrossed in resuming the practice of law, getting my first book published, writing a newspaper column, shooting off my face as a pundit on national media, and becoming a host on the VOCM morning call-in show.

I remember phoning Tobin at home from my radio show one morning, out of the blue at 7:30 Ottawa time, to ask him why he was supporting the way his government was screwing Newfoundland on the offshore oil. I quickly told him he was on the air so that he wouldn't say something inappropriate when he heard my voice. He chuckled, completely at ease with being taken by surprise by the early morning call and the awkward question, and said that I'd just done what he would do if he were still in the media. I don't recall his answer, but that's probably because he fielded the question as if it was child's play.

At some point over those four years, I had him on the radio show as a guest for an hour, and he was right in his element, sounding off and answering callers' questions. During a commercial break, he told me that he wanted to do something like this, hosting a radio or television show, when he got out of politics. It confirmed for me that he was finding his four years of toeing the line as an ordinary government backbencher less than fulfilling. For someone with flair and a yen for the dramatic, I suspect he understood, even if he didn't enjoy, Prime Minister Trudeau's gratuitous insult to the backbench that, when MPs were fifty yards from Parliament Hill, they were nobodies.

But whatever he was not able to do on the big stage in Ottawa, he was doing something right in his own Newfoundland riding.

When Trudeau resigned in 1984 and John Turner won the Liberal leadership against Jean Chrétien, with Tobin's support, the new prime minister looked at the polls showing the Liberals ahead and called an immediate federal election. Tory leader Brian Mulroney clobbered him. Turner's Liberals were reduced from 147 seats to forty, and the PC Party won 211 seats, one of the largest majorities in history.

In Newfoundland and Labrador, the Liberal Party, which in 1980 had won five seats to the PCs' two, now dropped to three while the Tories went up to four seats. And the total Liberal popular vote in the province declined substantially. Somehow, though, Brian Tobin was able to buck that trend. Not only did he get re-elected against the Mulroney onslaught, by a narrow margin, but he actually increased his percentage of the vote significantly and added over 4,000 votes to his total from the previous election. All his political life, federally, before he became premier, Tobin's personal election returns only went up. In 1980, he'd received about forty-two per cent. In this second election in 1984, he got nearly fifty per cent; and in 1988 and 1993, he would win by about sixty-eight per cent and eighty-four per cent, respectively.

The landslide election of the Mulroney Tories in 1984 became Liberal Tobin's salvation. He was now in Opposition, where he began to thrive. Except for the short span out of government in 1979, this was the first time the Liberal Party had been in Opposition since the Diefenbaker years, before Lester Pearson elected a minority government in 1963. Few of the senior members now remaining in the demoralized, nearly annihilated Official Opposition party in 1984 seemed to have a clue what to do.

If Turner was rusty when he returned to politics to take over as prime minister, he was worse as Leader of the Opposition. There was a vacuum on that side of the House of Commons. And politics, like nature, abhors a vacuum. A great fear reigned in the Liberal Party that the NDP under Broadbent would elbow the Liberals aside in the House and fill the emptiness. But, fortunately for the Liberal Party, into the void scuttled the Rat Pack.

The name, hardly original, was bestowed by a *Toronto Star* reporter on a group of young, relatively unknown Liberal backbench MPs. The core consisted of John Nunziata, Sheila Copps, Don Boudria, and Brian Tobin. It was supplemented, from time to time, by Quebecer Jean Lapierre and old-timer Herb Gray, who helped largely behind the scenes with memories of buried skeletons and cunning tactics. They lambasted the huge majority government indiscriminately, but mostly they concentrated on the patronage and freebies to PC supporters. They even created the Patronage Award of the Week and bestowed it on whatever government appointment or other reward to Tory cronies they judged the worst.

Nunziata seemed to be their de facto leader, judging by the number of times government members called him sleazy and slimy. But they all held their own in that department, including, or perhaps especially, Brian Tobin. And there was much tut-tutting by pundits in the media over their low and nasty insinuations. Tobin in particular had a penchant for the dramatic.

I recall one TV clip from the House featuring him haranguing the government during a controversy over conflict-of-interest allegations against Tory minister Sinclair Stevens. In his hands, Tobin brandished a copy of the Tory Party's conflict-of-interest guidelines. As his facial features went from merely grave to absolutely disgusted, he held up the document, ripped it in two, and flung the scraps and shreds into the air. For television screens it was an excellent image of the futility of expecting this government to abide by even its own undemanding rules of honesty.

So that got good coverage, as did the occasion in 1985 when he was kicked out of the House for calling Prime Minister Mulroney a liar. But even Tobin's antics were overmatched one time by the spectacle of his fellow Rats, Copps and Nunziata, scrambling over rows of chairs in their attempt to get physically at some minister who had displeased them. Brian Mulroney called the pack of them Nazis.

Leader John Turner was delighted that the Rat Pack let him off the hook over his own uselessness in Opposition, and he did nothing to rein in their excesses. Indeed, he actively encouraged them: I recall a picture of him becoming an honorary member of the Rat Pack, complete with his own ten-dollar Rat Pack T-shirt.

John Crosbie was a natural, hard-to-resist target. He claimed that the Speaker of the House allowed Question Period to become a circus under the domination of the Liberal Opposition Rat Pack. He yelled across the House at the attacking Sheila Copps, one time, "Quieten down, baby." Which caused Copps to yell the obvious right back, "I'm nobody's baby." This gave her a title for her bestselling memoirs, but I don't think she gave John a fifteen per cent agent's fee. Crosbie groused that he, and the prime minister, and the government generally, spent nine years fending off the sensationalist slander and untrue allegations of vicious little rodents like Tobin and Copps.

Some pundits deemed the antics of the Rat Pack to be so far over the top as to be demeaning to the House of Commons. And of course they were right. Any diminutive rump, as the Liberal MPs in the House then were, had to resort to unusual tactics to survive against the huge majority force which the PCs had become, and to hope to hold the otherwise unbridled government to account.

I believe the Rat Pack kept the Liberal Party alive in the public consciousness, particularly when it was needed most, during those first four years of Mulroney dominance and control. And there was a good Liberal precedent for their actions. During the similar supremacy of the Diefenbaker Tories from 1958 to 1962, Newfoundland MP Jack Pickersgill played the role of a one-man "rat pack," which held the government to account by his knowledgeable questions and oratory, and ultimately allowed the Liberals to regroup and lay Diefenbaker low.

I'd urge those who want a polite and courteous and tidy parliament, with no undignified or unbecoming criticism of the government, to look to Stalin's Kremlin or Hitler's Reichstag, rather than the Houses of Commons in Ottawa or London.

TWENTY-FIVE

Tobin's profile became high enough throughout Newfoundland and Labrador that, despite never having been in cabinet when the Liberal Party formed the government, and then having been only an Opposition maw-mouth during the party's fragile days, he was approached by the provincial Liberal caucus with a request that he run for the leadership.

A federal election was soon coming up in 1988, and Tobin must have thought that, this time, Turner would win it against Prime Minister Mulroney, who was declining in popularity. Turner appointed him chairman of the Liberal caucus, which indicated he'd get a cabinet position when the party returned to power. So Tobin visited Clyde Wells in Corner Brook and urged the still-reluctant holdout to run for the provincial leadership. But after the 1988 federal election, he must have kicked himself.

Mulroney and Crosbie were bringing in a free trade deal with the US, and canny Mulroney was able to divide the opposition to it between the Liberal Party and the NDP. In that way, he was able to win a reduced but still good majority of 169 seats, with forty-three per cent of the popular vote, against a combined opposition vote of well over fifty per cent.

The Liberal caucus more than doubled in size, but it would still be in Opposition for four more long years. Tobin's joy at being once more a gadfly pestering the government must have been wearing thin by now.

The Meech Lake debacle took place during that parliamentary term. Tobin was in favour of the Accord, which put him in opposition to Clyde Wells, and to the man he would soon support for national Liberal leadership, Jean Chrétien. Mulroney, whom Tobin had torn strips off in the House for years, was desperate enough in his desire to salvage Meech that he used Tobin as "an honest broker" on one occasion. He asked him not to persuade Wells over—that was out of the question—but simply to stop his countryman from walking out of the talks. Tobin did go to see Wells, despite the tension between them about Meech. This was a courageous act since, to meet privately with the premier, he had to get by the gatekeeper, Deborah Coyne, who considered Tobin an out-and out traitor to their cause and didn't mind telling him so.

Meanwhile, John Turner, defeated twice by Mulroney, finally got the message from central casting, the electorate, that he was never going to regain the star role of prime minister. He announced his retirement and called a leadership convention for June 23, 1990, to take place in Calgary.

Two Rat Packers in their mid-thirties jumped into the race, Sheila Copps and John Nunziata. I never heard that Tobin, thirty-six, was tempted to emulate them. A good thing, too. Despite having played a crucial part in saving the Liberal Party from starving to death during those lean years, neither of the two who did run was able to attract the support of any caucus members. And at the convention, Copps garnered less than eleven per cent of the votes of delegates, and Rat Pack leader Nunziata a dismal one per cent. Tobin probably learned a valuable lesson from that: over-the-top drama and histrionics may be useful for personal success in elections, but for the actor to be perceived as top leadership material, the dramatic activities have to signify a serious head and a composed heart fit and ready to govern.

Quebec MP Paul Martin, fifty-one, though elected to the House only a year and a half before, was already prominent and highly esteemed in the party as a result of his great success as CEO of Canada Steamship Lines and the political legacy of his stalwart Liberal father, Paul Martin, Sr. He was able to attract the support of over half a dozen fellow caucus members, most of them well regarded.

Jean Chrétien, fifty-six, although he wasn't an MP when this leadership convention took place, had been continually elected to the House from 1963 till 1986 and served in increasingly important portfolios under Lester Pearson and Pierre Trudeau. Leading up to 1982, he'd been, as Justice minister, responsible for the negotiations that brought Canada's constitution home from Great Britain and led to the ratification of our Charter of Rights and Freedoms.

Chrétien had been defeated fairly narrowly by John Turner at the earlier 1984 leadership convention. I was there at the civic centre in Ottawa and could see clearly that Turner had been put over the top by the ex officio delegates, mostly stuffed shirts from the past. They liked the respectable cut of his jib compared to the relatively uncouth Chrétien who, many Liberals as well as Tories joked, couldn't speak either official language, and looked like the driver of the getaway car.

But, truly, as Liberal Party president Iona Campagnolo said in her speech after Turner had won, Jean Chrétien may have been "second in the balloting, but first in our hearts." Turner chose a strange way to worm his way back into Iona's heart when, a little later, he was caught by television cameras patting her on the bum with his hand. Although she politely dismissed it as trivial, it was the beginning of a successful portrayal of Turner by opponents as a corporate neanderthal, out of touch with the modern world.

By 1986, Chrétien hadn't been able to stomach political life in the Opposition under Turner any longer and had resigned from the House. Yet, despite his absence for four years, he was still able to attract the support of many important members of the Liberal caucus, including MPs from Newfoundland and Labrador, George Baker, Bill Rompkey, Roger Simmons, and Brian Tobin.

Tobin played a significant role in organization, communications, and speechwriting for Chrétien's campaign. I could see his hand behind the positive attention paid to Chrétien by the media, including such favourable headlines as the one in the *Toronto Star* early in the year: "Thirty MPs endorse Chrétien."

Later, in spite of Chrétien's attempt to be quiet about it and glide past it, the Meech Lake Accord started to cause discord among the leadership candidates. A couple of days before the convention, a *Globe and Mail* story headlined that the candidates were fighting over Meech and that Chrétien was being scolded for his stance by Martin and Copps. From a man who would be painted by the media as remembering vindictively every slight he ever received, those two critics of Chrétien would later receive the highest positions in his cabinet. And it was an insight into the characters of both Chrétien and Tobin that they were able to work together on the campaign, despite their diametrically opposed views on something as crucial at the time as the polemical Meech Lake Accord. These two guys were exceedingly flexible pragmatists.

At the convention, Chrétien wiped out all the other candidates on the very first ballot, gaining nearly fifty-seven per cent of the votes cast, more than doubling second-place Martin's twenty-five per cent: a fabulous triumph for the little guy from Shawinigan. But for the next three years, that victory seemed to be the summit of his political progress. Because, before the election in 1993, he had started to go into steady decline. Stiff, glued to his script, over-regulated by handlers, many pundits did not believe he could possibly be headed for a win when the tainted Mulroney finally resigned and someone fresh and new would take over the Tories.

In February 1993, Brian Mulroney announced he'd be resigning as prime minister on June 25, and a Progressive Conservative leadership convention was called for earlier that month. Avril Phædra Douglas Campbell, better known as Kim, jumped into the race. Immediately she became the star candidate, and over half the Tory caucus lined up to support her. It looked like the convention was not going to be a contest but a coronation of Campbell.

Then, late in the game, Mulroney persuaded French-Irish, perfectly bilingual Quebecer Jean Charest (the separatists used his name's English version, "John," as an insult) to enter the competition. It was either an indication of Kim Campbell's essential weakness in the eyes of delegates, or Charest's dynamism and verve, that he kept gaining on her right to the very end. Commentators opined that with a few more days he would have won. But he'd jumped in too late. It took two ballots, but Kim Campbell won the leadership—by less than 200 votes of the nearly 3,500 cast.

After that victory, Campbell's popularity took off once more, spurred on by her activist reforms to her cabinet as prime minister and her non-stop barbecues across the nation that summer. By August, I recall a Canada-wide poll showing her with a fifty-one per cent approval rating, making her one of the most popular prime minister for years. She was way ahead of Liberal leader Jean Chrétien in personal popularity, and she'd all but effaced Preston Manning of the emerging Reform Party.

This was the situation when Brian Tobin and Jean Chrétien approached me in St. John's. Their first attempt to get together was amusing. I was alone in my house one Saturday afternoon, sitting in the living room with a book, when the front doorbell rang. Now, as *Open Line* host on VOCM Radio, I was used to occasional knocks at the door of my private residence by people who thought, wrongly, that I could somehow get them a job or overturn a negative decision by unemployment insurance authorities. I'd grown weary of trying to convince them that I was a guy who took calls for discussion on the public airwaves on weekday mornings, and that I had no authority, or right, to even raise hopes that I could solve their problems. They would look at me in the certain knowledge that I was indeed a miracle worker who could do exactly what they wanted, if only I wasn't such a prick.

I glanced out the window toward the door and could vaguely see two men standing there. They were either petitioners or missionaries, and I was determined not to have my own private time disturbed by either. The doorbell rang again, and again I buried my nose in my book. Then I saw one of them gesturing at me through the window and heard in the distance, "Is that you, Bill?" a formula used by *Open Line* callers. I kept still and quiet when the doorbell rang the third time: No, by God, I was not going to have my private-time agenda disrupted unilaterally by anyone! At last, the two doorbell ringers sauntered off down the road. I was proud of myself. My ruthlessness in defending my private space and time had paid off.

Fifteen minutes later, my phone rang. It was Brian Tobin. "What have you got against the next prime minister of Canada," he asked.

"What are you talking about?" I replied, as if the full realization was not dawning on me.

"That was you holed up there in the corner, wasn't it?"

"Jeez, Brian, why didn't you call?"

He was going to, he said, but he and Jean Chrétien were staying at the Hotel Newfoundland behind my house and were out for a stroll, when they decided spontaneously to drop in on me. Could I come over that afternoon before Jean had to get ready for a function that evening? Yes, I said, feigning delight. I knew what they wanted.

Tobin's good buddy, MHA for St. Barbe Chuck Furey, had already had me out for a coffee and urged me to run federally in St. John's East. I'd also received a long-distance telephone call from old-time friend and Liberal stalwart Joe Ashley with the same urgent suggestion, backed up by a call from his daughter, Bonnie Hickey, who was, I believe, president of her executive in the riding of St. John's East. All the ridings in the province had Liberal candidates by now, except for that one. It had been considered a Tory stronghold since Confederation, having elected Liberals only a couple of times long ago under special circumstances, and an NDP candidate once in a by-election. This riding where they all wanted me to run was the ancient burial ground for Liberal candidates. What did they think I was, cracked?

The incumbent in the district was federal cabinet minister Ross Reid. He had defeated NDP Jack Harris in 1988 and had been appointed minister of Fisheries by Prime Minister Campbell. I'd been partly responsible, indirectly, for Reid's victory in 1988. When a whispering campaign had started over Ross's sexual orientation, he flatly refused to comment publicly on something so politically vicious, yet completely irrelevant. I agreed with his stand, and I was outraged on principle by the injustice of anyone trying to turn something so private, yet so volatile in those benighted days, into a bigoted slur. So I'd voice this mantra on my *Open Line* show whenever the prejudiced insinuation came up: "It's not what an MP does in bed that counts. It's what he does in the House." This *Reader's Digest*–type chin-lifter took off like wildfire and defused the whole question of anyone's sexual propensities.

I went over to Brian Tobin's hotel room to meet with him and Chrétien. Brian was by himself. After we'd caught up a little, he put to me the question of running. I told him I thought Ross Reid was unbeatable, not only in his own right, but doubly so in such a Tory riding, and triply so considering Kim Campbell's popularity.

Tobin conceded it was a challenge but confirmed what I'd heard also: polls showed that, nationally, support for the Progressive Conservative Party itself was running behind Campbell's own popularity. The party had gone up during the weeks of Campbell's leadership, but it was still a few points behind the Liberals. And as for Campbell personally, Tobin said, not only were her numbers stalled, but Jean Chrétien was the most effective campaigner he'd ever seen. Just wait till the election writ was dropped and I would see that, too.

Besides, he flattered mercilessly, I was the perfect candidate—well known, respected, experienced, savvy, popular, and so on and so forth and et cetera. When the Liberals won the election, Tobin predicted, he himself would be minister for a couple of years while I got my feet wet, and then I'd go right in the cabinet. What was there not to love in this whole beautiful scenario?

I told Brian that my radio show was riding high in the ratings, I was being invited weekly to comment on national media, my law practice was flourishing, and I was in the middle of writing another book. I owed it to my family, and myself, not to disrupt all that for another futile go at politics. If I wanted a vacation from the real world, I'd embark on a Mediterranean cruise, not become cannon fodder for two months in a forlorn political cause.

Jean Chrétien now invaded the room. He always seemed to move at a run. We shook hands, and straight away, without any foreplay, he asked me to become his candidate. I sized him up. He was an imposing character, over six feet tall and bristling with energy and what seemed a lot like aggression. He filled the room with his presence. But his features were impassive and wooden. I think some of that was caused by powder or makeup applied for impromptu TV appearances. He didn't smile. His invitation to me seemed to be the pro forma duty of a defeated man. There was no way this guy was going to beat the animated Kim Campbell, I thought.

I politely declined his offer. I don't know if Tobin gave him a high sign that this was useless, but Chrétien didn't argue or try to persuade. He stuck out his hand and said thank you for coming over as he stared into my eyes fixedly from that deadpan face. It was almost unsettling. I could think of other things I'd rather be doing than—best-case scenario—sitting around a cabinet table with this guy as boss. I was glad to be out of there.

Kim Campbell called the election early in September 1993. Under the constitution, she had to. Mulroney's five-year mandate from 1988 had nearly run out, but the unpopularity he had bestowed on the Progressive Conservative Party had not. Campbell's flurry of personal approval as the new leader proved shallow. Her party's profound unpopularity broke through her surface veneer, and, moreover, earlier supporters were being drained away by the new party in Quebec, the Bloc Québécois, and by Preston Manning's Reform Party out west.

During her campaign visit to St. John's, Prime Minister Campbell came on my *Open Line* show as a guest. I thought she performed well—bright and vigorous and articulate. But support for her seemed muted. Political junkies, nationally, were deeming her straightforward frankness a liability in an election campaign. But probably more fatal for a woman in leadership in those days, some commentators were starting to give examples of her words and actions that insinuated flightiness and inconsistency.

One story making the rounds everywhere in the nation was that, between campaign stops, she was spending her time in the back of the campaign bus necking up a storm with her new boyfriend. I don't know if it was a symptom of a more widespread, inherent misogynistic reaction, but one caller to my show labelled her "just another flaky broad." Thankfully I was able to get the words cut by the alert control room technician before they went on the air.

Bonnie Hickey, rather than suffering the indignity of having no Liberal candidate in St. John's East, had finally put her own name forward as a last-minute contender. It was widely considered to be an act of desperate valour on her part.

I invited each of the candidates in the province to come on my show for an hour to field calls. Bonnie didn't really want to. She was not at all your typically extroverted public person as a candidate. But I prevailed upon her to come on, and she did a good job—understated, but sincere and honest. She didn't deny she was fighting an uphill battle. During off-air breaks, I mentioned her self-sacrifice in taking this on and her act of courage as a good party soldier. She laughed and said she'd call it more accurately an act of total madness. At least, I thought, she had the right attitude.

At one point during the campaign, Kim Campbell's brilliant strategists, including now Toronto mayor John Tory, who was then PC campaign director, had a brainwave: put an attack ad on television showing a photograph of Jean Chrétien's face distorted by the Bell's palsy that had afflicted him as a child, and ask voters if this was the prime minister we wanted to represent Canada on the international stage.

At the sight of the photo, every mother's heart in Canada broke and then turned to outrage at the mockery. The fury directed against the Tory Party was phenomenal, assisted by a phone-in campaign to all radio stations in Canada, substantially orchestrated by the Liberal Party. I saw Brian Tobin's hand in that as well as in Chrétien's measured response to the ad.

He alternated between moving audiences to tears and cracking them up with self-effacing humour. "God gave me a physical defect," he said, "and I've accepted that since I was a kid." The Tories were like the teasing bullies of his childhood, he went on: "When I was a kid, people were laughing at me. But I accepted that because God gave me other qualities and I'm grateful." And then he'd smile: "It's true that I speak on one side of my mouth. I'm not a Tory, I don't speak on both sides of my mouth." Voters loved both the tears and the laughs he evoked. Tobin had been right: Chrétien was the most effective campaigner he'd ever seen.

Campbell had the ad pulled as soon as she learned of it, she said, but it was too late.

A number of days before the election, Brian Tobin called to say he was flying to St. John's to campaign. When could he take his turn on my show? On the designated morning, I asked him on the air why, of all places in Newfoundland or Canada that might benefit from his skills, he'd chosen to come here to Tory St. John's to campaign. Because, he replied, party polls were showing that Bonnie Hickey was likely to win, and he was here to help put her over the top.

I'm not sure if I snorted my skepticism out loud or not, but I certainly did internally. And during a break I told him I realized he was a persuasive guy and all that, but he was straining listeners' credulity a teeny bit with his prediction. No, he said, it was true, and he told me that come election night I'd be really sorry I hadn't run in the district myself. Tobin and I parted company, agreeing to disagree on that one.

Election day was October 25. That evening, as the results rolled in, people sat in front of their TV sets dumbfounded. The volatility of the electorate was staggering. Over half the voters had switched parties from the last election. The Reform Party under Preston Manning, which had won no seats in the last election, took fifty-two ridings this time. The Bloc Québécois, which had only come into existence after the Meech Lake fiasco in 1990, won fifty-four seats under Lucien Bouchard's leadership. That was the second-highest number of seats in the House of Commons. The separatist party which fielded candidates only in Quebec, and which had utterly no presence anywhere else in Canada, and which was dedicated to breaking up the nation, and which despised the very notion of the monarchy in Canada, became Her Majesty's Loyal Opposition in the country's House of Commons.

The mighty Progressive Conservative Party under Kim Campbell dropped 167 seats from the last election, including her own, and came back with two MPs. The party received only sixteen per cent of the popular vote. In other words, despite a brief flurry of "Campbellmania" when she first took over as leader, the Tories had plummeted back down near to the all-time low of fifteen per cent polled by Brian Mulroney in surveys in 1991. No wonder Kim Campbell complained, after her utter rout, that Mulroney had set her up to take the fall for him in the 1993 election.

The NDP under Audrey McLoughlin dropped from its best showing ever of forty-three seats in the last election to nine now, its worst performance in its history. Jean Chrétien took the Liberal Party from eighty-three seats last time to a solid majority government of 177 seats in this election.

Cannon fodder Bonnie Hickey, the sacrificial Liberal candidate in St. John's East, got over forty-four per cent of the votes cast, to Ross Reid's forty-two per cent, and she beat him by more than a thousand votes to become the new MP.

TWENTY-SIX

Brian Tobin was re-elected in his district of Humber–St. Barbe–Baie Vert with over eighty-two per cent of the vote, a rather spectacular return, up from sixty-seven per cent in the previous election. He beat out Corner Brook native Margaret Ann O'Rourke, who would prove to be no slouch herself a few years later by getting elected to the legislature in New Brunswick, where she'd moved, and being appointed to the cabinet in that province.

New prime minister Jean Chrétien appointed Brian Tobin minister of Fisheries and Oceans. This appeared to many to be a thankless job so soon after the complete shutdown of the historic cod fishery. But Tobin turned it into the opportunity of a lifetime. To the many MPs in the House and the multitudes of citizens outside whose eyes normally went glassy and blank at the mere mention of an Atlantic fish, Tobin directed his rhetoric. His aggressive "posturing," as characterized by some, was aimed chiefly at the foreign overfishing on the Nose and Tail of our Grand Banks.

These two areas were located on the wrong side of Canada's exclusive economic zone (EEZ) of 200 nautical miles, which had been declared back in 1977. Foreign fishing fleets treated the Nose and Tail like the Wild West: they ravaged the stocks out there with impunity, without regard to any global laws or rules of conservation. Tobin railed at the illegality and at the uselessness of the international institutions when it came to quotas and law enforcement.

His descriptions of what was happening out there, and his fierce threats of action to be taken if it didn't stop, started to make the stolid citizenry of the nation sit up and take notice. No federal minister of Fisheries had assumed such a forceful position since the exclusive economic zone had come into effect, not even the bold and gutsy John Crosbie, who despite best efforts had been frequently stymied by the diplomatic (i.e. timorous) reaction of the mandarins in Foreign Affairs. They always wanted to maintain Canada's position as the nice guy of the western world.

I had said to Crosbie on *Open Line* once, when he'd been minister of Fisheries, that Canada's role in the world was to be everybody's pet declawed pussycat; I could see how much it galled him not to come right out and agree and go even further. Off-air, we agreed that the top brass in Canada's diplomatic corps were too polite (a.k.a. cowardly) to say "poop" if their mouths were full of Spanish trawlermen's shit. Crosbie maintained that there was no way to get effective action on foreign overfishing as long as their attitude was always allowed to take priority.

Perhaps their knowledge of that priority of the Department of Foreign Affairs was why many critics of Tobin's position considered it mere posturing bluster. He was playing to the home audience, they figured, simply to maintain his popularity with Newfoundlanders, who were suffering from the cod moratorium and the unemployment and economic devastation resulting from decades of federal mismanagement. But as John Crosbie would tell me on the air years later when he was flogging his memoirs, *No Holds Barred*, the difference between Tobin's strength in taking action and the relative weakness of earlier ministers of Fishery was that Tobin had his prime minister solidly behind him in whatever actions he chose to take to combat the problem.

It was true. Jean Chrétien was a political street fighter. Wishy-washiness disgusted him. He supported Tobin to the hilt by including in the new government's very first Throne Speech, at the beginning of 1994, a pledge to end foreign overfishing on the east coast. That spring, Tobin introduced in the House of Commons the Coastal Fisheries Protection Act, which would enforce rules protecting straddling fish stocks, that is, fish that swam back and forth between Canadian waters and the ocean beyond the 200-mile limit, including the Nose and Tail of the Grand Banks.

With the enthusiastic backing of Chrétien and all ministers, and even of the separatist Leader of the Opposition, Lucien Bouchard, whom Tobin personally briefed, the House quickly passed the act unanimously. The senate, led by Newfoundland senator Bill Petten, endorsed the legislation in short order. The European Union went off the head. The act was illegal, they ranted, because, under the very convenient international law in effect, enforcement beyond 200 miles could be done only by the country of the fleet that was busy raping the resource.

Some vessels were arrested and brought to shore for violations of the act, including a couple of American ones, which caused a racket in Washington, complete with patriotic protests from Senator Ted Kennedy. The problems were mostly ironed out by diplomatic talks. But that was before the "Turbot War" of the spring of 1995.

Among the European vessels suspected of violating quotas, net sizes, and other regulations on the Grand Banks was a Spanish trawler out of Vigo, the *Estai*. She was taking turbot on the Nose of the Banks, and as far as the Department of Fisheries was concerned, she was obviously serving as a deliberate provocation to Canada by the European Union.

On March 9, Tobin ordered that the *Estai* be arrested and escorted to St. John's. When the Canadian patrol vessels approached the trawler with a view to boarding her, the *Estai*'s officers told them to get lost, flung their ladders into the ocean, cut the *Estai*'s turbot nets, and took off across the North Atlantic. Three Canadian government ships, including the Coast Guard vessel *Sir Wilfred Grenfell*, pursued her, assisted by surveillance from the air conducted by Provincial Airlines. For several hours the pursuit continued, with the *Estai*'s captain defying all orders to heave to. At one point, other Spanish trawlers interfered in the chase, bringing Canadian water cannons into play. There were ominous reports that a Spanish vessel rigged with guns was heading for the scene.

With the support of Prime Minister Chrétien and the cabinet, Tobin now gave orders to warn the captain of the *Estai* that the Canadians were about to fire shots across her bow. But the *Estai* kept going. After four bursts of machine-gun fire and a warning that the Canadian gunner was about to disable the *Estai* by firing at her propellers, the Spanish trawler finally did heave to. Gun-bearing RCMP and fisheries officers boarded the *Estai*, took over, and turned her about for St. John's.

The European Union ambassador to Canada called the incident an act of piracy. Other European officials publicly deemed it an act of war. One of the more interesting representatives of the European Union was Emma Bonino, who was the EU Commissioner for Fisheries. Reporters often attached the adjective "fiery" to her name. Her credentials for political action included a stint as the chair of Italy's Radical Party. She declared that Canada's arrest of the *Estai* had nothing to do with fisheries conservation or supervision, but was designed merely to satisfy Canada's internal political needs and to distract attention from Canada's fisheries mismanagement.

When the *Estai* steamed in through the Narrows and docked in St. John's, many thousands of people had assembled at the harbourfront to cheer the Canadian seizure and to jeer the captain and crew. Tobin didn't come down to St. John's because, he said, he didn't want to appear to be gloating or have his presence provoke the already high feelings of the crowd. Besides, he was busy reporting to the world that the Spanish trawler was discovered to possess two sets of books, one containing the correct record of the catch for the owners, and one containing a much lower—fake—account for the regulatory authorities.

Moreover, the trawler had a false bulkhead, behind which tons of undersized turbot had been hidden. Fisheries officers also found a secret hold illegally filled with tons of another protected species. Soon, Canadian patrol vessels said they had located the net which the *Estai* had cut when first approached. Inspectors found that the openings in the net were far smaller than the minimum legal size and were obviously designed to catch smaller-than-regulation-sized fish. If that were not enough, the net also had a lining to keep anything at all from escaping.

While many European leaders blustered and threatened Canada, the prime minister of Great Britain dithered. At first John Major hardly knew what to say or do. Would he side with his EU partners and condemn Canada? Or would he follow (i.e. appear to lead) the growing numbers in England and Scotland who supported the actions of his respected sister nation in the British Commonwealth? The issue was decided for him by the British media and public.

A goodly part of the media reaction there was caused by a journalist with a Newfoundland connection by the name of David Twiston-Davies. David and I became friends before and during the *Estai* fuss, and I learned of his background and what he was doing to support Canada's action. He was related by family marriage to Newfoundland's Lord Morris. Edward Morris had been prime minister of Newfoundland during most of the First World War. He retired in 1917, and a year later he was elevated to the British peerage as the first Baron Morris. He moved to London and took his seat in the House of Lords.

David Twiston-Davies was extremely proud of this link to Newfoundland, and soon after the *Estai* action, he called me in St. John's on *Open Line* to talk about it. He also wanted to obtain names of contacts here, from whom he could receive comments and letters to the editor. He was, of all things, renowned as the chief obituary writer of the *Daily Telegraph*, a London newspaper owned by Conrad Black, but more important for our purposes, he was letters editor for the paper as well.

As such, he also invited letters to the editor from all over England about Britain's oldest colony, Newfoundland, and particularly Newfoundland's outstanding contribution to the mother country during the First and Second World Wars. Newfoundland had stood by Great Britain in her hours of greatest need, he pointed out far and wide, and now it was the duty of Great Britain to stand by Newfoundland and Canada in their own hour of need. The thing took off like a house afire.

Newspapers all over the United Kingdom got behind Canada. Fishermen, fish sellers, and shops in the West Country of England, and in Scotland, and in Ireland, flew Canadian flags everywhere and were loud in their support. MPs in the British House of Commons called the EU's attacks on Canada deeply offensive and intimated that if the British navy was going to be employed it must be with the Canadian navy, just like in World War Two, and not with this modern Spanish armada.

On a television news clip in the UK, I saw one magnificent old government backbencher rise in the British House of Commons and declaim, "Can that indeed be what the Honourable Member on the other side is suggesting? That we take action against *Canada*? Join the *Spaniards* in retaliation against our Queen's fellow subjects? *Not bloody likely, suh*!" The roar of "Hear, hear," was deafening.

The uprush of British sentiment forced Prime Minister John Major's besieged government to ditch its professed neutrality and grudgingly come on side. Major stood in the House of Commons and stated, "Canada is quite right to take a tough line on enforcement." Spain was demanding that the EU impose economic sanctions against Canada, but Britain's threatened veto of such measures as unthinkable thwarted that.

A Canadian journalist who was touring Ireland at the time told me that he'd been told—whether it was true or whether people were taking the mickey out of him he wasn't sure—that legends were already springing up among fishermen around the Irish coast about how one day "the mighty Brian Og Toibin" was going to return to Ireland and defeat her enemies to the last man.

In Canada, one of the few sour notes was sounded by the Reform Party. Its spokesman described the Canadian action as absolutely disgusting and a mere PR exercise. Lucien Bouchard of the Bloc Québécois, on the other hand, said that protection of the turbot was imperative and that Canada, the country he wanted to leave, had done what was necessary.

If Tobin's actions were a mere PR exercise, though, it was not yet complete. He wanted to bring the *Estai*'s recovered net, twenty storeys high and wider than a football field, to the United Nations in New York for display. He saw his chance later in April, when the UN would be discussing fisheries issues. The icing on Tobin's cake was that his would-be avenger in the EU, Commissioner for Fisheries Emma Bonino, was due to speak there. The Canadian Department of Foreign Affairs, of course, wouldn't hear of his mad venture. Canada risked losing all it had gained, they said, by trivializing the overfishing with a transparent media spectacle and, heaven forbid, by hurting the feelings of other nations.

Tobin was called on the carpet by Chrétien. But on hearing the plan, the prime minister seemed to like the way Tobin's media-know-how mind worked and, in any event, tended to appreciate any dramatic, bare-knuckles approach. Having won the Turbot War thus far, "don't give up now" was his attitude. Chrétien gave his imprimatur to Tobin's intended histrionics . . . but on the condition that, if the mission flopped or threatened to embarrass Canada, he would leave Tobin hanging out there, twisting in the wind all by himself. The PM had been watching *Mission Impossible*.

Tobin sent the net to New York and had his people set the scene so that the huge contraption would be displayed in its full monstrous glory on a barge in the East River across from the United Nations building. Evidently Signora Bonino didn't have very good surveillance or intelligence on what those pesky Canadians were up to, because in her speech on behalf of the EU at the UN, she sleepwalked right into a farcical PR disaster. As if she was Tobin's vaudeville straight woman, she accused Canada of fabricating the evidence of a net. Nobody except the delusional Canadians, she suggested, had seen any such net. She expected Canada to plant evidence of heroin or cocaine as well, next.

Tobin asked the media at the UN, already all excited by Bonino's accusations, if they would like to see the net. Yes, they said. Tobin had arranged for chartered buses, naturally, to be waiting outside the UN front door, and the international press brigade boarded them and headed for the river barge. There, Premier Clyde Wells and Minister of Fisheries Tobin held a news conference in front of the enormous, expanded web of diminutive meshwork, with an illegal liner backing, hoisted high on a colossal crane. Was there any wonder, they queried, that this lethal apparatus left behind it a silent, empty ocean devoid of all life?

Tobin held up a tiny turbot less than the size of his hand and proclaimed, "We are down to the last, lonely, unloved, unattractive little turbot clinging by its fingernails to the Grand Banks of Newfoundland, saying, 'Someone reach out and save me in this eleventh hour as I'm about to go down to extinction.'" That picture and the over-the-top but highly effective quote became a lead story in practically all news media in North America and Europe. A commentator or two in Canada, ignoring the international effect of the event, decried the tone and content of Tobin's statement as ludicrous. A talking turbot with fingernails, clinging on to the Grand Banks? Preposterous!

They seemed to be the same people who had earlier deplored Tobin's general tendency toward rhetoric of biblical proportions: when he'd been appointed minister in 1993, he rose in the Commons and intoned, "I speak for those who have no voice—the fish." One visiting Ottawa journalist asked me at the time, "Who does this guy think he is, St. Francis of the Flatfish?"

Meanwhile, back in New York in 1995, after her turbot net debacle, Bonino was raging that the press were unfair to her, and picked on her, and never believed a word she said. Thereupon, apparently, she stomped out of the UN session. Tobin reported that a newspaper characterized her reaction as "Bonino goes Bananas."

However, it's important to note that anyone observing Bonino at this period, particularly from a biased Canadian standpoint, would get the completely wrong idea about her. In fact, a little research will show that she was a vastly esteemed and accomplished stateswoman in Italian, European, and international affairs. She would become Italian minister of European Affairs and International Trade, and minister of Foreign Affairs, and occupy high office in the European Union. She'd also win several prestigious awards for her accomplishments in the protection of human rights, pluralistic democracy, and the improvement of North-South relations.

In other words, a little objectivity and perspective are needed in these matters. The international achievements of her career were greater than any minister in the Chrétien cabinet. But for a short time—and this was also a measure of Tobin's achievement—this formidable woman had the ill luck of coming up against a Canadian minister whose flair and media savvy in the Turbot War would make him a household name and celebrity at home and abroad. In the British Isles he was called "Terrific Tobin," and in his home country he was awarded the monikers "The Tobinator" and "The Turbotonator"—neither of them quite as catchy as Arnold Schwarzenegger's "Terminator," but they got the idea across—and perhaps most evocatively, "Captain Canada."

Meanwhile, members of the cabinet and the House of Commons were frankly astonished by what Tobin had been able to pull off. Flowers were delivered to him in his place in the House. Colleagues joked that the whole caper had been an Academy Award performance, and I kidded on *Open Line* that MPs figured his frolic on the East River barge was Tobin's "Oscar-winning clip."

At one point I had a chat with a friend, the wife of a highly esteemed cabinet minister in Ottawa. We talked about Tobin's actions and his media triumph. The minister's wife, while full of admiration for her own husband's achievements and capabilities, stated candidly that her husband "would never be able to do that."

I happened to be in London, England, in the summer of 1995, and went up the Thames by boat, from Charing Cross to Canary Wharf on the Isle of the Dogs, to meet with David Twiston-Davies. He was at the *Daily Telegraph* in One Canada Square, a building which had been developed by the Canadian company Olympia and York and was then the tallest in the United Kingdom. We had lunch in a restaurant on the riverbank and had a great chat about the Turbot War.

David told me that Brian and Jodean Tobin were visiting Devon and Cornwall in the West Country of England that summer and were being cheered and feted and lionized by officials and ordinary citizens alike, as if they were royalty. They were special guests of the Fisheries Festival down there, and Canadian flags were flying everywhere. David himself revelled in the role he had played in the ecstatic reaction of Britons to Canada's high-seas actions and in bringing on side the UK government.

The next year, I would talk to David on *Open Line* again, this time about his new 1996 book, *Canada from Afar: the Daily Telegraph Book of Canadian Obituaries*. It was a fascinating piece of work, containing scores of notable Canadian lives, including Newfoundlanders Billy Browne, Joey Smallwood, Eugene Forsey, Bob Furlong, Don Jamieson, and George Story. I was always moved by the emotional connection of this thoughtful Englishman from afar to Newfoundland in Canada, and the contribution he always wanted to make to our well-being, and our standing in Great Britain and globally. Brian Tobin's caper was right up his alley.

After much more to-ing and fro-ing across the Atlantic, and threats from Canada to remove Spanish fishing vessels by force, and the cutting of nets, and negotiations aborted by Spain, and pressure from the UK and Ireland, the EU pushed Spain into some kind of a settlement. Canada paid back the half-million dollars of bond money which had been put up for the *Estai*'s earlier release. Canada repealed the provision of the Coastal Fisheries Protection Regulations, enacted under the Coastal Fisheries Protection Act, that had allowed the arrest of Spanish vessels, and Canada agreed to a reduction of Canada's own turbot allocation.

Compromises or giveaways by Canada made some observers claim that Tobin's actions were nothing but a PR flash in the pan and mere political sizzle from the get-go, with little of substance ultimately accomplished. Tobin maintained that Canada continued to play hardball with the European Union and did finally reach a deal to protect different species of fish, with a new system to monitor Canadian and EU fishing vessels also set up.

Former Newfoundland premier Brian Peckford's take on the Turbot War was one of contempt for the national press's infatuation with Tobin's silly public relations efforts. It concerned, he said, a minor turbot species flap, long after the cod had disappeared, an issue on which Tobin had done precious little when he was MP.

My reaction to all of it then and now is that I couldn't care less what was compromised or given back by Canada in the short term. The point is that Tobin's actions did kick-start serious talks about moronic fishing practices in international waters, backed by a realization that Canada was no longer every nation's nice-guy buddy or a declawed international pussycat.

If irresponsible nations were going to take thuggish advantage of something as stupid as an exclusive economic zone, which only extended out an arbitrary 200 miles, instead of encompassing the entire continental shelf including the Nose and Tail of the Grand Banks, then such nations could expect Canada to enforce international law with patrol vessels bearing arms. That global realization of Canada's new fight-not-flight stance in itself encouraged sensible talks.

Also important at home in Canada was how the Department of Fisheries' bold facing down of European Union arrogance was a jolt of adrenalin to a Canadian citizenry disheartened and exasperated by Ottawa's cut-everything budget just a month before and by yet another separation referendum upcoming in Quebec.

TWENTY-SEVEN

During the 1994 provincial election in Quebec, the Parti Québécois, led by Jacques Parizeau, had promised to hold a referendum on sovereignty during his term as premier. With less than forty-five per cent of the popular vote, the PQ won a majority government, and they set the voting on a sovereignty question for October 30, 1995. The leader of the sovereignty "Yes" side was initially Premier Parizeau, and the leader of the federalist "No" side was Quebec Liberal leader Daniel Johnson, who mostly tried to squeeze Prime Minister Chrétien and other federal politicians out of the "No" campaign.

The referendum question was made public early in September 1995, and the English version asked: "Do you agree that Quebec should become sovereign, after having made a formal offer to Canada for a new economic and political partnership, within the scope of the bill respecting the future of Quebec and of the agreement signed on June 12, 1995?"

Of course, nobody in the rest of Canada had the slightest notion what this question meant, with its reference to some mysterious bill and agreement or other, and probably not 100 people in Quebec understood it clearly. No one on the federalist side had been asked to contribute to the question. And what, demanded Canadian leaders, was all this bafflegab about a new economic and political partnership? No political leader in the rest of Canada had evinced the least interest in, let alone agreed to, negotiating any partnership with an autonomous Quebec.

A bizarre campaign of about eight weeks now ensued on this convoluted, incomprehensible question.

During the first days, polls showed the sovereigntist "Yes" movement to be lagging behind the federalist "No" camp by single digits, and even more solidly if, as pundits suggested, the substantial "Undecided" vote went largely over to the "No" side. Premier Parizeau, though a long-time strong separatist of impeccable credentials, possessed little charisma and was viewed by many as divisive and generally obnoxious. He did not seem capable of fanning the sovereigntist spark into a blazing flame. I don't recall many pundits or politicians in the rest of Canada sounding, at the time, a split-up alarm.

Then, just over three weeks before voting day, Parizeau was coerced into doing something diabolically cunning. He announced that Bloc Québécois leader Lucien Bouchard had been appointed "Chief Negotiator" for those (imaginary) partnership talks that would follow the "Yes" vote for sovereignty.

No action by separatist pushers could have been more effective. Not only was Bouchard a forceful reminder of how *les maudit Anglais* had treated Quebec with contempt during the Meech Lake debacle, but his natural charisma had been raised to the level of messianic following his earlier, nearly lethal attack of flesh-eating disease, necrotizing fasciitis, in which he'd lost a leg. And his title confirmed in the minds of the Québécois that they would have the best of both worlds: independence *and* an economically beneficial association with Canada. Bouchard was the dramatic new leader of a campaign soon perceived to be the winning one.

Nothing negative stuck to Bouchard. Federalists found him impossible to attack. Even when he stated that the Québécois were the "white race" with the lowest rate of reproduction, which would have smacked of racism or ethnic bias in the mouth of anyone else, it slid off him, harmlessly. Pollsters found that when they repeated to Quebecers any remark by Bouchard that they disagreed with, they typically replied that they didn't think he really meant that.

In the days right after Bouchard's appointment, there was some see-sawing in the polls between the percentages of Quebecers favouring the yes and no sides. But soon the sovereignty "Yes" side was staying consistently ahead by up to six or seven per cent. Brian Tobin has said he saw one poll, a private one, I think, just days before the referendum, which recorded the federalist side as lagging behind the separatists by between seven and fourteen percentage points.

The meteoric upsurge of the "Yes" campaign following Bouchard's galvanic speeches, and the useless impotence of everyone leading the "No" campaign, generated anxiety in Ottawa. Or, as one Liberal MP personalized it for me, "At our last caucus meeting, Chrétien was up there shittin' shrapnel."

The transformed atmosphere caused strange twists and turns of desperation.

The official brochure of the "No" federalist side, written by the Quebec Liberals, recognized Quebec as a "distinct society" and accorded Quebec full autonomy in areas of provincial jurisdiction. Nine days before the vote, the "No" leader, Daniel Johnson, demanded out of the blue that Prime Minister Chrétien state his position on distinct-society status for Quebec. Chrétien, who'd been elbowed to the sidelines by the "No" team, was at the United Nations in New York and replied that he wouldn't do it: "We're not talking about the constitution, we're talking about the separation of Quebec from the rest of Canada." This response was interpreted by the Quebec media as a continued stark refusal of recognition by Ottawa and as showing the hopeless confusion and conflict among those touting the federalist cause.

Then, three days later, less than a week before the vote, Chrétien spoke at a sizable federalist rally in Montreal and startled Canada by proclaiming his support for Quebec as a distinct society, along with other reforms to the Canadian constitution to please Quebec. This abrupt

180-degree reversal of Chrétien's rigid stance from Meech Lake times, plus his reported ashen face and panicky appearance on the podium, gave credibility to my MP friend's shrapnel wisecrack.

As Fisheries minister, Brian Tobin had no direct involvement with the referendum, but as a member of the federal cabinet and a Canadian citizen, he was disquieted enough by the polls that he felt impelled to do something to clearly express to Quebecers how much the rest of Canada loved them.

His staff told him about a basically token rally for business persons to take place on October 27 in Montreal's Place du Canada. That square was bordered, ironically enough, by René Lévesque Boulevard. Tobin had the inspired brainwave to invite Canadians in the rest of Canada to this rally. Walking a tightrope through Quebec's referendum laws, he urged members of his own caucus to encourage as many people as they could to travel to Montreal and take part.

I gathered at the time that some Quebec members of the federal cabinet didn't like at all what Tobin was up to. They probably feared a backlash. But Chrétien was more fearful of leaving a legacy as the prime minister who had presided over the breakup of Canada. Like someone diagnosed with a fatal illness, he was game to try anything.

Tobin got him to override the opposition of ministers from Quebec and then went on television—*Canada AM*. There he denied any link with the official, federalist "No" team. That was technically correct, perhaps, but rather disingenuous. Because he thereupon announced that the "No" side was planning the rally in Montréal on October 27 and beseeched everyone all over the country to go there and get behind the "crusade for Canada."

Aircraft were being chartered, he said, and Canadian Airlines was offering what they called a "unity" sale of ninety per cent off. Then he cajoled—as a private citizen, mind—the head of Air Canada to provide planes at the same low rate. Bus companies proffered their buses by the score to transport Canadians to Montreal. Via Rail jumped in. Travel agencies and hotel companies extended deep discounts on travel to Montreal for the weekend. Some telephone companies allowed free five-minute long-distance calls all day. MPs reported that Tobin's TV appearance caused a deluge of calls to their offices from eager would-be participants.

Dubbed the "Unity Rally," the numbers drawn to Place du Canada that Friday depended on whether the count was conducted in French or English: only 30,000 bodies according to a French-language radio station; more than 150,000, to listen to an English-language station in Montreal. Conventional wisdom seems to have zeroed in on a compromise crowd of about 100,000.

Whatever the number, it was reported to be the largest political rally in the history of Canada till then, complete with a gargantuan Canadian flag undulating, and an ebbing and flowing throng celebrating a Canada containing Quebec. "We Care" was the slogan dreamed up by Tobin, to counteract the notion successfully perpetrated so far by Bouchard to francophones that the rest of Canada just didn't give a damn about Quebec. Several provincial premiers, whom the federalist "No" committee in Quebec had earlier barred from the campaign, went to the rally: Mike Harris, John Savage, Frank McKenna, Catherine Callbeck. I didn't hear that Clyde Wells was there.

The rally must have been perceived by the "Yes" side as giving a boost to the federalist "No" cause, if an article in Montreal's sovereigntist newspaper, *Le Devoir*, felt the need to scoff at the event as "*Les touristes du fédéralisme*." Daniel Johnson was quoted as suggesting, though, that the gathering, at which he spoke himself only made worse the tensions with English Canada. But that was an understandable reaction from the leader of the federalist side, who had seen his campaign heading for disaster. He obviously wanted to blame others for a possible defeat, or claim credit for himself in the event of victory. On the other hand, federalist Jean Charest, leader of the national PC Party, and very much in tune with the Quebec electorate, also spoke at the rally, and he felt the demonstration lent momentum to the "No" campaign.

Professional opinions on whether the rally had an impact were mixed, because its timing made it so hard to evaluate: the rally took place right in the middle of the last polls before the referendum. One big poll I saw, by Leger and Leger, which had been completed on the day of the rally, showed the sovereigntist vote ahead by six per cent, with an undecided vote of twelve per cent.

Meanwhile, leading up to the rally, Tobin was appearing on other media and phoning call-in shows, including my own. The reaction among Newfoundlanders and Labradorians was so great that we decided to hold a special *Open Line* show on Sunday afternoon, the day before the vote, with a hookup to a station in Montreal. The calls back and forth were phenomenal in support of the Canadian union.

The turnout of voters in the referendum was higher than in any election, provincial or federal, in the history of Canada. 93.52 per cent of registered Quebec voters went to the polling booths. 49.42 per cent voted "Yes" for sovereignty, and 50.58 per cent voted "No." The sovereignty proposal was just barely rejected. Francophones voted "Yes" to sovereignty by a margin of about sixty per cent. English speakers, and those who spoke neither English nor French as a first language, voted "No" by a majority of ninety-five per cent.

Bouchard made a speech in which he accepted this particular result. But he went on to describe his dream of victory in the next referendum. This sent shivers down many an anglophone spine at the thought of another ten or fifteen years of this. "And remember," some sadistic sovereigntist smirked, "we only have to win once; you guys have to win every time."

One fed-up Newfoundlander "joked" on my show: "I hope to God Quebec does leave Canada—it'll make the drive to Toronto shorter."

On referendum night, a drunk Premier Parizeau blamed the defeat on "money and ethnics," demonstrating yet again how close to the surface a racist or tribal prejudice existed in some segments of the separatist movement. The remark caused such outrage, even among his own crowd, that he resigned as premier the next day, although he insisted that he intended to resign anyway in the event of a referendum defeat.

The usual fuss and turmoil ensued after the vote, with accusations of wrongdoing from both sides: outside interference and illegal contributions alleged against the federalists, widespread illegal ballot rejections alleged against the separatists. Evidently, it was all true.

Tobin himself was reported as acknowledging that Canadian corporations had funded his Montreal love-in project. And a university investigation showed that polling booths with a large number of "No" votes also had elevated percentages of rejected ballots. Tom Mulcair, then a member of the Quebec National Assembly, claimed that there was "an orchestrated attempt to steal the vote" in his district. Charges were contemplated, and in a few cases even laid, against the outside meddlers and interlopers, but ultimately they all came to nothing.

Parizeau would disclose later just how close the country came to breakup on referendum day: with a "Yes" result of fifty per cent plus one, his government fully intended to proceed quickly with a unilateral declaration of Quebec independence, knowing full well that any talk of negotiations with Ottawa to remain in Canada was a sham. Jacques Chirac, the president of France, had even been primed to recognize Quebec's independence, immediately.

Most objective commentators I talked to, or heard or read, conceded that the rally initiative Brian Tobin conceived and orchestrated had a favourable impact that contributed, just three days later, to the narrow "No" vote victory. Among the federalists there seemed to be no doubt whatsoever that he'd done it. Even a previous political opponent, the formidable John Crosbie, was in awe of the former Rat Packer's media savvy. The little rodent had saved Canada.

Crosbie one time constructed from his experience the ideal political leader. He or she would possess the iron will of Peter Lougheed, the common touch of Ralph Klein, the ruthlessness of Brian Peckford, the aura of unflappable confidence of Bill Davis, the ability of Clyde Wells to comprehend and articulate complicated issues, and the media savvy of Brian Tobin. It's interesting that three of the ideal components belonged to Newfoundlanders who had caused him so many years of excruciating torment.

But chief among the Tobin aficionados after the Quebec referendum was Jean Chrétien. My favourite Liberal MP informant in Ottawa told me that, when the close victory was finally known on the night of the referendum, the prime minister was heard screeching, "I love you, Brian Tobin," from the bathroom, where he was changing his soiled underwear.

The referendum victory, heaped on top of his triumphant PR from the "Turbot War," burnished even more the shine on Tobin's "Captain Canada" image. All the fame and popularity led the Liberal Party of Newfoundland to crave the hero as premier once Clyde Wells retired. And after six challenging years, that was exactly what Wells was contemplating.

One Liberal, who never liked Clyde, told me that his real incentive for getting out was the fact that, earlier in the year, his nemesis, Lynn Verge, had won the leadership of the provincial PC Party. She was the first woman to become leader of the Official Opposition, and the way she habitually laced into him in the House of Assembly reduced him, on occasion, to a blustering heap of Y-chromosome protoplasm. The fear that she might upend him and his party in the next election, as she had done to him personally in 1989 in Humber East, was giving the poor guy deja vu nightmares. Wells hastened to ask Tobin if he was interested in coming back.

Brian let him know that he might consider running for the provincial leadership if Wells got out before the end of the year, i.e. in the next few weeks. Otherwise, he had other fish to fry: Chrétien had big moves in store for him. Meanwhile, Tobin had a chat on the subject with fellow Newfoundlander John Crosbie, veteran leadership candidate at both federal and provincial levels.

Crosbie evoked his well-known Julius Caesar complex: Caesar, on passing through a tiny Alpine village, said to Mark Antony, "I'd rather be first man here than the second man in Rome." So Crosbie advised Tobin to go for it. He'd be far better off as the big fish in the little puddle—number one in Newfoundland—than even as number two in the Ottawa Government.

Wells seemed eager to accommodate Tobin and announced his resignation between Christmas and New Year's, on December 29. But Tobin would force him, against his will, to be more accommodating still. Around January 8, 1996, Tobin announced he'd be running for the Liberal leadership and moved to St. John's for the race. He wanted to lead in developing, for the province's benefit, he said, Newfoundland and Labrador's enormous oil and mining potential. Some members of the mainland media, however, speculated that he wanted the premiership as another stepping stone to becoming prime minister. If that was his motive, I remember thinking at the time, the shrewd and savvy Tobin should ask himself how many premiers have ever become prime minister.

There was no great interest shown by others in taking on the wildly popular Tobin, although I vaguely recall that someone else did throw his hat in. I think it was one of the MHAs later convicted of fraud and breach of trust, but whoever it was, just before the deadline for nominations on 17 January, the other name was unaccountably yanked out of the running. Brian Tobin became leader, and premier-to-be, by acclamation. The message was clear: no one could or would run against Captain Canada; there'd be no contested leadership convention.

Now matters came quickly to a head. Tobin was in St. John's without his wife and kids, who were back in Ottawa finishing out the school year. He was ready and waiting to take over as premier. He did not want to hang around all alone in his flat, twiddling his thumbs and cooling his heels as the time crawled by.

The message went through loud and clear to Wells from party bigwigs: get the hell out. This was around the time that the Liberal organizer told me Clyde was lucky he didn't find his belongings on the steps of Confederation Building after being flung out of a window of the premier's office. In a speech at a later function honouring his premiership, Wells himself would refer to his unceremonious exit, when he described how one minute he was premier, and then, all of a sudden, he wasn't.

Maybe Tobin's speedy takeover did not in fact indicate that he wanted to even the score with Wells. Perhaps it was just a matter of his simply wanting to get on with the job. But recalling his request to Clyde Wells for help as a young, forlorn federal candidate on the west coast back in 1980, and being snubbed by Wells in his hour of need, he must have derived some small satisfaction now as the party gave the once illustrious but current has-been, Clyde Wells, the bum's rush to make way for the famous Captain Canada.

A little over a week after his coronation as leader, Tobin was sworn in on Friday, January 26, as premier. He managed to let the weekend go by, but on Monday, three days later, he visited the lieutenant-governor to call a winter election for four weeks down the road, on February 22, 1996. This was a man in a hurry.

TWENTY-EIGHT

The leader of the Progressive Conservative Party heading into the election was Lynn Verge. She'd won the leadership the year before by three votes over Loyola Sullivan. Earlier, in her late twenties, she'd been one of the first two female cabinet ministers in our history.

For this election, Tobin recruited a number of female candidates, including Judy Foote, Julie Bettney, Joan Marie Aylward, Anna Thistle, Sandra Kelly, and Mary Hodder. This added to his lustre as a modern leader, especially when they got elected. And the fact that there weren't more females running for the party was not for his lack of trying. A number of women told me they'd been personally called by Tobin to run but weren't able to.

Sadly, though, there was one incident in the campaign, I recall, where Tobin's conduct in an encounter with Lynn Verge left a bad taste in my mouth. It was captured in TV footage. Tobin and Verge happened to cross paths by chance one night and got into an argument. Normally, two leaders meeting randomly like that would exchange greetings, or perhaps throw a wisecrack at each other, and vamoose. These two, however, went at it hammer and tong.

I don't know who started it or even what they were scrapping about.

I have the feeling, though, that it was Tobin who raised a contentious issue—maybe the fuss the PCs were causing about his federal pension. In any event, as picked up on the TV video and audio, Tobin used his big baritone voice—media-trained and Rat Pack–practised—plus his outstanding oral skills, to talk over Verge's remarks and try to drown her out.

Watching them there in the dark with the glaring television lights reflecting off their eyes, I felt the episode making me wince in discomfort. Of course, Lynn Verge doesn't, and didn't, need me or anyone else to stand up for her. That was proved by her debating skills in the House of Assembly when she frequently reduced Premier Wells to blithering status. So my comment is about Tobin, not her. She may not even remember the incident, and it was no big deal. But I still have the clear image of someone using his great gifts gratuitously, a bit like a macho bully. It reminded me of Shakespeare's line: "It is excellent to have a giant's strength, but it is tyrannous to use it like a giant."

The main PC strategy in the campaign was to criticize Tobin for taking his federal MP pension when he'd resigned from the House of Commons. Tobin confronted the issue head-on. He didn't apologize. He had earned it, he was entitled to it, and he was accepting it. He was not going to donate it to charity; he was going to keep it and spend it for the benefit of his family. He reminded voters that there was an election on, and if they didn't like it, they knew what they could do on voting day.

One Liberal organizer, worried about the pension issue during the campaign, told me after the election: "The little frigger is all balls, and they must be made of Teflon. Who else but Brian would, or could, not only defend drawing down a federal pension at the age of forty-two, on top of a premier's salary, but get away with it completely and win the election by a landslide?"

On election night, the Liberals increased their seats in the House, bettering Wells's big 1993 victory by two and winning thirty-seven out of the forty-eight districts, with over fifty-five per cent of the popular vote. Brian Tobin became the first premier of Newfoundland and Labrador to have been born after Confederation with Canada.

The Progressive Conservatives suffered their worst defeat in thirty years, ever since Joey Smallwood nearly removed the party from the House of Assembly altogether back in 1966, leaving them just three seats. This time they won in nine districts, drawing about thirty-nine per cent of the votes cast. The NDP took one seat, re-electing leader Jack Harris in Signal Hill–Quidi Vidi. And one independent MHA got elected, Yvonne Jones in Cartwright–L'Anse au Clair, but she later joined the Liberal caucus to begin a sterling career with the party in provincial and federal politics.

Sadly, Lynn Verge was personally defeated in Humber East, losing by only fourteen votes, and soon resigned as Tory leader. I didn't know her well, but I was well aware of her many achievements, and admired her performance in the House and whenever she was on *Open Line* as my guest. She was a genuine trailblazer for women in politics and a huge asset, of either gender, to the governance of the province.

Brian Tobin was certainly no laissez-faire premier. He was obviously determined to portray himself as an activist, and during his less than five years, which were both economically slow and politically turbulent, I was struck by how much he tried to do. But compared with other premiers, how much did he in fact accomplish?

A review of the province's finances right after the election revealed to him that—surprise!—the financial and economic situation was far worse than he'd been led to believe. The province had an $8 billion debt, and counting. The budget, due in a few weeks, predicted a deficit far larger for the 1996–97 fiscal year than he'd thought: at least $290 million in the hole. And since he'd taken over from his Liberal colleagues, many of whom would be in his own cabinet, he didn't even have the comfort of being able to blame a wicked Tory "previous administration."

A member of his inner circle told me of visiting Tobin in his eighth-floor office early in his first term and finding him taking peeks out the window at a massive protest rally below while banging his head against the wall and muttering to staff, "What have I done? What have I done?"

My informant thought that, knowing Tobin's sense of humour, he was merely exaggerating, for amusement, the gravity of his situation. If so, what happened next probably stopped the laughter.

His federal government buddies in Ottawa drastically reduced the amount of funding traditionally transferred to the provinces for infrastructure projects, health care, education, and other social programs. Paul Martin was federal minister of Finance, and his policy of slashing federal payments to the hinterland and boonies imperilled the ability of the poorer provinces, like Newfoundland, to provide vital government services. How successful Martin would be in butchering these dependent provincial services would be seen from the fact that, after some eight solid years of it, an international business and financial body, the World Economic Forum in Davos, Switzerland, would list Martin as a member of their "dream cabinet" and name him among the top world leaders.

As a result of Martin's lauded good works, Tobin had to come to grips with the financial forecast that, during his first fiscal year, 1996–97, Newfoundland would get from Ottawa some $45 million less than it received the year before.

Malcolm Rowe became Tobin's chief executioner in effecting cutbacks to cope with the deficits. For his efforts, many in the media and public service dubbed him "Malcolm *Axe*."

Rowe's background of national and international experience made him a rather over-skilled choice to help a government of a small province wrestle its deficit to the ground. Perhaps he saw it as his duty, as a Newfoundlander, to answer Tobin's call to perform the necessarily ruthless actions.

I'd known him briefly back in the 1970s when, as a young lawyer, he became assistant clerk to the Newfoundland House of Assembly. I recall my Opposition colleagues on the Public Accounts Committee saying what a great help he was to them.

Later he became an adviser to John Crosbie, when he was a top Tory minister in Ottawa. Then he worked with the Department of External Affairs at the United Nations, and later practised law in Ottawa with one of Canada's leading firms, as well as teaching at the University of Ottawa Law School, while performing various projects for the Government of Canada, and then becoming an adviser to Tobin as federal minister.

He is the former husband of fellow Newfoundlander Moya Greene, a high-powered Canadian public servant who was recruited by the United Kingdom government to head the Royal Mail, its first female and non-Briton CEO since the agency was established by Henry VIII. There she became the highest-paid public servant in the UK, with an income equivalent to several million dollars a year.

Meanwhile, back in 1996, Malcolm Rowe accepted Tobin's invitation to become clerk of the Newfoundland and Labrador Executive Council and secretary to the cabinet. After Tobin's departure as premier, Rowe would be appointed to the Supreme Court of Newfoundland and Labrador.

The deficit problem confronting him after his first election, Tobin concluded, could only be met, among other brutal means, by cutting ten per cent of the jobs in the public service. In his very first budget, he and Malcolm Rowe chopped 1,000 government jobs, and union leaders thundered and raged. He also banged a surtax on incomes over $60,000, causing the middle-income class, and above, to screech and howl.

If there was anyone else left in the province not infuriated, he fixed that by boosting fees for government services, including core necessities like marriage licences, drivers' licences, and birth certificates. These draconian measures succeeded in lowering the budget deficit to less than $50 million.

In his second year, Tobin slashed again. The government got rid of a score of its agencies and stated that over the next three years more than a thousand additional employees would be let go. He softened the impact by promising that nearly all those laid off would qualify for retirement benefits and that this go-round of cuts would be the last. The 1997–1998 budget increased various fees again by nearly $20 million but forecast that the hurting would end with a balanced budget in just three years.

Throughout it all, Tobin's charismatic leadership managed to keep a note of optimism alive in the province. His campaign slogan had been the buoyant "Ready for a Better Tomorrow." And he kept urging that theme for the future. Which, of course, didn't stop sarcastic jibes from commentators, like myself: "Right. Jam tomorrow, always jam tomorrow, but never jam today."

In fact, for all the pain and suffering he was forced to inflict, Tobin and his government, from the outset, engaged in a remarkable number of positive actions and took full advantage of some lucky breaks.

While unemployment persisted at high levels, especially rurally, as the cod moratorium dragged on, and the packages of federal compensation to fishermen dwindled, the shellfishery started to develop and flourish and fill the void.

And back in August 1996, just six months after he was elected, Tobin's government signed a deal with Petro-Canada to get the Terra Nova offshore oil field going. He raised spirits by forecasting the production of oil from that field in just five years, with well over $1 billion in royalties and taxes to the provincial coffers during its lifetime.

Also in 1996, the Tobin government announced a new, simplified, generic royalty regime for offshore oil developments. By December, less than a year after his election, Husky Oil had put together a consortium of corporations to exploit the White Rose oil field.

Having to rely on Ottawa for money to survive was still the perennial bugbear of Newfoundland. Tobin's stated hope was to diminish our addiction to federal handouts by encouraging homegrown businesses. The government sent a positive message by cutting payroll taxes, but it was in the sphere of tourism, especially related to historical celebrations, that the Liberal administration went wild.

The year 1997 was the five hundredth anniversary of John Cabot's landfall somewhere in North America. Ignoring the competing claims of historians that he'd first hit Cape Breton Island, or St. John's, or Labrador, or Maine, the governments in Ottawa, London, and St. John's confirmed Cape Bonavista, for the purposes of the big celebration, as the "official" place of Cabot's arrival in the western hemisphere in 1497.

Queen Elizabeth II was invited, as was the president of Italy, since Cabot's real name was *Giovanni Caboto* in Italian, or *Zuan Chabotto* in his hometown, Venice. Tobin also invited John Bruton, the prime minister, or taoiseach, of Ireland. Both the president and the taoiseach accepted with alacrity. Whereupon government underlings in London reacted with something like, "What? The Queen of England share the stage with the president of, sniff, Italy and the prime minister of, splutter, Ireland! Are you colonials completely bonkers?" They insinuated that unless that pair were *un*invited, it was highly unlikely that Her Majesty could even come.

Tobin refused to uninvite them. But the president of Italy withdrew, apparently under diplomatic pressure, and sent a large Italian delegation instead. A UK government official was then dispatched to St. John's to chastize Tobin into cancelling John Bruton, too. Tobin told the lackey that if the Queen didn't attend as a result of the taoiseach's presence, he would hold a news conference and explain her absence to the world in most negative terms: a clique of British bureaucrats had twisted a Newfoundland celebration to suit their own perverse agenda.

The Queen came. Likewise the Irish prime minister. As a footnote, though, when John Bruton rose to speak in Bonavista, the Queen's entourage hustled her off the stage in an official rebuff. I recall thinking at the time: wasn't 900 years of that crap enough?

Meanwhile, a less official royal reaction involving Her Majesty's backside had taken place in St. John's. During the Queen's week-long visit to the province, Tobin escorted her and Prince Philip up the steps to the front door of Confederation Building. Television cameras captured him placing his hand a number of times on Her Majesty's lower back.

Tobin's story, and he stuck to it, was that because the steps were tricky to negotiate, his gesture was a precautionary and protective one. But the British tabloids went off their heads at his *lèse-majesté*, verging on high treason. Happily, Prince Philip was able to rescue the British

Empire's honour by reportedly growling at Premier Tobin, "You there, take your bloody hand off my woman's arse!"

There were other diversions and entertainments. Concerts, times, and plays led up to the showpiece of the festivities, the arrival in Bonavista on June 24 of a replica of Cabot's vessel, the *Matthew*. The weather was wintery, the worst June day in living memory. But thousands jammed roads and massed in the town to see the end of the craft's much-documented voyage across the Atlantic from Bristol, England. The ocean passage duplicated what had perhaps been the first expedition by Europeans to "Canada" since the Vikings had been driven out of Vinland, 500 years before, by the Aboriginal inhabitants they called Skraelings.

Modern-day leaders of First Nations people deplored the Cabot commemoration for disregarding the brutal effects of the European collision with indigenous peoples in the Americas. But the tourism industry lauded it as a financial success, estimating that some 70,000 people had visited the province and poured tens of millions of dollars into the economy.

It was the start of the Tobin government's future celebrations of momentous historical events: the fiftieth anniversary in 1999 of Confederation; the one thousandth anniversary in the year 2000 of the Vikings' landing at L'Anse aux Meadows and Leif Ericsson's settlement there, and the later birth of Snorri, the first European baby born in North America; the hundredth anniversary in 2001 of the first wireless radio transmission, allegedly received on Signal Hill, across the Atlantic from Cornwall, UK, by Guglielmo Marconi.

These were the beginnings of an aggressive and shrewd marketing campaign to bring tourists to the province, much of it based on our remarkable history and geography, as well as our genius in arts and crafts, which has been going on ever since.

TWENTY-NINE

In 1997, when the Roman Catholic Church, the Pentecostal Assemblies, and some parents went to the Supreme Court of Newfoundland to challenge the very limited changes to denominational education brought in by Clyde Wells, their successful legal action pointed the way, paradoxically, to the complete annihilation of church control over schools. The churches only seemed to win the battle in court, because, in reality, they would lose the war.

Mr. Justice Leo Barry, early in July 1997, ruled that the provincial government did not have the legal right to close denominational schools without the consent of the denominations. He stated, "We've accepted a less than optimal standard of education by opting to preserve at least some of the denominational system of education. This statement is made not as a criticism but as a matter of fact."

Low-key though it was, Barry's opinion was both a slap at the half-hearted, hybrid initiative of Clyde Wells and the death knell of control over schools by religious denominations. The outrage of the vast majority of parents over the way the churches were clinging on to a system of education that was undemocratic, uselessly expensive, discriminatory, not to mention dim-witted and archaic, was intense and almost palpable.

Strongly anti–denominational education himself and, according to reports, supported in this by his even more passionately opposed wife, Jodean, Tobin was ready to act by the end of the same month as Barry's decision. And his assault on the structure pulled no punches. It was perhaps helpful to his cause that Tobin was Roman Catholic and his minister of Education, Roger Grimes, was Pentecostal, the same denominations that they were effectively joining battle with.

On the evening of July 31, I was in Woody Point, Bonne Bay, my mother's hometown, when Premier Tobin came on the air. He was making a province-wide broadcast. My brother, Bud, from Toronto and I were on our annual week-long hiking tour of Gros Morne National Park. But instead of driving to wherever we had planned to go, I pulled the car over in a parking lot and listened to Tobin's speech. It was exceedingly impressive, so much so that I obtained a copy and have kept it to this day, because it is a historic document.

He started by declaring that the time had come to end the confusion and chaos and conflict that has gripped our education system, and its never-ending debate about how to reconcile the need for reform with the rights of the religious denominations. He didn't believe we could achieve necessary education reform if we continued to tie that reform to a denominational system. Clyde Wells had attempted a compromise solution to this problem. Wells proposed a constitutional amendment which altered, but did not eliminate, denominational rights. It didn't work. The churches exercised their remaining constitutional rights in a manner that frustrated reform.

Tobin said he believed the rights of our children to be given a full opportunity to live together, and to learn together, were the really important rights, which could not be fulfilled if the denominational rights which existed today continued into the future. Did we want to continue a system of education that separated our children, that hired or fired teachers, that elected school boards, all on the basis of religion?

It was time to allow our children of every denomination to sit in the same classroom, in the same schools, to ride the same bus, to play on the same sports teams, to live and to learn together in the same community. It was time to hire our teachers because they were competent, caring, and committed to our children . . . not because of their religion, and to elect our school board members because they would exercise their best judgment on behalf of all of us, not just on behalf of some of us.

The province hadn't been able to find a consensus between the conflicting parties because, as long as it had a system which fundamentally divided its people, real consensus wasn't possible.

The government had listened to their constituents, Tobin said, and they were telling the government to stop navigating between the denominations, trying to seek compromise after compromise in the name of a false consensus, but to put an end to a denominational system that pulled us apart.

The government had the will and desire to take decisive and swift action to bring about a new education system for our province, but it needed the authority to act, and that could only come from the people. He announced a referendum for September 2, just over a month away, in which the government sought a mandate to end the denominational school system and to create a new single school system where all of our children, regardless of their religious affiliation, would attend the same schools.

Here was the question: "Do you support a single school system where all children, regardless of their religious affiliation, attend the same schools where opportunities for religious education and observances are provided?"

Opportunities for religious education, he said, meant an opportunity for religious education for all of our students . . . not on a denominational basis, but on the basis of an approved curriculum common to all of our students. Opportunity for observances meant that provision would be made for Christmas concerts, plays, for a nativity scene or a Christmas tree in the class or the school lobby.

Tobin hammered home that there would be no constitutional rights for the churches in the new school system. Parents, not the churches, would have the ultimate right and responsibility to direct their children's education. Unelected and unaccountable church representatives would have no special rights and no special role. It would mean nothing less than the removal of the churches from the governing of schools.

Tobin mentioned that Mr. Justice Leo Barry's judgment reminded us that the denominational system of education carried with it limitations. Tobin believed these limitations were no longer acceptable. He wasn't discounting the contribution of those who taught or administered the denominational system, but he was saying firmly that we had grown beyond such a system.

The province didn't reserve seats in the House of Assembly or in the cabinet room or in the courts or in the workplace on the basis of religion. Did we have to go on reserving seats in our schools on the basis of religion? "The choice is yours," he told the province. "You know where I stand."

Tobin had made it clear to his caucus that if his referendum was defeated, he would quit as premier. A Liberal MHA told me at the time that this promise galvanized all his colleagues to get out there and campaign. Tobin beat around the province himself, together with Roger Grimes, talking up the benefits of the change.

Personally, as I watched and listened, I did not consider victory for the referendum to be a sure thing, even though the public opinion surveys seemed to be very much on side. I'd been constantly amazed at how adamant in their religious loyalties, or bias, some people were. Among many I talked to was a highly intelligent, female, Roman Catholic teacher whom I knew through a professional relationship to be gay.

She had to keep her orientation secret from the religious authorities or she would have been fired from her position, no questions asked. We often discussed the prejudice, the unfairness, the tyranny of that religious power over her. Yet when I assumed, during one of our conversations, that she would be voting in favour of Tobin's changes, she brought me up solid: she'd be voting against the proposal, she said. She was a faithful Catholic and she believed the Church should be allowed to maintain its rights in our education system. Go figure.

Another example occurred when a good friend of mine, a senior

Pentecostal layman, came to see the producer of VOCM *Open Line*, Pat Murphy, and me as host, to request that a certain spokesman for his denomination be allowed to go on the show as a guest the next morning. We told him we couldn't do it. We had imposed a deadline a couple of days before the referendum on all guest appearances, in order to avoid an unholy scramble and claims of unfairness from spokespersons trying and failing to get on during these last days. The deadline had already passed.

But, my friend urged, this spokesperson had important new information that had to be put out in the public domain, and he had to take calls on it and discuss it thoroughly for the benefit of all, for at least an hour. Pat and I told him gently to invite his man to phone in to chat for a few minutes, but we couldn't have him on as a guest; it would be unfair to the others. But, my friend sputtered, he'd already told his man he'd get his good friend Bill Rowe to have him on; Bill Rowe would understand how important it was that he go on.

Pat and I looked at each other. Good heavens, man, we said, not so gently now, we had announced a deadline. The answer was no. We couldn't make any exceptions. Couldn't he see that? My friend's lips quivered in frustration and his eyes blazed at us in righteous rage for several seconds. Then he turned and stomped away. He remained distant from me for the rest of his life.

The PC caucus under leader Loyola Sullivan were split on the question. Sullivan himself was against the proposed reform. The lone NDP Member in the House, Jack Harris, also Catholic, I believe, was all for it.

In Clyde Wells's earlier referendum two years before, which had proposed incomprehensible half-measures and which Wells didn't personally campaign for, 54.4 per cent of the voters had supported some kind of change. In Tobin's new referendum, the clear, revolutionary changes he proposed were approved by seventy-three per cent of the voters.

In Loyola Sullivan's own district, which was over ninety per cent Catholic, two thirds of his constituents voted for the reform. Forty-seven of the forty-eight districts voted for the proposed reform. On referendum night, Tobin said, he was able to discard the speech in which he announced his resignation.

Some Catholic leaders denounced Tobin for his failure of leadership as premier. The Catholic Church went to court to have the referendum question and the result ruled unconstitutional. Their action was dismissed at every judicial level all the way up to and including the Supreme Court of Canada.

Term 17 of Newfoundland's Terms of Union with Canada was amended by due process, granting the House of Assembly exclusive power over education matters. Despite differences of position in the Opposition caucus before the referendum, the provincial House now passed the necessary legislation unanimously. By the very next school year, 1998, the new non-denominational system was in effect.

Years later, during a chat with one of Tobin's colleagues at the time of the reform, I told him I thought that Tobin had shown real courage to take that on so frontally and to carry it through relentlessly to completion. The former minister nearly scoffed me out of the room we were in. "Courage?" he pooh-poohed. "Our polls in favour of getting rid of denominational education were so high it would have taken courage *not* to do it."

Perhaps so. But the fact is Tobin did do it, when it would have been much easier not to do it, to avoid the hassle and let the matter lie. I'd had reports from inside the Liberal caucus that, despite what the polls said, some MHAs thought that a referendum battle to the death, to get rid of the churches entirely in education administration, could very well fail in the face of an all-out church campaign, or be won by a majority so slight as to cause rancour and discord forever.

Yet Tobin did it, and not in a wishy-washy, weasel-worded, half-surrendering way, but forthrightly, directly, and openly. The referendum result itself was, I believe, even larger than the poll numbers leading up to it. His campaign seems to have paid off. But whatever the case, Tobin's referendum, and the people's response to it, were great historic accomplishments.

Many felt that the notorious Mount Cashel Orphanage scandal had an effect on the outcome of the referendum. And yes, I'd be surprised if the outrage and disgust experienced by people of all religious or non-religious views didn't have an impact on it. Brian Tobin has stated, though, I suspect a little disingenuously, that the scandal did not prompt him to push for the education reforms. But regardless of the reality of his motives there, he took equally forthright action concerning the compensation of men who'd been abused as boys by the Christian Brothers at Mount Cashel.

Tobin insisted that, according to the government's legal advisers, the government had no legal liability regarding the sexual and physical abuse suffered by the boys at Mount Cashel. I was startled to hear that at the time. Not only did the Christian Brothers own and run Mount Cashel under government auspices, jurisdiction, and child welfare laws, but there was so precious little surveillance or enforcement by the government under such laws as to amount to a dereliction of duty. Moreover, some high officials of the Department of Justice and its police agency were aware of the abuse and actively covered it up.

But whatever the technical correctness or not of the legal advice, Tobin bypassed it. Some forty male victims had retained lawyers like Danny Williams, later PC premier of the province, and Jack Harris, leader of the NDP and former and future federal MP, to seek compensation. The Christian Brothers and their insurance companies denied, roadblocked, and dug in their heels. It was obvious from statements of both lawyers, Williams and Harris, and their clients, on *Open Line* and elsewhere, that the Brothers and their insurers were intent on dragging out the process till doomsday.

So, Tobin and his cabinet approved an order to grant to the victims, and divide equitably among them, several million dollars in compensation. The men then passed over to the government their right of action against the Christian Brothers. From my knowledge of Tobin, this was the kind of arrangement he would have come up with on his own. But judging by the utter disdain he described his wife, Jodean, as expressing to discredited former Archbishop of Newfoundland Alphonsus Penney, when she later met him by chance in Ottawa, I wouldn't be amazed if she had actively encouraged her husband to do it. When the priest accompanying Penney had said to her, "You must know the archbishop," she'd glared into Penney's eyes and said scathingly, "Indeed I do; I know all about the archbishop." Archbishop Penney scarpered away without a word.

Six more years would grind by, after the government's payment to the victims, before the government finally got its money back from the Christian Brothers.

THIRTY

Tobin was equally forthright, but far less successful, in approaching the major economic developments in Labrador—hydroelectricity on the Lower Churchill River and the enormous nickel deposit at Voisey's Bay.

Three years into his term as premier, Tobin called a snap election for February 9, 1999. He gave as his reason for the early election that he wanted a strong mandate from the people to shore up his bargaining position on Voisey's Bay. He'd been getting nowhere in his negotiations with Inco, which owned the deposit. The company was playing hardball with the government, mainly because it had nearly bankrupted itself by its excessively huge payout of $4.3 billion in acquiring it.

Few people believed Tobin's rationale for the election. Rumours were making the rounds that he wanted to get out of provincial politics and go back to Ottawa, so that he could get cracking on becoming Liberal leader and prime minister of Canada.

The provincial election was a rough one for Tobin, especially because the nurses' union dogged him at every turn over their wage and benefits demands, converting his campaign stops into bitter confrontations. The spectacles made great television viewing—especially for people sympathetic to the nurses' position, a number that seemed to go up throughout the campaign.

But still, Tobin's general popularity and campaigning skills managed to dominate the media against the PCs under leader Ed Byrne. A few days before the election, Tobin came on *Open Line*, and I asked him during a break if he thought he was going to win every seat. I was only half joking. But Tobin didn't joke at all. He looked at me with distraught eyes I'd seldom seen before and replied, "Win every seat? We'll be lucky to win the damned election."

It didn't turn out that bad for him, but it was *relatively* bad, compared to last time. He won a second majority, but a reduced one. The Progressive Conservatives gained five seats for a total of fourteen, and the New Democrats went from one to two. Tobin's Liberals dropped from thirty-seven in 1996 to thirty-two this time.

On March 24, the nurses went on strike. Although the other public service unions had accepted a seven per cent increase in their new collective agreements with the government, the nurses demanded seventeen per cent. And public opinion largely sided with them, as highly regarded and essential medical practitioners. The strike continued the acrimony and bitterness that had been directed at Tobin and the government during the election.

To add to the government's torture, the nurses would congregate in the lobby of Confederation Building, just outside the House of Assembly, and hammer on the hard floor with the ends of the sticks that their placards were attached to. I went up there once to see and hear the uproar, and once was enough. The noise and vibration were excruciating. As one TV journalist reported from there on the air, "Jeez, the deafening racket would drive ya" (i.e. insane).

After ten days of it, Tobin had the House of Assembly legislate the nurses back. He always said that if you weren't prepared to take the kind of pressure he'd suffered from nurses, you were not suited for public office. Funny, though—regulations were passed, soon afterwards, controlling public access to Confederation Building and banning demonstrations in the lobby.

The election result was hardly the strengthened mandate Tobin wanted, to be able to hold like a bludgeon over Inco's head. Because of the inflated, multi-billion dollar purchase price for Voisey's Bay that Inco was saddled with, and the collapse of nickel prices the year before, the company had reneged on its earlier proposed $1.5 billion smelter and refinery to be built in Newfoundland.

And encouraged by their running dogs on Bay Street and in the Ontario Government, the corporation insisted on processing the resource in Sudbury. Tobin advised Inco's hysterical cheerleaders in Ontario media and government "to take a pill" and remained adamant that all the ore from Voisey's would be refined in Newfoundland; none of it would leave the province: "Not one teaspoonful." No deal was struck on Voisey's Bay before the end of his premiership. That would be left to his persevering successor, Roger Grimes.

The other colossal project Tobin wanted to see launched while he was premier was the Lower Churchill hydroelectrical project. To that end, he initiated intensive discussions with Premier Bouchard and Hydro-Québec. In the summer of 1997, the CEO of Hydro-Québec called a news conference to say the talks were going smoothly and harmoniously.

In light of the Upper Churchill contract, utterly lopsided in favour of Quebec, the thought that Hydro-Québec's CEO was now pleased with the Lower Churchill talks sent shivers up many a Newfoundland and Labrador spine. But Tobin assured everybody of his tough stance in the best interests of the province. In conjunction with the new project, Bouchard even appeared interested in negotiating changes to the Upper Churchill deal.

By the spring of 1998, Tobin and Bouchard were all set to announce a mega hydroelectric project. News had "leaked out" that backroom deliberations were going on over a $12 billion plan of development. The Parti Québécois caucus was said to be delighted when Bouchard told them that good work had already been done to help make the project a reality and that he was quite hopeful. And in this province, people were quivering with anticipation. Finally, the quarter of a century of hostility between the two neighbouring provinces would be over and they'd be working co-operatively, pulling together at last, as they should.

On March 9, 1998, I was sitting in a CBC Television studio in St. John's with Doug Letto, waiting for the momentous joint announcement from the town of Churchill Falls. Bouchard and Tobin had travelled there for the purpose, and the cameras were ready to roll. Letto was going to report on the proceedings and I was going to comment on what it all meant. We waited and waited. Then we waited some more.

What we saw and heard was an Innu demonstration that blocked the premiers from making their announcement at their intended locale. The Innu were protesting that they had been excluded from government talks to develop the Lower Churchill. Their concerns were understandable, credible, and reasonable. The Upper Churchill development in the 1970s had created the Smallwood Reservoir, the second-largest man-made reservoir of water on the face of the earth. It had flooded 2,500 square miles of Innu ancestral lands without Innu discussion or permission or so much as a "by your leave."

At length, too late for Letto and me to pontificate on it, the two premiers did make an announcement. It was a broad framework of an agreement to agree, with the details to be concluded after nine months of formal negotiations. A $12 billion project was proposed, second only in size in the world to the Three Gorges development in China, comprising a $3 billion dam on the Lower Churchill. Included was a diversion of water from two Quebec rivers into an enhanced Upper Churchill power station, billions of dollars of transmission lines in both provinces, and shared financial arrangements that made the Upper Churchill deal more equitable for Newfoundland.

From the start there were murmurings of media doubt. Tacked onto most references to the project were qualifiers like "if it goes ahead," "if finalized by the target date," "provided all continues to go well," "possible hurdles in the way from Aboriginals, the federal government, and the unpredictable marketplace." For two years, there were reports of progress from the two governments but with ominous signs in the media of some see-saw ups and downs, including threats from Quebec Innu to stop the project.

In September 2000, Tobin and Bouchard met in Montreal and agreed to restart talks that had somehow stalled. Tobin introduced a note of foreboding, just before the meeting, by commenting that a number of US partners were interested in participating in the project if Quebec was not. The hope of a far-sighted, mammoth, joint project seemed to have largely evaporated.

A month later, Tobin himself evaporated. In the middle of October 2000, out of the blue, he resigned as premier, to be appointed as minister of Industry in Jean Chrétien's cabinet, and to run again for the House of Commons in a snap federal election.

Within another month, a pathetic news report appeared about this Churchill Falls project that had been all but assured by Tobin for the past two and a half years. On November 9, Newfoundland Mines and Energy minister Paul Dicks verified that the power development had been downgraded from Tobin and Bouchard's visionary $12 billion megaproject and was now going to cost $3.7 billion. It would be financed, he said, by the province of Newfoundland and Labrador.

Not a few people in the province went, "What the hell happened?" If you look for the answer in Tobin's memoirs, *All in Good Time*, you will look in vain. I couldn't find one word on the deal. I recall thinking during the period of negotiations, though, how unsettling it was that the mainland press always referred to the project as Tobin's "sweetheart deal from Bouchard," or "very favourable financial terms from Quebec," or "in return for putting up 35% of the equity capital, Newfoundland will reap . . . possibly as much as 80% of the profits." It could only be a matter of time, I figured, before Quebec politicians, hearing and reading that incessantly, would lurch away from the deal and flee for their lives.

Brian Tobin was premier for less than five years, but he always seemed to have a pretty clear political map of where he wanted to go in the job and what he wanted to do there. One of his colleagues told me that he had a technique for keeping his schedule of policy initiatives uncluttered and free of convoluted meanderings. If he himself, or anyone else, wanted to propose a policy, it had to be presented on one side of a three-inch-by-five-inch index card; the other side of the card had to contain the plan for the effective public communication of the initiative.

Sir Winston Churchill had a similar technique whereby any proposal to him, however important or complicated, during the height of the Second World War, if it was going to be read at all, had to be contained on a side and a half of one sheet of paper. The requirement was said to concentrate the minds of long-winded advisers marvellously.

In Tobin's case, it may have contributed to the successful implementation of a number of other important undertakings whose time had finally come:

In 1997, the government brought Newfoundland up to speed with most of the rest of Canada by establishing the Newfoundland and Labrador Film Development Corporation. It was to foster and encourage the film and video industry in the province and increase its national and international visibility as a location for film and television production. It has added to the overall success of the industry here, achieved in the face of unremitting worldwide competition.

During his term of office, Tobin passed amendments to the Newfoundland Human Rights Act, banning discrimination on grounds of sexual orientation.

The Morgentaler abortion clinic had opened in St. John's in 1990. But women had to pay for abortion services there themselves. MCP, the Newfoundland Medical Care Plan, paid for abortions performed only at the Health Sciences Centre. At the beginning of 1998, Tobin brought the Morgentaler clinic under MCP, so that full funding was provided at a saving of hundreds of dollars to women concerned.

First oil from the Hibernia offshore field flowed late in 1997. There was a public announcement when the first royalty was received by the government. But the payment was so small, as a result of the low price of oil internationally, I said on the air with unpardonable sarcasm that the embarrassment made Tobin sneak the cheque into his hand behind his back so as not to draw attention to it. And wild horses couldn't make him confess the amount.

But he was able to show a surplus in the 1998–99 budget for only the second time since Confederation, it was said, and Newfoundland was predicted to be number one in Canada in economic growth.

The reform to the education system wasn't the only constitutional change Tobin brought about. In 1999, he steered the House of Assembly into joining with the House of Commons to change the province's name from just Newfoundland to "Newfoundland and Labrador." The formal amendment to the Canadian constitution, which was far from every Newfoundlander's liking, took place in 2001.

In February 2000, Tobin announced that the government would build a $40 million cultural facility in St. John's to bring together, protected by modern technology, the art gallery of Newfoundland and Labrador, the provincial museum, and the provincial archives. The new building would rescue them from their existing dilapidated surroundings. The idea of this edifice, to be designed by renowned architect Philip Pratt, and to be called The Rooms, caused the usual fuss: why was the government spending all the money on that frivolity while they were closing down hospital beds and couldn't fill in the potholes?

When he was beginning to falter on proceeding, as he has stated publicly since, he received encouragement and moral support from Jodean: the province should not curtail all spending on arts and culture and history on the grounds that it couldn't fulfill every other important demand. So Tobin persisted in the face of the criticism, and The Rooms opened next to the historic Basilica of St. John the Baptist in 2005. Many people have given it high grades since for its many positive features, although for a long while the tired local joke was that it looked like the box the Basilica came in.

THIRTY-ONE

I once or twice claimed on *Open Line* that Liberal Party headquarters in Newfoundland and Labrador, under Tobin's leadership, was being run in a Stalinist fashion. I seem to recall that my disparagement had to do with the provincial party's perceived attempt to control who got nominated as Liberal candidates to run in federal elections in the ridings of Labrador and of Humber–St. Barbe–Baie Verte.

First, the party seemed to be trying to keep Lawrence O'Brien from being nominated Liberal candidate for a Labrador by-election, and although I didn't know O'Brien, I condemned the attempt on principle. My own brother, Fred, was the executive director of the party at the time, and Lawrence O'Brien emphasized to me later that it was in fact Fred's fairness and rigorous adherence to proper procedure that allowed him to overcome attempts by the political brass to shut him out and to win the nomination. I've been apologizing to big brother ever since.

A later effort by Tobin to keep Gerry Byrne out of the party nomination in Humber–St. Barbe–Baie Verte really brought out my Stalinist accusation. I didn't know Gerry Byrne at the time, either, but I didn't like what was being done, and of course *Open Line* never saw an underdog it didn't love.

On one of his visits to VOCM, Tobin and I had words. He thought it was unfair to be called Stalinist, and he resented it. And of course he was right. It was an offensive insult to the millions of victims of that psychotic monstrosity to compare him to any leader in our democracy, however authoritarian he seemed to be becoming.

At Brian and Jodean's Christmas party that year, a friend and I looked around at the invited guests, and I joked that we had definitely been dropped from last year's A-list party down to the B-list. We figured that I was being punished for my Stalinist insult. Or maybe it was for the time I said on *Open Line* that Tobin possessed "short man syndrome," like Napoleon. I believe that callers and I had been talking about the impressively aggressive stand he'd taken on Voisey's Bay and Inco. Or maybe it was during his battle with the nurses. Whatever—being a host with a big, loose mouth on *Open Line* was a hazardous occupation when it came to schmoozing privileges over cocktails with the mighty.

We couldn't zero in on what my friend's crime had been, but we agreed that it was obviously atrocious, because here he was right now, reduced to having to converse with a fallen subversive as punishment.

Brian Tobin's abrupt resignation as premier in October 2000, only twenty months after his last election and less than five years in office, was at the urging of Jean Chrétien. The prime minister was said to be eager to shore up support for his government in Atlantic Canada. But in reality he wanted some stronger countervailing forces in the government to offset the power of the man who'd become the tail wagging the dog in the Chrétien cabinet—Paul Martin. And having been very impressed with Tobin's media successes in the "Turbot War," and during the Quebec referendum five years before, Brian seemed to be Chrétien's man.

The PM appointed him, without a seat in the House of Commons, as minister of Industry, one of the most important and senior portfolios. This bumped George Baker out as this province's cabinet minister.

No argument from long-time MP Baker, though: Chrétien would later elevate him to that Valhalla of deserving party warriors, the Senate of Canada. Never having to run for election again after more than a quarter of a century of campaigning—what's not to love? And George used the senate properly—to speak and advocate regarding key public concerns, just as he'd done in the Commons.

Chrétien called the snap election in November 2000, just days after Tobin's appointment as minister. Tobin had no trouble winning his seat with a majority of about fifty-four per cent against all other candidates, including PC and NDP heavyweights Jim Morgan and Fraser March in the Newfoundland riding of Bonavista–Trinity–Conception. Still, it was hard not to notice that the result was far from the enormous majority of eighty-two per cent he'd received in his most recent federal election in Humber–St. Barbe–Baie Verte in 1993. There seemed to be a widespread bad taste in some people's mouths over his sudden abandonment of the premiership.

Beaton Tulk became caretaker premier while a Liberal leadership convention was called for February 3, 2001. Roger Grimes, John Efford, and Paul Dicks, cabinet ministers from Tobin's government, jumped into the race. Grimes, who'd been the reliable point man for premiers during a decade of challenging portfolios, and who now attracted massive support from caucus and party establishment, led the pack.

Efford was a populist and appealed to the party's grassroots. A couple of years before, he'd stood in the House of Assembly and declared that he "would like to see the six million seals . . . out there, killed and sold, or destroyed or burned. . . . The more they kill, the better I will love it." This was great ammunition for the anti–seal hunt gang, and therefore it caused the more thoughtful among strong supporters of the seal hunt to grieve. But Joey Smallwood's "ragged-arsed artillery" in the party seemed to go for it. They also liked his announcement that he was going to lead riots in the streets if the federal Fisheries minister, a fellow Liberal, didn't overturn his grant of a shrimp licence to Prince Edward Islanders to fish off Newfoundland.

Tobin came down from Ottawa to attend the convention at the Mount Pearl Glacier. I was at the convention all day as a commentator on CBC Television with Doug Letto. I don't recall if Tobin had formally endorsed Grimes or not, but I could see that he was clearly backing him. At one point he asked me worriedly, off the air, if I thought Roger was going to win. I said it looked like it, but really, neither I nor anyone else I talked to had any idea that the race had become so close.

Grimes won on the second ballot—by fourteen votes. And he inherited a party in which, because of the vicious trench warfare between the leadership camps, the atmosphere remained toxic. Neither Efford nor Dicks would join his cabinet. Tobin's former provincial seat, The Straits–White Bay North, one of the most Liberal districts in Newfoundland, went Tory in a by-election, as did nearby St. Barbe District.

Then, newly acclaimed Tory leader Danny Williams won by a landslide in Paul Dicks's former Liberal district of Humber West, while the Liberals barely managed to hang on in Efford's former seat, the powerful Liberal district of Port de Grave, by ninety-eight votes. The backlash against Tobin's unsinkable Liberal Party was setting in with a vengeance.

The provincial Liberal Party would not recover for years from Tobin's brusque departure and the noxious leadership race. Within three years, despite the best efforts of his first-rate successor as premier, Roger Grimes, the Progressive Conservatives, headed by Danny Williams, were elected to government with a large majority. Indeed, back at the time of Tobin's resignation, there had been speculation that he'd gotten out while the going was good: the thought of Williams as Tory leader, with Tobin's probable defeat at his hands, some said, was what had made Captain Canada bolt for Ottawa like a scalded cat.

Other Newfoundlanders were more positive, or forgiving, and contributed to the pervasive conjecture, locally and across Canada, that he'd left as premier because Chrétien would soon be retiring: Tobin was going to run for leader of the federal Liberal Party. People in this province could forgive a lot at the thought of a Newfoundlander becoming prime minister of Canada.

He started working assiduously on his French. Combining work with pleasure, he reportedly travelled to the South of France for a total immersion French course. And he seemed to take to it. When he came back, I heard him in television clips occasionally, emitting French idioms and colloquialisms like a pro.

Plus, Chrétien had put him in the Industry Department, the more cynical observers were surmising, where he'd be rubbing shoulders with the business leaders who'd be financing his leadership campaign. It was when he was minister of Industry that Fred Hutton, of the NTV *Evening News* in St. John's at the time, created a fascinating documentary on Tobin called *Destination PMO*, which zeroed in on his unquestionably high ambitions for himself. I recall that, watching the video, I wondered why Tobin seemed to portray himself as going flat out, non-stop, all the time. Travelling from point A to point B, he would move so quickly, he always looked like he was on the verge of breaking into a run.

Clearly this was a man with a precise blueprint of his path to greatness ahead. And he was going to get there fast. His momentum was such that nothing could stop him.

So, what went wrong?

Prime Minister Chrétien had been emasculated and converted into a eunuch in his own cabinet harem. He could no long perform as The Man. Despite the inordinate time and energy Tobin spent in the House passionately defending Chrétien against accusations that he had enriched himself as prime minister over a land deal in his riding, the so-called Shawinigate scandal, Chrétien could not even reciprocate by backing Tobin's pet government project. Instead, he left Brian humiliated.

This pet project of Tobin's as Industry Minister was his Broadband Initiative, basically the support and financing by the federal government of the high-speed connecting of every person, business, and community in the country, many rural and northern, to the Internet. Chrétien told Tobin that as prime minister he was right behind his broadband initiative and would make sure its first phase of $100 million or so was in that year's budget.

When Paul Martin brought down his budget in December 2001, Tobin heard for the first time, like everyone else, that his project had been watered down to the point of extinction. Publicly embarrassed, Tobin confronted the prime minister on reneging on his commitment, and Chrétien told him frankly that Paul Martin had not followed his instructions. Tobin snapped that, if that was so, Chrétien had a bigger problem than he himself had: the Finance minister had grown more powerful than the prime minister.

Chrétien undermined Tobin's position and prestige further by appointing Tobin's predecessor in the Department of Industry, John Manley, as deputy prime minister. Deliberately or inadvertently, Chrétien appeared to be signalling Manley as his preference over Tobin as his successor. Clearly, Chrétien's original, mentor-like enticement of Brian back to federal politics had grown decidedly less warm and cuddly. All this had an adverse effect on Tobin's earlier buoyant leadership aspirations.

Even before Tobin had resigned as premier, he has acknowledged, he was quietly contemplating his federal Liberal leadership bid and making preliminary moves in that direction. Before the end of 2000, around and after the time of his appointment as minister of Industry, he was unobtrusively putting together a campaign organization and a fundraising apparatus. Newfoundland senator George Furey became chair of the campaign, and Newfoundland business magnate Craig Dobbin helped head up the fundraising operation.

Other Canadian tycoons and entrepreneurs joined the campaign, and enough money flooded quickly in to allow him to open offices in Toronto and Montreal and to employ a dozen workers. Tobin has protested that great care was taken to ensure that the fundraising caused no conflict of interest with his powerful public position of minister of Industry in the federal cabinet. Evidently it never occurred to anyone, or if it did it was blithely ignored, that the whole shebang was inherently a conflict of interest, and that anyone actively seeking the leadership of the party and the prime ministership should resign from government decision-making capacity.

During 2001, Tobin was gradually concluding that Paul Martin had a death grip on the leadership. Not only had Martin easily blindsided him on his Broadband Initiative, which was unnerving enough, but the advice he was getting, based on the polls, was that Martin's advantage was insurmountable. Personally, unlike so many others, I never believed that Martin was uncatchable.

I should say that, by this time, Brian Tobin and I, except for the occasional mob-scene social event, or media chat, hadn't had anything to do with each other on a personal basis for years. I had no great desire to change that, and particularly because of my *Open Line* comments, the feeling was no doubt mutual. But my own indifference in that regard was greatly overbalanced by my general esteem for him as a political leader, and by the hope of myself and many others that we might have a Newfoundlander as prime minister. So I phoned him.

I told him that I would do everything in my power, at home and across Canada, to help him win the leadership. His response, though appreciative, was less upbeat than I'd grown used to expecting from the old Brian Tobin. Suspecting that he had already, in his own mind, given up, I argued that Martin's lead was a house of cards.

The man had no charisma, and no media sense or attractiveness, and little to draw people to him besides the Bay Street crowd who had loved his slash-and-burn budgets. He was ahead in the leadership by default. I instanced the Kim Campbell phenomenon, when the polls and the hype had scared off all Tory leadership hopefuls, until Jean Charest jumped in and gained on her in leaps and bounds and would have won if he hadn't held off entering the race until it was too late. Tobin could do the same thing, I argued, regardless of what the polls were saying about Martin's lead. He would run circles around Martin in the media and on the hustings.

Brian listened without great enthusiasm. Not long after, he announced he was quitting the race and resigning from the cabinet and the House of Commons.

His reason seemed to be that he was fed up with politics after twenty-five five years in the federal and provincial trenches. He'd done nothing else with his life since the age of twenty-three. It was important to him that he spend more time with his wife and children. I seem to recall that he rhapsodized about being in the bosom of his family, under the comforting glow of the Christmas tree.

One theory about Tobin's psychology is that, from the start, he was always a quitter when it came to hard, executive, decision-making challenges over the long haul. His modus operandi was to dive into a project headfirst and give it everything he had, hammer and tong, for a while, and then bail out fast. His first demanding executive job was as minister of Fisheries in Chrétien's first cabinet. He lasted there for two or three years of dramatics and then couldn't get out fast enough to waltz into the premiership of Newfoundland.

He lasted as premier for three years or so of progressive activism, before calling an unnecessarily premature election as an excuse to walk out a short while after that, and go federal again. He stayed on as minister of Industry, trying to move heaven and earth, before abruptly resigning after a couple of years.

He took on the federal Liberal leadership competition with his eyes wide open about Paul Martin's ascendancy, before quitting because of the magnitude of the challenge after a few months. Next, he took on a demanding CEO position with Frank Stronach's Magna empire but bailed out after less than a year in a golden parachute worth a couple of million dollars or more.

The man was always a flash in the pan, some have argued. He was lazy when it came to stick-to-it-iveness regarding a taxing, trying responsibility over a marathon run. He was only in his element in a milieu like the Rat Pack during the long Mulroney years, where all he had to do was shout his diatribes without accountability from the Opposition benches.

Since his resignations, he has been happiest of all pontificating on the media; or sitting on corporate boards; or plotting with Belinda Stronach her jump from the Tories to the Liberals; or joining a big law firm as senior business adviser (a.k.a. new business rainmaker); or landing up in the think tank which, when they had criticized him as premier for wanting benefits from Voisey's Bay, he'd called "the most right-wing, Looney Tune institute" in Canada.

My own conclusion about Tobin's psychology and makeup is that none of that is true. He is what a lot of successful, intelligent, energetic people are, namely a person who wants to tackle projects. He likes to take on and complete individual, challenging tasks. He's not content to be tied to the same thing for an extended period. He wants to undertake a challenge, sink his teeth into it, and get it done. Then he wants to move on to the next challenge. He is not a quitter, in my view—far from it. Whenever he has shouldered a project—first running for MP, or individual challenges as federal minister or premier—some of them verging on the impossible, he's done it with enthusiasm, toiled at it, and seen it through as far as he can take it, usually to success.

THIRTY-TWO

Throughout 2005, with Prime Minister Paul Martin's shaky leadership in question, there was speculation that Tobin would contemplate running for it again if Martin faltered in the next election. Some people in St. John's surmised such a possibility when Liberal Tobin came down to Tory premier Frank Moore's funeral at Cochrane Street United Church on July 14, 2005. He must have wanted to be seen on television for that reason, they figured. But I think his attendance was a purely personal sentiment. Janice Wells, in her excellent book *Frank Moores, The Time of His Life* in 2008, mentioned that Tobin had called Frank's wife privately, a week before he died, to say he felt strongly that Frank should have a state funeral.

When Stephen Harper's Conservatives won a minority government in the general election of January 23, 2006, Martin announced his resignation as Liberal Party leader. The pressure came on Tobin again to run for the leadership. He must want it, people said. After all, he'd entitled his 2003 autobiography *All in Good Time.* Wasn't that a clear reference to his intention of going for it again when the right time came?

Myself, I'd seen the handwriting on the wall when a couple of good Tobin supporters told me in dismay that he'd stopped taking his French lessons, a sure sign in today's Canada that he'd given up any thought of the country's top job. Then Tobin allayed all doubt just one week after Martin's resignation in 2006 by announcing emphatically that he would not be a candidate for the federal Liberal leadership.

One never knows what personal considerations motivate or discourage a person. I'd heard earlier from someone politically close to Tobin for years that after he completed some demanding task, which he'd applied himself to for weeks on end, working flat out on it day and night, body and soul, till it was finished in either success or failure, he often suffered from a migraine headache. The headache happened not when he was engaged in the massive effort itself, but when he was coming down from it, the person told me: sort of a decompression migraine after dealing with an exceedingly challenging issue. So, no wonder, at this stage of his life, the supporter surmised, that he'd steered clear of the greatest, unending series of monumental tasks to decompress from—those in the office of the prime minister of Canada.

I had never seen that affliction in Tobin during my own time with him, but when I mentioned it during a conversation with a mutual acquaintance, a national political figure, he said that if it was true then he was full of sympathy and empathy for Tobin. He too was subject to the same condition, he said, when he finished some big important case after working flat out on it day after day. It never happened when he was actually involved in the challenging task, but only when he had completed it and was coming down from it. And it was a physical reaction that was far from pleasant: Brian may have made a well-considered move out of top leadership to avoid that miserable torment.

When Tobin became an Officer of the Order of Canada in 2013, he was listed as residing in Manotick, Ontario. Many have found it passing strange that, of the five elected premiers, up to and including him, since Confederation—Smallwood, Moores, Peckford, Wells, Tobin—only two stayed in the province after their premiership: Smallwood and Wells.

Even Smallwood spent substantial time down in Clearwater, Florida, immediately after resigning, but came back in his seventies to enter politics again, and then to work on his great project, *The Encyclopedia of Newfoundland*. And Wells remained here to accept from Prime Minister Chrétien the top judicial job, chief justice of the province; that was good reason for staying put.

The other three premiers sought their fortunes outside the province, causing some sarcastic Newfoundlanders to sum it up: they did such a good job here as premier they had to leave the province themselves to keep body and soul together. But another argument might be that the field of activity here was too small for their talents.

Tobin has been awarded honorary doctorates from universities. But he never completed his undergraduate degree. In fact, three of our province's most successful politicians never earned a university degree, Joey Smallwood provincially, Don Jamieson at the federal level, and Brian Tobin at both. They were among the most articulate and informed and savvy politicians our province has produced—able to walk and talk equally with kings and queens, or fishermen, or prime ministers, or social service recipients.

When I chatted about that to a fellow lawyer recently, we laughed about our backload of undergraduate and graduate and professional school degrees, and we agreed that Brian Tobin and the other two were walking advertisements for the advantages of *not* wasting your productive years on a higher education. The only caveat for those contemplating that perilous route, without benefit of academic tickets, would be that you have to be sure you possess exceptionally great talent.

The citation for Tobin's Order of Canada award touched on some of his accomplishments. As minister of Fisheries he got the Oceans Act passed, which was described as providing "a unique framework for modern ocean management." He was also lauded for his "strong stance against offshore overfishing by foreign fleets," which was a nice way of describing what others have characterized as the first act of war on the high seas by Canada since the Second World War, or more bluntly, as an act of outright piracy. He was praised as premier for "important economic reforms to traditional industries, the modernization of the educational system, and the development of the offshore oil and gas industry." As a corporate leader, "he is known for his commitment to sound governance and corporate social responsibility."

Many people acknowledge these achievements, and more, on Tobin's part. Others carp and quibble over their accuracy. But assuming them all correct, and the credit well deserved, there can be no doubt he would gladly have relinquished all of it in a second if only he could have prevented Christmas Eve, 2010, from ever arriving.

That night before Christmas, Brian and Jodean Tobin's younger son, Jack, while performing drunken stunts with a pickup truck, killed his own best friend. After a night on the town with his buddies, twenty-four-year-old Jack was doing doughnuts in his pickup on top of an Ottawa parking garage when, somehow, Alex Zolpis got pinned under the vehicle and died.

I didn't know the Tobin children, Heather, Adam, and Jack, very well. I'd met them maybe a couple of times at the Christmas parties at their Waterford Bridge Road house when Brian was premier, where they were chipping in on the chores of keeping the guests happy. They seemed to be lovely, intelligent kids who made their parents, and rightly so, inordinately proud.

Then, a decade later, I was as shocked and heartbroken as anyone else outside the families themselves by news of the traumatizing event. It was sad beyond words to see the utter devastation on the faces of Alex Zolpis's family and girlfriend, and on the faces of Jack and Jodean and Brian. Jack was ordered by the court to reside with his parents. Friends of the family were aware that his mother and father had to stay close to their inconsolable son to prevent him from doing harm, or worse, to himself.

In May of 2011, Jack pleaded guilty in court to impaired driving causing death. At the sentencing hearing, he wished, in tears, that it had been himself instead of his friend who'd died as a result of his unforgivable actions that night.

Brian Tobin told reporters afterwards, "We believe in Jack. I can tell you that he is a good son and a good brother. He's made a serious mistake and he's going to pay the price of that mistake."

The judge sentenced Jack to three years in prison and banned him from driving for seven years. A year later, he walked out with full parole, but carrying with him a whole lifetime ahead to contemplate every day the ghastly tragedy he'd visited upon his best friend's family and loved ones, and upon his own. Many people have noted the strength and dignity of family members as the tragedy and its consequences unfolded and have felt the unspeakable sadness that such a tribute would ever have been required to be paid.

AFTERWORD

As a political participant and close observer of the political scene, I've been amazed at the quality and ability of the leadership that has sometimes emerged from the tiny population of this province. I believe that two of the three premiers depicted here, Clyde Wells and Brian Tobin, and a third portrayed in one of my earlier books, Danny Williams, possessed the national popularity based on their actions, as well as the ability and charisma, to have become prime minister of Canada. Perhaps the timing wasn't right, or perhaps none of them possessed the overriding "will to power" to go for it. But I do think that with the reputations they had created and the qualities they possessed, each of them had an excellent shot at the top job.

Among the premiers of Newfoundland and Labrador so far, which of them might be considered the most significant of our political leaders? Who among them has made the greatest historical impact? That would be, largely, a subjective judgement and a tentative one: I've found my opinions altering somewhat with the passage of time and the ability to view each leader in the changing perspective of history.

If we bring into play their political accomplishments outside as well as inside their premierships, then Joey Smallwood's Confederation victory was so powerful and unique in our history that I'd have to place him at the top of the roster. But Frank Moores's achievement in breaking at last Joey's insufferably long grip on power, and ushering in a new political era, would have to bring him near the head of the list as well.

Then, Brian Peckford's ferociously fought battle to obtain his 1985 Atlantic Accord must also rank him close to the top, just as Danny Williams's addendum, the 2005 Atlantic Accord, would similarly elevate him. If Danny's Lower Churchill initiative should happen to pan out rewardingly in years to come—seemingly an ever-diminishing likelihood as I write—then he would bode fair to be considered one of our most noteworthy leaders in vision, tenacity, and actual accomplishments.

What about Brian Tobin? I believe that in the public consciousness he's our most underrated political leader since Confederation. Perhaps a perceived slickness, plus a residue of bitterness from the manner of his leaving the premiership, led to that. But I consider the reality of his leadership, in Ottawa as well as St. John's, to be far different and much more positive.

His actions in the federal Department of Fisheries—viewed by some as mere showmanship and pizzazz—had in fact a substantial effect, far beyond anything achieved by his predecessors, on the morale of the nation and on the world's approach to the oceans' fishery. And as a federal minister, he probably turned the tide in favour of keeping Canada united, as a result of that hair's-breadth win of the 1995 Quebec separation referendum.

Add to all that his demolition of denominational education, and his other accomplishments and directions during just five years as premier, and I view Brian Tobin as one of our province's pre-eminent political leaders so far. But stay tuned.

ACKNOWLEDGEMENTS

Once more, my heartfelt gratitude to Garry Cranford, Margo Cranford, Jerry Cranford, Laura Cameron, Bob Woodworth, Peter Hanes, Gerard Murphy, and Jennifer Konieczny, all of Flanker Press, for contributing in so many ways to the creation of the book and its presentation to readers. And again, my sincere thanks to graphic designer Graham Blair for producing the striking covers.

Born in Newfoundland, Bill Rowe graduated in English from Memorial University and attended Oxford University as a Rhodes Scholar, obtaining an Honours M.A. in law.

Elected five times to the House of Assembly, Rowe served as a minister in the Government of Newfoundland and Labrador and as leader of the Official Opposition. He practised law in St. John's for many years and has been a long-time public affairs commentator, appearing regularly on national and local television, as well as hosting a daily radio call-in show on VOCM and writing weekly newspaper columns.

Rowe has written ten books: *Clapp's Rock*, a bestselling novel published by McClelland & Stewart and serialized on CBC national radio; *The Temptation of Victor Galanti*, a second novel published by McClelland & Stewart; a volume of essays on politics and public affairs published by Jesperson Press of St. John's; the critically acclaimed political memoir *Danny Williams: The War With Ottawa*, which appeared on the *Globe and Mail*'s bestsellers list; *Danny Williams, Please Come Back*, a collection of newspaper articles covering social, political, and economic issues; *Rosie O'Dell*, a critically acclaimed crime novel published by Pennywell Books, a literary imprint of Flanker Press; *The Premiers Joey and Frank*, a *Globe and Mail* bestseller and selected by the *Hill Times* as one of the Best 100 Books in Politics, Public Policy, and History in 2013; *The Monster of Twenty Mile Pond*, the much-loved novel of a legendary monster who engulfed the lives of two teenaged girls; *The True Confessions of a Badly Misunderstood Dog*, a fictionalized account of the frantic years when a Labrador retriever and two cats lived with the author's family; and now *No Punches Pulled: The Premiers Peckford, Wells, and Tobin*, a political memoir that lives up to its title.

Rowe is a member of the Writers' Union of Canada and has served on the executive of the Writers' Alliance of Newfoundland and Labrador. He is married to Penelope Ayre Rowe CM of St. John's. They have a son, Dorian, a daughter, Toby, and three grandchildren, Rowan, Elizabeth, and Phoebe.

INDEX

Abbott, Beaton 96
Abitibi Price 27
Aboriginal 138, 140, 142, 143, 161, 220, 232
Academy Awards 200
Africa 36, 146, 147
Air Canada 206
Alberta (AB) 28, 64, 126, 148
"Anglican Archbishop" 113
Anglican Church 102, 113
"Anglo-Saxon Route" 16
Angus Reid Institute 142
Ashley, Joe 186
Atkins, Norman 26
Atlantic Accord (1985) 51-56, 60, 77, 252
Atlantic Accord (2005) 56, 252
Atlantic Agricultural Hall of Fame 65
Atlantic Canada 133, 237
Aylward, Joan Marie 213

"Bad Boy of Confederation" 4
Baker, George 146, 176, 183, 237, 238
Ballam, Charlie 79, 80
Barry, Leo 17, 29, 53, 54, 61, 63, 73, 110, 119, 221, 222, 224
Basilica of St. John the Baptist 235
Bay of Islands, NL 120
Bay Street, Toronto 231, 242
Bell Island, NL 80
Beothuk 58
Bettney, Julie 213
Black, Conrad 196
Bloc Québécois 134, 144, 188, 190, 197, 204
Bonaparte, Napoleon 137, 237
Bonavista, NL 219, 220

Bonino, Emma 195, 198, 199
Bonne Bay, NL 222
Bouchard, Lucien 128, 134, 143, 144, 190, 194, 197, 204, 205, 207, 208, 231-233
Boudria, Don 179
Bourassa, Robert 39, 121, 123, 131-135
Bowater 82, 108
Brace, Jeff 33
Bristol, England 220
British Columbia (BC) 49, 75, 76, 115, 126, 141
British Commonwealth 122, 196
British Isles 200
Broadband Initiative 240, 242
Broadbent, Ed 178
Browne, William Joseph "Billy" 31, 201
Bruton, John 219
Burgess, Tom 96
Butler, Joe 32
Byrne, Ed 230
Byrne, Gerry 236

Cabot, John 218-220
Cabot Strait 16
Caesar, Julius 17, 210
Calgary, AB 64, 72, 142, 154, 182
Calgary Herald 72
Callahan, William R. "Bill" 80, 93
Callbeck, Catherine 207
Cameron, Margaret 61
Campagnolo, Iona 183
Camp Associates 26
Campbell, Avril Phædra Douglas "Kim" 184-191, 242
"Campbellmania" 191
Canada Act (1982) 37
Canada AM 206
Canada Day Royal Visit (1983) 43
Canada House 31
Canada-Newfoundland Offshore Petroleum Board (CNOPB) 51
Canada Revenue Agency (CRA) 81
Canada Steamship Lines 183
Canadian Airlines 206
Canadian Armed Forces (CAF) 82
Canadian Bar Association 135, 155
Canadian Broadcasting Corporation (CBC) 76, 92, 96, 103, 105, 136, 232, 239
Canadian Charter of Rights and Freedoms 126, 135, 183
Canadian Officer Training Corps 82
Canadian Union of Public Employees (CUPE) 151
Canary Wharf, London 200
Cape Bonavista, NL 219
Cape Breton Island, NS 218
"Captain Canada" 200, 210-212,

239
Carney, Pat 51
Carter, John 57
Carter, Walter 17
Cashin, Richard "Rick" 29, 46, 73, 113, 146, 148
Cayman Islands 43
Chalker, Jim 111
Chamberlain, Neville 48
Charest, Jean 185, 207, 242
Charing Cross, London 200
Charlottetown Accord 143
China 232
Chirac, Jacques 209
Chrétien, Jean 21, 38, 47, 51, 137, 142-144, 163, 178, 182-195, 198, 199, 203, 205, 206, 209, 210, 233, 237-241, 243, 247
Christian Brothers 227, 228
Chronicle Herald 141
Churchill Falls, NL 14, 28, 33-35, 56, 106, 135, 159, 232, 233
Churchill Falls (Labrador) Corporation 106
Churchill River, NL 31, 35, 229
Churchill, Winston 29, 234
CJON Television 167
Clark, Joe 19, 20, 24, 27, 28, 30, 62, 63, 73, 172, 173, 176
Clearwater, FL 246
"Clyde Lied" 151, 152, 163
Coastal Fisheries Protection Act 194, 201
Coastal Fisheries Protection Regulations 201
Cochrane Street United Church 245
"Cod Wars" 146
Come by Chance, NL 60, 88, 92, 97
Conception Bay, NL 101
Confederation 4, 31, 33, 35, 40, 49, 61, 63, 71, 79, 90, 94, 116, 172, 186, 214, 220, 235, 246, 251, 252
Confederation Building 1, 2, 7, 12, 58, 162, 173, 211, 219, 230
Conservative Party of British Columbia 76
Conservative Party of Canada 143, 144, 245
Consolidated Bathurst 26
Controlled Ecological Life Support System 75
Cook, Joan 21
Copps, Sheila 137, 179, 180, 182, 184
Corner Brook, NL 23, 61, 78-82, 85-87, 90, 98, 99, 101-103, 108, 109, 120, 152, 175, 176, 181, 192
Cornwall, England 200, 220
Court of Appeal (Newfoundland and Labrador) 49, 105, 106, 163, 166
Court of Appeal (Quebec) 35
Court of St. James 30

Coyne, Deborah 130, 182
Cree 140
Critch, Mike 154
Crosbie, Ches 94
Crosbie, Jane 73
Crosbie, John 5-8, 11, 12, 17, 20, 24, 27-29, 39-41, 51, 55, 56, 60, 62, 63, 73, 80, 88-94, 96-98, 105, 125-128, 132, 141, 147, 148, 154, 155, 172, 180, 181, 193, 209, 210, 216
Curtis, Dave 112, 150

Daily Telegraph 196, 200, 201
Dalhousie University 122
Davies, Brian 108
da Vinci, Leonardo 165
Davis, Bill 209
Davos, Switzerland 216
Decima Research 114
Deer Lake, NL 79, 80, 175
Deer Lake Airport 79, 80
Dempster, Michael 155
Denominational Education Councils 160
Desmarais, Paul 26
Destination PMO 240
Devon, England 200
Dicks, Paul 233, 238, 239
Diefenbaker, John 31, 173, 176, 178, 180
Diocese of Western Newfoundland 102, 103
Dobbin, Craig 241
Doer, Gary 136, 138
Doody, Bill 17, 24
Doucet, Fred 40
Doyle, John C. 105

East River, NY 198, 200
École Polytechnique de Montréal 150
Economic Recovery Commission 156
Edmonton Eskimos 136
Efford, John 146, 238, 239
electoral districts (Federal)
  Humber–Port au Port–St. Barbe 172
  Humber–St. Barbe–Baie Vert 192, 236, 238
  St. John's East 186, 189, 191
  St. John's West 11
electoral districts (Provincial, Newfoundland and Labrador)
  Bonavista North 48
  Bonavista–Trinity–Conception 238
  Cartwright–L'Anse au Clair 215
  Gander 61
  Green Bay 1, 5, 10, 11
  Humber East 60, 81, 85, 98, 118, 210, 215
  Humber West 81, 98, 99, 118, 239
  Labrador 236
  Naskaupi 149
  Port au Port 95

Port de Grave 239
St. Barbe 186, 239
St. Barbe South 85
St. George's 61
St. John's 82, 190
Signal Hill–Quidi Vidi 158, 215
Straits–White Bay North 239
Twillingate 22, 24, 48, 171
White Bay North 80
White Bay South 1, 5, 98, 99
Windsor–Buchans 63, 112
Electric Reduction Company of Canada Industries Ltd. (ERCO) 71
Elizabeth Towers 104, 175
England 59, 69, 78, 133, 196, 197, 200, 219, 220
Epp, Jake 142
Ericsson, Leif 220
Estai 194-197, 201
Europe 13, 37, 38, 146, 147, 194-196, 199, 201, 202, 220
European Union (EU) 146, 147, 194-199, 201, 202
(*Evening*) *Telegram* 42, 59, 104, 105, 111, 115, 148
exclusive economic zone (EEZ) 192, 193, 202

Faour, Fonse 173
Farrell, Tom 98, 103-106, 175
"Father of Confederation" 90
Fenwick, Peter 54
"fighting Newfoundlander" 14, 47, 48
Filmon, Gary 126
First Nations 126, 220
Fisheries Festival, England 200
Fishery Products International (FPI) 70, 40, 146
Fish, Food and Allied Workers Union (FFAW-Unifor) 40, 46, 113, 145
Fleur de Lys, NL 116
Flight, Graham 63
Foote, Judy 213
Forsey, Eugene 130, 201
Fortis Inc. 158
Fraser, John 40
Fraser River, BC 76
Furey, Chuck 186
Furey, George 241
Furlong, Bob 201

Gatineau Hills, QC 121
George Street Church 165
Getty, Don 136, 137
Ghiz, Joe 135
Glacier Arena, Mount Pearl 239
Glenridge Crescent 137
Globe and Mail 102, 184
Glynmill Inn 99
Goulds, NL 157
government departments (Canada)
Energy 47, 51
External Affairs 40

Finance 20, 24, 216, 241
Fisheries 20, 28, 40, 147, 186, 193-195, 198, 202, 206, 238, 243, 247, 252
Fisheries and Oceans 192
Foreign Affairs 193, 198
Health 76
Industry 233, 237, 240, 241, 243
Justice 51, 183
government departments (Newfoundland and Labrador)
Agriculture 69
Consumer Affairs and Environment 61
Education 60, 222
Energy 51, 53, 170, 233
Environment 61
Finance 11
Justice 61, 104, 120, 150, 227
Labour 79-81, 84, 86
Mines and Energy 11-14, 17, 233
Municipal Affairs and Housing 11
Welfare 4
government departments (Quebec)
Intergovernmental Affairs 121, 134
government departments (United Nations)
External Affairs 216
Government House, St. John's 79
Grand Banks of Newfoundland 12, 49, 145, 146, 192, 194, 199, 202
Grand Falls, NL 78, 84, 93
Grant Collegiate 5, 6
Gray, Herbert Eser "Herb" 179
Great Northern Peninsula, NL 149
Green Bay, NL 1, 5, 8, 10, 11, 18, 42
Green Bay Integrated School Board 5
Green Bay Liberal Association 5
Greene, Graham 165
Greene, Moya 217
Grimes, Roger 222, 224, 231, 238, 239
Gros Morne National Park 149, 222
Guardian 146
Gzowski, Peter John 67

Halifax, NS 122, 141
Halley, Hickman, Hunt and Steele 86
Hall's Bay, NL 42
Harper, Elijah 126, 140, 142
Harper, Stephen 76, 144, 245
Harris, Elmer 32, 154
Harris, Jack 157, 186, 215, 225, 227
Harris, Michael "Mike" 44, 207
Harvard University 135
Hawaii (HI) 94

Health Sciences Centre 33, 234
Here and Now 103
Hibernia oil field 12, 27, 54, 55, 153-155, 234
Hickey, Bonnie 186, 189-191
Hickey, Jim 43
Hickey, Tom 17
Hickman, T. Alex 24, 47, 80, 88, 89
Hickman, Tom 111
Hitler, Adolf 96, 180
Hodder, Mary 213
Hong Kong, China 94
Hosea 159
Hôtel Château Laurier 38, 169
Hotel Newfoundland (now Sheraton Hotel, St. John's) 52, 186
House, Doug 64, 66, 166
House of Assembly 1, 4, 5, 8, 11, 16, 19, 24, 25, 29, 30, 48, 53-55, 57-61, 63, 74, 79, 80, 82, 84-86, 89, 90, 92, 93, 95-99, 102, 104, 106, 111, 118-120, 124, 127, 138, 140, 141, 144, 150, 152, 160, 165, 168, 170, 171, 210, 213-216, 224-226, 230, 235, 238
House of Commons (Britain) 180, 197
House of Commons (Canada) 125, 134, 144, 153, 176, 178-180, 182, 183, 187, 190-192, 194, 200, 214, 233, 235, 237, 240, 242
House of Lords 196
Hoy, Claire 117, 119
Hughes Commission 120
Hughes, Samuel 120
Hull, QC 138
Husky Oil 218
Hutton, Fred 240
Hydro-Québec 33-35, 231

Iceland 146
Inco Limited 229, 231, 237
Innu 58, 232, 233
International Fund for Animal Welfare (IFAW) 108
International Woodworkers of America (IWA) 84
Inuit 58
Iran 22
Ireland 197, 201, 219
Isle of the Dogs, London 200
Ivany, George 78

Jamieson, Don 20-24, 29-31, 48, 90, 110, 115, 172, 173, 201, 247
John Lewis Paton Society Award 78
Johnson, Daniel 203, 205, 207
Johnson, Lyndon B. 79
Jones, Yvonne 215
Joyce, Eddie 120
Judge Advocate General's Office 82

Kelland-Dyer, Sue 159
Kelland, Jim 149, 150
Kelly, Sandra 213
Kennedy, Ted 169, 194
Khomeini, Sayyid Ruhollah Mūsavi 22
King Henry VIII 217
Klein, Ralph 209
Knights of Columbus Hall 174, 175
Kremlin 180
Kuwait 31

La Forest, Gerard 135
Lalonde, Marc 28
Langevin Block 41
L'Anse aux Meadows, NL 220
Lapierre, Jean 179
Laschinger, John 22, 23, 26, 73, 74, 114, 117
Laval University 122
Law Society of Newfoundland and Labrador 86, 87
"Lawyers' Union" 86
Leclair, Joseph 105
Le Devoir 207
Leger and Leger 208
Legislative Assembly of Manitoba 140
Legrow, A. S. 105
Lépine, Marc 150
Lesage, Jean 34
Letto, Doug 232, 239
Lévesque, René 14-16, 206
Liberal Party of Canada 14, 19, 20, 24, 27, 30, 31, 33, 46, 48, 50, 90, 114, 137, 142, 144, 169, 172-174, 178-183, 185-187, 189, 191, 205, 209, 215, 229, 236, 238, 239, 241, 243, 245, 246
Liberal Party of Newfoundland and Labrador 1, 4-6, 10, 11, 16, 17, 19-26, 28-30, 41, 42, 47, 48, 53-55, 61, 63, 66, 72-74, 78, 79, 81, 84, 87, 89, 90, 92-96, 98, 99, 105, 107, 110-112, 114, 115, 117-121, 124, 158, 159, 162, 164, 166-168, 170-173, 175, 176, 178, 181, 210, 211, 214, 215, 218, 224, 226, 230, 236, 238, 239
Liberal Party of Quebec 34, 203, 205
Liberal Reform Party 5, 11, 96
Little, Philip Francis 18
Locke, Wade 154
London, England 30, 31, 180, 196, 200, 218, 219
Long Harbour, NL 71
Long Range Mountains 149
Los Angeles, CA 94
Lougheed, Peter 209
Lower Churchill River 35, 229
Lundrigan, Harold 111
Lundrigans Inc. 79
Lundrigan, W. J. 102
Lynx, The 59

Maclean's 4, 141
Magna International Inc. 243
Mahoney, John 105
Maine (ME) 218
Major, John 196, 197
"Make Work Not War" 48
"Male Menopause Manor" 42
Malone, Greg 159
Manitoba (MB) 126, 136, 140-142
Manley, John 241
Manning, Preston 153, 185, 188, 190
Manotick, ON 246
March, Fraser 53, 118, 151, 238
Marconi, Guglielmo 220
Marine Institute 62
Marshall, Jack 172
Marshall, Tom 23, 24
Marshall, William 51
Martin, Cabot 102
Martin, Paul Jr. 137, 182, 216, 237, 241-243, 245
Martin, Paul Sr. 183
Marx, Karl 153
Matthew 220
Maynard, Ed 17
McCarthy, Jack 175
McGrath, Jim 20, 28
McIsaac, Hazel A. 61
McKenna, Frank 126, 136-138, 140, 207
McLoughlin, Audrey 191
McMurtry, Roy 38
McTeer, Maureen Anne 63
Medical Care Plan (MCP) 234
Meech Lake, QC 80, 121
Meech Lake Accord 39, 112, 121, 122, 124-139, 141-145, 147, 153, 159, 163, 166, 182, 184, 190, 204, 206
"Meech Lake Monster" 121, 122
Meek, Jim 141
Member of Parliament (MP) 5, 17, 134, 172, 173, 176, 180, 182, 183, 187, 191, 201, 205, 206, 209, 214, 227, 238, 244
Member of the House of Assembly (MHA) 4, 5, 21, 54, 57, 59, 60, 63, 70, 73, 79-82, 85, 95, 96, 99, 102, 103, 111, 112, 120, 124, 140, 141, 149, 168, 170, 171, 186, 211, 215, 224, 226
Memorial Stadium 95
Memorial University of Newfoundland (MUN) 64, 68, 78, 115, 154, 168
"Million Dollar Pickles" 70
Mission Impossible 198
"Mr. Cucumber" 115
Montebello, QC 131
Montreal, QC 69, 122, 205-209, 233, 241
Montreal Gazette 42, 121, 129
Moores, Frank 1, 10-12, 14-17, 19, 20, 23-27, 29-31, 45, 53, 63, 73, 75, 98, 99, 103, 110, 115, 130, 245, 246, 252
Morgan, Jim 17, 238

Morgan, Mose 82
Morgentaler, Henry 234
Morningside 67
Morris, Edward 196
Mosher, Terry "Aislin" 121
Mount Cashel Orphanage 104, 120, 226, 227
Mount Pearl, NL 64, 69, 157, 239
Mount Scio House 25, 41
Mulcair, Tom 209
Mulroney, Brian 30, 34, 39, 40, 50-52, 55, 56, 62, 63, 73, 114, 121, 122, 127-129, 133, 135, 137-143, 146, 178-182, 184, 185, 188, 191, 243
Mulroney, Milica "Mila" 73
Murphy, Noel 81, 82
Murphy, Pat 225
Murphy, Rex 22, 43, 92, 119, 120
Murray, Lowell 133
Murray Premises 164
Museum of Civilization 133
Muskrat Falls 16, 159
Myrden, Gerald "Gerry" 85, 96

Nalcor 35, 159, 160
Narrows, St. John's 195
National Aeronautics and Space Administration (NASA) 75
National Convention 79
National Magazine 155
National Research Council 68
Neary, Peter 78
Neary, Steve 11, 42, 80, 82, 86, 87, 93, 98, 111, 118
New Brunswick (NB) 126, 136, 140, 192
New Democratic Party (NDP) of Canada 173, 178, 181, 186, 191, 238
New Democratic Party (NDP) of Manitoba 126
New Democratic Party (NDP) of Newfoundland and Labrador 12, 54, 66, 118, 120, 157, 174, 215, 225, 227, 230
New England 69
"Newfie Bullet" 35
Newfoundland and Labrador Arts Council 61
Newfoundland and Labrador Film Development Corporation (NLFDC) 234
Newfoundland and Labrador Hydro 7, 14, 158, 159, 163
Newfoundland and Labrador Association of Public Employees (NAPE) 53, 112, 118, 151, 152
Newfoundland Energy Limited 60
Newfoundland Enviroponics Limited 65, 70
Newfoundland Federation of Labour 80, 112
Newfoundland Fisheries Development Authority 7
Newfoundland Human Rights Act 234

Newfoundland Light and Power 109
Newfoundland Ocean Industries Association (NOIA) 76
Newfoundland Power 158
Newfoundland Power Commission 80
Newfoundland T'Railway Provincial Park 36
Newfoundland Transportation Initiative 35
Newhook, Hazel 60
New World Island, NL 22
New York, NY 146, 197-199, 205
Nicholson, Jack 169
Nigeria 13
Noel, Wally 159
"Noisy Six" 90
Nolan, John 80, 93
North America 13, 199, 218, 220
Nose and Tail of the Grand Banks 145, 147, 192, 194, 212
Nova Scotia (NS) 16, 39, 90, 115
NTV *Evening News* 240
Nunziata, John 179, 182

O'Brien, Lawrence 236
Ocean Drilling & Exploration Company (ODECO) 47
Ocean Ranger 47, 50
Oceans Act 247
O'Flaherty, Patrick 78
Olympia and York 200
Olympic Saddledome 142
One Canada Square, London 200
Ontario (ON) 67, 90, 120, 125, 131, 132, 134, 136, 147, 231, 246
Open Line 22, 32, 40, 64-66, 68, 111, 113, 116, 133, 146, 147, 149, 153, 154, 158, 185-188, 193, 196, 200, 208, 215, 225, 227, 230, 236, 237, 242
Opposition party (Canada) 144, 178-183, 191, 194, 243
Opposition party (Newfoundland and Labrador) 1, 11, 16, 24, 29, 30, 54, 55, 63, 81, 92, 96, 104, 111-113, 124, 167, 168, 172, 174, 176, 210, 216, 226
Order of Canada 246, 247
O'Regan, Seamus Sr. 74
O'Rourke, Margaret Ann 192
Osgoode Hall 130
Ottawa, ON 9, 13, 14, 17, 19, 21, 24, 28, 31, 33-35, 37, 39-41, 45-48, 51, 52, 55, 56, 72, 90, 106, 122, 127, 130, 133-135, 138, 140, 142, 147, 148, 153, 154, 169, 176, 177, 180, 183, 199, 200, 202, 205, 209-211, 216-218, 227, 229, 239, 248, 252
Oxford University 130

Paddon, Anthony 38
Paris, France 40
Parizeau, Jacques 203, 204, 208, 209

Parliament Hill 177
Parti Québécois 131, 203, 231
"Patronage Award of the Week" 179
Pearson, Lester B. 34, 178, 183
Peckford, Alfred Brian 1, 3-57, 59-77, 102, 106, 110-115, 118, 119, 124, 148, 149, 153, 155, 164, 170, 172, 201, 209, 246, 252
Peckford, Carol 75
Peckford, Marina 42
Penney, Alphonsus 227, 228
Pentecostal Assemblies 161, 221
Peterson, David 131, 136, 137, 140
Petro-Canada Exploration Inc. 60, 218
Petten, Bill 194
Pickersgill, Jack 133, 180
Place du Canada, Montreal 206, 207
Placentia, NL 22
Port aux Basques, NL 102
Portugal Cove Road, St. John's 65
Power, Charlie 69
Pratt, Christopher 57-59
Pratt, Philip 235
Prime Minister's Office (PMO) 39-41, 240
Prince Charles 43
Prince Edward 67, 68
Prince Edward Island (PEI) 90, 135, 143, 238
Prince Philip 219
Princess Diana 42, 43
Progressive Conservative (PC) Party of Canada 19, 20, 24, 27, 30, 34, 39, 50, 55, 62, 121, 172-174, 178-180, 184, 187-189, 191, 207
Progressive Conservative (PC) Party of Newfoundland and Labrador 1, 6, 7, 10-12, 14, 16, 17, 20, 23-25, 41, 48, 53, 54, 64, 70, 81, 95, 98, 99, 105, 110, 112, 114, 115, 117-120, 155, 166, 168, 178, 210, 213-215, 225, 227, 230, 238, 239
Provincial Advisory Council on the Status of Women 61
Provincial Airlines 194
Prowse, Kenneth 17
Public Accounts Committee 25, 216
Public Tendering Act 163, 164
Public Utilities Board (PUB) 109

Qualicum Beach, BC 75
Quebec (QC) 14-16, 28, 33-35, 39, 49, 56, 67, 90, 121-123, 125-132, 134, 135, 137, 139, 140, 142-144, 147, 163, 179, 182, 185, 188, 190, 197, 202-209, 231-233, 237, 252
Quebec City, QC 122
Quebec National Assembly 209
Queen Elizabeth II 31, 39, 67, 99,

133, 134, 197, 219
Queen's University 130
Question Period 180

Radical Party (Italy) 195
"Rat Pack" 178-180, 182, 209, 214, 243
Reader's Digest 187
"Ready for a Better Tomorrow" 218
Reform Party of Canada 153, 185, 188, 190, 197
Reichstag 180
Reid, Ida 48
Reid, Ross 186, 187, 191
Reid, Wally 14
Renaissance 165
René Lévesque Boulevard, Montreal 206
"Rest of Canada, the" (RoC) 127
Riche, Nancy 103
Rideout, Tom 114-120
River Thames 200
Roaches Line, NL 26
"Roads for Rails" 35
Roberts, Edward 10, 80, 88, 93, 95, 99, 149, 150
Robin Hood Bay, NL 67
Rolling Stones 169
Roman Catholic Church 43, 83, 116, 117, 161, 174, 175, 221, 222, 224-226
Romanow, Roy 38
Rome, Italy 17, 134, 210
Rompkey, Bill 78, 176, 183
Rooms, The 235
Roosevelt, Franklin D. 29
Rowe, Bud 222
Rowe, Fred Jr. 236
Rowe, Frederick William Sr. 78, 83, 90, 149, 165
Rowe, Malcolm 216, 217
Royal Canadian Legion 58
Royal Canadian Mounted Police (RCMP) 195
Royal Commission on Education in Newfoundland (1992) 160
Royal Commission on Employment and Unemployment (1986) 64, 156
Royal Commission on Newfoundland and Labrador's Place in Canada 7
Royal Commission on the *Ocean Ranger* Marine Disaster 47
Royal Mail 217
Royal Newfoundland Constabulary 3, 104
Royal Trust 106
Ryan, Frank 164

St. Anthony, NL 149
St. Barbe, NL 85, 172, 174, 186, 192, 236, 238, 239
"St. Francis of the Flatfish" 199
St. John's, NL 2, 7, 11, 13, 14, 17, 21, 23, 25, 30, 44, 47, 49, 52, 54, 55, 64, 65, 67, 76, 79, 80, 82, 85,

86, 94, 95, 99, 100, 102, 104, 108, 109, 112, 117, 130, 137, 139, 152, 157, 164, 175, 185, 186, 188-191, 194-196, 211, 218, 219, 232
St. John's International Airport 21, 139
Saint-Pierre and Miquelon, NL 40
Sauvé, Jeanne 133
Savage, John 207
School Construction Board 161
School of Fine Arts 61
Schwarzenegger, Arnold 200
Scotland 196, 197
Senate of Canada 21, 24, 122, 125, 131, 133, 134, 138, 143, 172, 194, 238, 241
Shaheen, John 88, 89, 97, 105
Shakespeare, William 214
Shawinigan, QC 184
"Shawinigate" scandal 240
Ship Inn 107
Signal Hill, NL 158, 215, 220
Simmons, Roger 5, 80, 81, 107, 176, 183
Simms, Len 114, 157
Simms, Randy 167
Simoni, Michelangelo di Lodovico Buonarroti 165
Simpson, Jeffrey 129
Sir Richard Squires Building 152
Sir Wilfred Grenfell 194
Sir Wilfred Grenfell College 61
Skanes, Graham 78
Smallwood, Bill 94
Smallwood, Clara 26
Smallwood, Joey 5, 7, 25, 26, 29, 31, 33, 34, 58, 69, 71, 73, 78, 79, 94, 96, 99, 102, 108, 118, 149, 154, 157, 163, 201, 215, 232, 238, 246, 247, 251
Smallwood Reservoir 232
Snorri 220
Society of United Fishermen (SUF) 171
South America 36, 146
South Brook, NL 18, 42
South of France 240
Spain 197, 201
Speaker of the House of Assembly 114
Speaker of the House of Commons 180
Speech from the Throne 124, 194
Springdale, NL 5
Sprung, Beverly 70
Sprung, Dawn 65
Sprung greenhouse 66-69, 71, 72, 77, 112, 114, 148
Sprung Group of Companies 65, 70
Sprung, Philip 64, 65, 67, 68, 72, 74
Sprung Structures 72
Squires, Richard 10
Stagg, Fred 94, 95, 163
Stalin, Joseph 180, 236, 237

Stanfield, Robert 133
Starkes, Harold 10
Star Wars 66
Statistics Canada 67, 156
Steele, Harry 44, 111
Stephenville, NL 26, 94, 172
Stephenville Crossing, NL 83, 100
Sterrett, Carl 32, 33
Stevens, Geoffrey 22
Stevens, Sinclair 179
Stirling, Geoff 167
Stirling, Len 20, 22, 48, 110
Story, George 201
Strait of Belle Isle 16
Stronach, Belinda 243
Stronach, Frank 243
Studio 54 169
Sudbury, ON 231
Sullivan, Loyola 213, 225
Sunday Express 44, 115
Supreme Court of Canada 15, 34, 35, 49, 50, 61, 106, 107, 120, 122, 135, 226
Supreme Court of Newfoundland and Labrador 24, 61, 82, 109, 144, 161, 163, 164, 217, 221
Swift Current, NL 30
Switzerland 165, 216

Terms of Union 37, 49, 51, 160, 226
Terra Nova oil field 155, 218
Third Man, The 165
Thistle, Anna 213
Thoms, Fowler, Rowe and Barry 61
Three Gorges 232
Titanic 47
Tobin, Adam 248
Tobin, Brian Vincent 26, 29, 30, 55, 117, 144, 146, 155, 156, 162, 167-190, 192-195, 197-201, 205-220, 222-227, 229-249, 251, 252
Tobin, Heather 248
Tobin, Jack 248, 249
Tobin, Jodean (Smith) 174, 200, 222, 227, 235, 237, 248
Toronto, ON 26, 81, 94, 169, 179, 184, 189, 208, 222, 241
Toronto Star 179, 184
Tory, John 189
Trans Canada Trail 36
Trans City Holdings Limited 164
Trans-Labrador Highway 60
Trask, Ralph 17
Traverse, Ross 64, 65
Triple-E Senate 125
"Trudeaumania" 90
Trudeau, Margaret 169
Trudeau, Pierre Elliott 5, 12, 14, 19, 20, 24, 27, 28, 30, 33, 34, 37, 38, 46-49, 51, 54, 61, 73, 81, 90, 114, 121-123, 128, 130, 137, 143, 144, 163, 169, 170, 172, 173, 176-178, 183
Tulk, Beaton 238

"Turbot War" 194, 198, 200, 201, 210, 231
Turner, John 50, 114, 178, 179, 181-183
Twiston-Davies, David 196, 200

Union Jack 57, 58
United Fishermen of Newfoundland and Labrador 146
United Kingdom (UK) 38, 146, 196, 197, 200, 201, 217, 219, 220
United Nations (UN) 146, 197-199, 205, 216
United States Coast Guard 51, 52
"Unity Rally" 207
University of Ottawa 217
Upper Churchill Falls 14, 15, 28, 34, 35, 56, 77, 106, 135, 231, 232
Upper Churchill Water Rights Reversion Act 106

Venice, Italy 219
Verge, Lynn 60, 61, 101, 118, 120, 149, 150, 210, 213-215
Victoria, BC 141
Vigo, Spain 194
Vikings 220
Vinland 220
VOCM Radio 32, 40, 154, 167, 177, 185, 225, 237
Voisey's Bay, NL 229, 231, 237, 244

Washington, DC 194
Waterford Bridge Road, St. John's 248
"We Care" 207
Wedgewood Park, St. John's 157
Welles, Orson 165
Wells, Clyde Kirby 5, 24, 26, 29, 39, 41, 50, 63, 66, 72-75, 78-82, 84-99, 101-103, 105-166, 176, 181, 182, 198, 207, 209-212, 214, 221, 222, 225, 246, 247, 251
Wells, Eleanor 79, 89, 113, 137
Wells, Janice 245
Wells, Karl 96
West Country of England 197, 200
Western Star 80, 81
White, Homer 97
White Rose oil field 155, 218
Williams, Danny 8, 9, 16, 56, 117, 155, 227, 239, 251, 252
Williams, Leonard 160
Winnipeg, MB 142
Winter, Gordon 20
Woodward, Mel 111
Woody Point, NL 174, 222
World Economic Forum 216
World War I 58, 196
World War II 58, 196, 197, 234, 247
Wyatt, Dorothy 17

Young, Graham 8

Young, Howie 8
Young Liberals Association 78, 93
Young, Robert 8
Young, Ross 7, 8
Young, Vic 7, 15, 146

Zolpis, Alex 248